LOST
IN THE
CITY

STORIES

Edward P. Jones

 Amistad   *An Imprint of* HarperCollins*Publishers*

HarperCollins books may be purchased for educational, business, or sales pro-motional use. For information, please write: Special Markets Department, HarperCollins Publishers, Inc., 10 East 53rd Street, New York, NY 10022.

Originally published in a different format in 1992 by William Morrow and Company, Inc. First published in paperback by HarperPerennial in 1993.

FIRST AMISTAD EDITION—2003

Designed by Stephanie Tevonian Design

Printed on acid-free paper

Library of Congress Cataloging-in-Publication Data
Jones, Edward P.
    Lost in the city : stories / Edward P. Jones.—1st Amistad ed.
      p.   cm.
    ISBN 0-06-079528-X (acid-free paper)
      1. Washington (D.C.)—Fiction.   2. African Americans—Fiction.   I. Title.
PS3560.O4813L67   2003
813'.54—dc21   2003048034

    11   12   BVG/RRD   20   19   18   17   16   15   14   13   12

To the memory of my mother,
Jeanette S. M. Jones

CONTENTS

The Girl Who Raised Pigeons ▪ 1

The First Day ▪ 27

The Night Rhonda Ferguson Was Killed ▪ 33

Young Lions ▪ 55

The Store ▪ 77

An Orange Line Train to Ballston ▪ 105

The Sunday Following Mother's Day ▪ 117

Lost in the City ▪ 141

His Mother's House ▪ 151

A Butterfly on F Street ▪ 177

Gospel ▪ 183

A New Man ▪ 203

A Dark Night ▪ 217

Marie ▪ 229

A Selection from All Aunt Hagar's Children:
A Rich Man ▪ 245

LOST
IN THE
CITY

THE GIRL WHO RAISED PIGEONS

Her father would say years later that she had dreamed that part of it, that she had never gone out through the kitchen window at two or three in the morning to visit the birds. By that time in his life he would have so many notions about himself set in concrete. And having always believed that he slept lightly, he would not want to think that a girl of nine or ten could walk by him at such an hour in the night without his waking and asking of the dark, Who is it? What's the matter?

But the night visits were not dreams, and they remained forever as vivid to her as the memory of the way the pigeons' iridescent necklaces flirted with light. The visits would begin not with any compulsion in her sleeping mind to visit, but with the simple need to pee or to get a drink of water. In the dark, she went barefoot out of her room, past her father in the front room conversing in his sleep, across the kitchen and through the kitchen window, out over the roof a few steps to the coop. It could be winter, it could be summer, but the most she ever got was something she called pigeon silence. Sometimes she had the urge to unlatch the door and go into the coop, or, at the very least, to try to reach through the wire and the wooden slats to stroke a wing or a breast, to share whatever the silence seemed to conceal. But she always kept her hands to herself, and after a few minutes, as if relieved, she would go back to her bed and visit the birds again in sleep.

What Betsy Ann Morgan and her father Robert did agree on was that the pigeons began with the barber Miles Patterson. Her father had known Miles long before the girl was born, before the thought to marry her mother had even crossed his mind. The barber lived in a gingerbread brown house with his old parents only a few doors down from the barbershop he owned on the corner of 3rd and L streets, Northwest. On some Sundays, after Betsy Ann had come back from church with Miss Jenny, Robert, as he believed his wife would have done, would take his daughter out to visit with relatives and friends in the neighborhoods just beyond Myrtle Street, Northeast, where father and daughter lived.

One Sunday, when Betsy Ann was eight years old, the barber asked her again if she wanted to see his pigeons, "my children." He had first asked her some three years before. The girl had been eager to see them then, imagining she would see the same frightened creatures who waddled and flew away whenever she chased them on sidewalks and in parks. The men and the girl had gone into the backyard, and the pigeons, in a furious greeting, had flown up and about the barber. "Oh, my babies," he said, making kissing sounds. "Daddy's here." In an instant, Miles's head was surrounded by a colorful flutter of pigeon life. The birds settled on his head and his shoulders and along his thick, extended arms, and some of the birds looked down meanly at her. Betsy Ann screamed, sending the birds back into a flutter, which made her scream even louder. And still screaming, she ran back into the house. The men found her in the kitchen, her head buried in the lap of Miles's mother, her arms tight around the waist of the old woman, who had been sitting at the table having Sunday lunch with her husband.

"Buster," Miles's mother said to him, "you shouldn't scare your company like this. This child's bout to have a heart attack."

Three years later Betsy Ann said yes again to seeing the birds. In the backyard, there was again the same fluttering chaos, but this time the sight of the wings and bodies settling about Miles intrigued her and she drew closer until she was a foot or so away, looking up at them and stretching out her arm as she saw Miles doing. "Oh, my babies," the barber said. "Your daddy's here." One of the birds landed on Betsy Ann's shoulder and another in the palm of her hand. The gray one in her hand looked dead at Betsy Ann, blinked, then swiveled his head and gave the girl a different view of a radiant black necklace. "They tickle," she said to her father, who stood back.

For weeks and weeks after that Sunday, Betsy Ann pestered her father about getting pigeons for her. And the more he told her no, that it was impossible, the more she wanted them. He warned her that he would not do anything to help her care for them, he warned her that all the bird-work meant she would not ever again have time to play with her friends, he warned her about all the do-do the pigeons would let loose. But she remained a bulldog about it, and he knew that she was not often a bulldog about anything. In the end he retreated to the fact that they were only renters in Jenny and Walter Creed's house.

"Miss Jenny likes birds," the girl said. "Mr. Creed likes birds, too."

"People may like birds, but nobody in the world likes pigeons."

"Cept Mr. Miles," she said.

"Don't make judgments bout things with what you know bout Miles." Miles Patterson, a bachelor and, some women said, a virgin, was fifty-six years old and for the most part knew no more about the world than what he could experience in newspapers or on the radio and in his own neighborhood, beyond which he rarely ventured. "There's ain't nothing out there in the great beyond for me," Miles would say to people who talked with excitement about visiting such and such a place.

It was not difficult for the girl to convince Miss Jenny, though the old woman made it known that "pigeons carry all them diseases, child." But there were few things Jenny Creed would deny Betsy Ann. The girl was known by all the world to be a good and obedient child. And in Miss Jenny's eyes, a child's good reputation amounted to an assent from God on most things.

For years after he relented, Robert Morgan would rise every morning before his daughter, go out onto the roof, and peer into the coop he had constructed for her, looking for dead pigeons. At such a time in the morning, there would be only fragments of first light, falling in long, hopeful slivers over the birds and their house. Sometimes he would stare absently into the coop for a long time, because being half-asleep, his mind would forget why he was there. The murmuring pigeons, as they did with most of the world, would stare back, with looks more of curiosity than of fear or anticipation or welcome. He thought that by getting there in the morning before his daughter, he could spare her the sight and pain of any dead birds. His plan had always been to put any dead birds he found into a burlap sack, take them down to his taxicab, and dispose of them on his way to work. He never intended to tell her about such birds, and it never occurred to him that she would know every pigeon in the coop and would wonder, perhaps even worry, about a missing bird.

They lived in the apartment Jenny and Walter Creed had made out of the upstairs in their Myrtle Street house. Miss Jenny had known Clara, Robert's wife, practically all of Clara's life. But their relationship had become little more than hellos and good-byes as they passed in the street before Miss Jenny came upon Clara and Robert one rainy Saturday in the library park at Mt. Vernon Square. Miss Jenny had come out of Hahn's shoe store, crossed New York Avenue, and was going up 7th Street. At first, Miss Jenny thought the young man and woman, soaked through to the skin, sitting on the park bench under a blue umbrella, were feebleminded or straightout crazy. As she came closer, she could hear them laughing, and the young man was swinging the umbrella back and forth over their heads, so that the rain would fall first upon her and then upon himself.

"Ain't you William and Alice Hobson baby girl?" Miss Jenny asked Clara.

"Yes, ma'am." She stood and Robert stood as well, now holding the umbrella fully over Clara's head.

"Is everything all right, child?" Miss Jenny's glasses were spotted with mist, and she took them off and stepped closer, keeping safely to the side where Clara was.

"Yes, ma'am. He—" She pushed Robert and began to laugh. "We came out of Peoples and he wouldn't let me have none a the umbrella. He let me get wet, so I took the umbrella and let him have some of his own medicine."

Robert said nothing. He was standing out of the range of the umbrella and he was getting soaked all over again.

"We gonna get married, Miss Jenny," she said, as if that explained everything, and she stuck out her hand with her ring. "From Castleberg's," she said. Miss Jenny took Clara's hand and held it close to her face.

"Oh oh," she said again and again, pulling Clara's hand still closer.

"This Robert," Clara said. "My"—and she turned to look at him—"fiancé." She uttered the word with a certain crispness: It was clear that before Robert Morgan, *fiancé* was a word she had perhaps never uttered in her life.

Robert and Miss Jenny shook hands. "You gonna give her double pneumonia even before she take your name," she said.

The couple learned the next week that the place above Miss Jenny was vacant and the following Sunday, Clara and Robert, dressed as if they had just come from church, were at her front door, inquiring about the apartment.

That was one of the last days in the park for them. Robert came to believe later that the tumor that would consume his wife's brain had been growing even on that rainy day. And it was there all those times he made love to her, and the thought that it was there, perhaps at first no bigger than a grain of salt, made him feel that he had somehow used her, taken from her even as she was moving toward death. He would not remember until much, much later the times she told him he gave her pleasure, when she whispered into his ear that she was glad she had found him, raised her head in that bed as she lay under him. And when he did remember, he would have to take out her photograph from the small box of valuables he kept in the dresser's top drawer, for he could not remember her face any other way.

Clara spent most of the first months of her pregnancy in bed, propped up, reading movie magazines and listening to the radio, waiting for Robert to come home from work. Her once pretty face slowly began to collapse in on itself like fruit too long in the sun, eaten away by the rot that despoiled from the inside out. The last month or so she spent in the bed on the third floor at Gallinger Hospital. One morning, toward four o'clock, they cut open her stomach and pulled out the child only moments after Clara died, mother and daughter passing each other as if along a corridor, one into death, the other into life.

The weeks after her death Robert and the infant were attended to by family and friends. They catered to him and to the baby to such an extent that sometimes in those weeks when he heard her cry, he would look about at the people in a room, momentarily confused about what was making the sound. But as all the people returned to their lives in other parts of Washington or in other cities, he was left with the ever-increasing vastness of the small apartment and with a being who hadn't the power to ask, yet seemed to demand everything.

"I don't think I can do this," he confessed to Miss Jenny one Friday evening when the baby was about a month old. "I know I can't do this." Robert's father had been the last to leave him, and Robert had just returned from taking the old man to Union Station a few blocks away. "If my daddy had just said the word, I'da been on that train with him." He and Miss Jenny were sitting at his kitchen table, and the child, sleeping, was in her cradle beside Miss Jenny. Miss Jenny watched him and said not a word. "Woulda followed him all the way back home. . . . I never looked down the line and saw bein by myself like this."

"It's all right," Miss Jenny said finally. "I know how it is. You a young man. You got a whole life in front a you," and the stone on his heart grew lighter. "The city people can help out with this."

"The city?" He looked through the fluttering curtain onto the roof, at the oak tree, at the backs of houses on K Street.

"Yes, yes." She turned around in her chair to face him fully. "My niece works for the city, and she say they can take care of chirren like this who don't have parents. They have homes, good homes, for chirren like her. Bring em up real good. Feed em, clothe em, give em good schoolin. Give em everything they need." She stood, as if the matter were settled. "The city people care. Call my niece tomorra and find out what you need to do. A young man like you shouldn't have to worry yourself like this." She was at the door, and he stood up too, not wanting her to go. "Try to put all the worries out your mind." Before he could say anything, she closed the door quietly behind her.

She did not come back up, as he had hoped, and he spent his first night alone with the child. Each time he managed to get the baby back to sleep after he fed her or changed her diaper, he would place her in the crib in the front room and sit without light at the kitchen table listening to the trains coming and going just beyond his window. He was nineteen years old. There was a song about trains that kept rumbling in his head as the night wore on, a song his mother would sing when he was a boy.

The next morning, Saturday, he shaved and washed up while Betsy Ann was still sleeping, and after she woke and he had fed her again, he clothed her with a yellow outfit and its yellow bonnet that Wilma Ellis, the schoolteacher next door, had given Betsy Ann. He carried the carriage downstairs first, leaving the baby on a pallet of blankets. On the sidewalk he covered her with a light green blanket that Dr. Oscar Jackson and his family up the street had given the baby. The shades were down at Miss Jenny's windows, and he heard no sound, not even the dog's barking, as he came and went. At the child's kicking feet in the carriage he placed enough diapers and powdered formula to last an expedition to Baltimore. Beside her, he placed a blue rattle from the janitor Jake Horton across the street.

He was the only moving object within her sight and she watched him intently, which made him uncomfortable. She seemed the most helpless thing he had ever known. It occurred to him perversely, as he settled her in, that if he decided to walk away forever from her and the carriage and all her stuff, to walk but a few yards and make his way up or down 1st Street for no place in particular, there was not a damn thing in the world she could do about it. The carriage was facing 1st Street Northeast, and with some effort—because one of the wheels refused to turn with the others—he maneuvered it around, pointing toward North Capitol Street.

In those days, before the community was obliterated, a warm Myrtle Street Saturday morning filled both sidewalks and the narrow street itself with playing children oblivious to everything but their own merriment. A grownup's course was generally not an easy one, but that morning, as he made his way with the soundless wheels of the carriage, the children made way for Robert Morgan, for he was the man whose wife had passed away. At her wake, some of them had been held up by grownups so they could look down on Clara laid out in her pink casket in Miss Jenny's parlor. And though death and its rituals did not mean much beyond the wavering understanding that they would never see someone again, they knew from what their parents said and did that a clear path to the corner was perhaps the very least a widow man deserved.

Some of the children called to their parents still in their houses and apartments that Robert was passing with Clara's baby. The few grownups on porches came down to the sidewalk and made a fuss over Betsy Ann. More than midway down the block, Janet Gordon, who had been one of Clara's best friends, came out and picked up the baby. It was too nice a day to have that blanket over her, she told Robert. You expectin to go all the way to Baltimore with all them diapers? she said. It would be Janet who would teach him— practicing on string and a discarded blond-haired doll—how to part and plait a girl's hair.

He did not linger on Myrtle Street; he planned to make the visits there on his way back that evening. Janet's boys, Carlos and Carleton, walked on either side of him up Myrtle to North Capitol, then to the corner of K Street. There they knew to turn back. Carlos, seven years old, told him to take it easy. Carleton, younger by two years, did not want to repeat what his brother had said, so he repeated one of the things his grandfather, who was losing his mind, always told him: "Don't get lost in the city."

Robert nodded as if he understood and the boys turned back. He took off his tie and put it in his pocket and unbuttoned his suit coat and the top two buttons of his shirt. Then he adjusted his hat and placed the rattle nearer the baby, who paid it no mind. And when the light changed, he maneuvered the carriage down off the sidewalk and crossed North Capitol into Northwest.

Miles the barber gave Betsy Ann two pigeons, yearlings, a dull-white female with black spots and a sparkling red male. For several weeks, in the morning, soon after she had dutifully gone in to fill the feed dish and replace the water, and after they had fortified themselves, the pigeons took to the air and returned to Miles. The forlorn sound of their flapping wings echoed in her head as she stood watching them disappear into the colors of the morning, often still holding the old broom she used to sweep out their coop.

So in those first weeks, she went first to Miles's after school to retrieve the pigeons, usually bringing along Ralph Holley, her cousin. Miles would put the birds in the two pigeon baskets Robert would bring over each morning before he took to the street in his taxicab.

"They don't like me," Betsy Ann said to Miles one day in the second week. "They just gonna keep on flyin away. They hate me."

Miles laughed, the same way he laughed when she asked him the first day how he knew one was a girl pigeon and the other was a boy pigeon.

"I don't think that they even got to the place of likin or not likin you," Miles said. She handed her books to Ralph, and Miles gave her the two baskets.

"Well, they keep runnin away."

"Thas all they know to do," which was what he had told her the week before. "Right now, this is all the home they know for sure. It ain't got nothin to do with you, child. They just know to fly back here."

His explanations about everything, when he could manage an explanation, rarely satisfied her. He had been raising pigeons all his life, and whatever knowledge he had accumulated in those years was now such an inseparable part of his being that he could no more explain the birds than he could explain what went into the act of walking. He only knew that they did all that birds did and not something else, as he only knew that he walked and did not fall.

"You might try lockin em in for while," he said. "Maybe two, three days, however long it take em to get use to the new home. Let em know you the boss and you ain't gonna stand for none a this runnin away stuff."

She considered a moment, then shook her head. She watched her cousin peering into Miles's coop, his face hard against the wire. "I guess if I gotta lock em up there ain't no use havin em."

"Why you wanna mess with gotdamn pigeons anyway?" Ralph said as they walked to her home that day.

"Because," she said.

"Because what?" he said.

"Because, thas all," she said. "Just because."

"You oughta get a puppy like I'm gonna get," Ralph said. "A puppy never run away."

"A puppy never fly either. So what?" she said. "You been talking bout gettin a gotdamn puppy for a million years, but I never see you gettin one." Though Ralph was a year older and a head taller than his cousin, she often bullied him.

"You wait. You wait. You'll see," Ralph said.

"I ain't waitin. You the one waitin. When you get it, just let me know and I'll throw you a big party."

At her place, he handed over her books and went home. She considered following her cousin back to his house after she took the pigeons up to the coop, for the idea of being on the roof with birds who wanted to fly away to be with someone else pained her. At Ralph's L Street house, there were cookies almost as big as her face, and Aunt Thelma, Clara's oldest sister, who was, in fact, the very image of Clara. The girl had never had an overwhelming curiosity about her mother, but it fascinated her to see the face of the lady in all the pictures on a woman who moved and laughed and did mother things.

She put the pigeons back in the coop and put fresh water in the bath bowls. Then she stood back, outside the coop, its door open. At such moments they often seemed contented, hopping in and out of cubicles, inspecting the feed and water, all of which riled her. She would have preferred—and understood—agitation, some sign that they were unhappy and ready to fly to Miles again. But they merely pecked about, strutted, heads bobbing happily, oblivious of her. Pretending everything was all right.

"You shitheads!" she hissed, aware that Miss Jenny was downstairs within earshot. "You gotdamn stupid shitheads!"

That was the fall of 1957.

Myrtle Street was only one long block, running east to west. To the east, preventing the street from going any farther, was a high, medieval-like wall of stone across 1st Street, Northeast, and beyond the wall were the railroad tracks. To the west, across North Capitol, preventing Myrtle Street from going any farther in that direction, was the high school Gonzaga, where white boys were taught by white priests. When the colored people and their homes were gone, the wall and the tracks remained, and so did the high school, with the same boys being taught by the same priests.

It was late spring when Betsy Ann first noticed the nest, some two feet up from the coop's floor in one of the twelve cubicles that made up the entire structure. The nest was nothing special, a crude, ill-formed thing of straw and dead leaves and other, uncertain material she later figured only her hapless birds could manage to find. They had not flown back to Miles in a long time, but she had never stopped thinking that it was on their minds each time they took to the air. So the nest was the first solid indication that the pigeons would stay forever, would go but would always return.

About three weeks later, on an afternoon when she was about to begin the weekly job of thoroughly cleaning the entire coop, she saw the two eggs. She thought them a trick of the light at first—two small and perfect wonders alone in that wonderless nest without any hallelujahs from the world. She put off the cleaning and stood looking at the male bird, who had moved off the nest for only a few seconds, rearrange himself on the nest and look at her from time to time in that bored way he had. The female bird was atop the coop, dozing. Betsy Ann got a chair from the kitchen and continued watching the male bird and the nest through the wire. "Tell me bout this," she said to them.

As it happened, Robert discovered the newly hatched squabs when he went to look for dead birds before going to work. About six that morning he peered into the coop and shivered to find two hideous, bug-eyed balls of movement. They were a dirty orange and looked like baby vultures. He looked about as if there might be someone responsible for it all. This was, he knew now, a point of no return for his child. He went back in to have his first cup of coffee of the day.

He drank without enjoyment and listened to the chirping, unsettling, demanding. He would not wake his daughter just to let her know about the hatchlings. Two little monsters had changed the predictable world he was trying to create for his child and he was suddenly afraid for her. He turned on the radio and played it real low, but he soon shut it off, because the man on WOOK was telling him to go in and kill the hatchlings.

It turned out that the first pigeon to die was a stranger, and Robert never knew anything about it. The bird appeared out of nowhere and was dead less than a week later. By then, a year or so after Miles gave her the yearlings, she had eight birds of various ages, resulting from hatches in her coop and from trades with the barber ("for variety's sake," he told her) and with a family in Anacostia. One morning before going to school, she noticed the stranger perched in one of the lower cubicles, a few inches up from the floor, and though he seemed submissive enough, she sensed that he would peck with all he had if she tried to move him out. His entire body, what little there was left of it, was a witness to misery. One ragged cream-colored tail feather stuck straight up, as if with resignation. His bill was pitted as if it had been sprayed with minute pellets, and his left eye was covered with a patch of dried blood and dirt and decaying flesh.

She placed additional straw to either side of him in the cubicle and small bowls of water and feed in front of the cubicle. Then she began to worry that he had brought in some disease that would ultimately devastate her flock.

Days later, home for lunch with Ralph, she found the pigeon dead near the water tray, his wings spread out full as if he had been preparing for flight.

"Whatcha gonna do with him?" Ralph asked, kneeling down beside Betsy Ann and poking the dead bird with a pencil.

"Bury him. What else, stupid?" She snatched the pencil from him. "You don't think any a them gonna do it, do you?" and she pointed to the few stay-at-home pigeons who were not out flying about the city. The birds looked down uninterestedly at them from various places around the coop. She dumped the dead bird in a pillowcase and took it across 1st Street to the grassy spot of ground near the Esso filling station in front of the medieval wall. With a large tablespoon, she dug two feet or so into the earth and dropped the sack in.

"Beaver would say something over his grave," Ralph said.

"What?"

"Beaver. The boy on TV."

She gave him a cut-eye look and stood up. "You do it, preacher man," she said. "I gotta get back to school."

After school she said to Miss Jenny, "Don't tell Daddy bout that dead pigeon. You know how he is: He'll think it's the end of the world or somethin."

The two were in Miss Jenny's kitchen, and Miss Jenny was preparing supper while Betsy Ann did her homework.

"You know what he do in the mornin?" Betsy Ann said. "He go out and look at them pigeons."

"Oh?" Miss Jenny, who knew what Robert had been doing, did not turn around from the stove. "Wants to say good mornin to em, hunh?"

"I don't think so. I ain't figured out what he doin," the girl said. She was sitting at Miss Jenny's kitchen table. The dog, Bosco, was beside her and one of her shoes was off and her foot was rubbing the dog's back. "I was sleepin one time and this cold air hit me and I woke up. I couldn't get back to sleep cause I was cold, so I got up to see what window was open. Daddy wasn't in the bed and he wasn't in the kitchen or the bathroom. I thought he was downstairs warmin up the cab or somethin, but when I went to close the kitchen window, I could see him, peekin in the coop from the side with a flashlight. He scared me cause I didn't know who he was at first."

"You ask him what he was doin?"

"No. He wouldn't told me anyway, Miss Jenny. I just went back to my room and closed the door. If I'da asked him straight out, he would just make up something or say maybe I was dreamin. So now when I feel that cold air, I just look out to see if he in bed and then I shut my door."

Sometimes, when the weather allowed, the girl would sit on the roof plaiting her hair or reading the funny papers before school, or sit doing her homework in the late afternoon before going down to Miss Jenny's or out to play. She got pleasure just from the mere presence of the pigeons, a pleasure that was akin to what she felt when she followed her Aunt Thelma about her house, or when she jumped double dutch for so long she had to drop to the ground to catch her breath. In the morning, the new sun rising higher, she would place her chair at the roof's edge. She could look down at tail-wagging Bosco looking up at her, down through the thick rope fence around the roof that Robert had put up when she was a year old. She would hum or sing some nonsense song she'd made up, as the birds strutted and pecked and preened and flapped about in the bath water. And in the evening she watched the pigeons return home, first landing in the oak tree, then over to the coop's landing board. A few of them, generally the males, would settle on her book or on her head and shoulders. Stroking the breast of one, she would be rewarded with a cooing that was as pleasurable as music, and when the bird edged nearer so that it was less than an inch away, she smelled what seemed a mixture of dirt and rainy air and heard a heart that seemed to be hurling itself against the wall of the bird's breast.

She turned ten. She turned eleven.

In the early summer of 1960, there began a rumor among the children of Betsy Ann's age that the railroad people were planning to take all the land around Myrtle Street, perhaps up to L Street and down to H Street. This rumor—unlike the summer rumor among Washington's Negro children that Richard Nixon, if he were elected president, would make all the children go to school on Saturday from nine to twelve and cut their summer vacations in half—this rumor had a long life. And as the boys scraped their knuckles on the ground playing Poison, as the girls jumped rope until their bouncing plaits came loose, as the boys filled the neighborhood with the sounds of amateur hammering as they built skating trucks, as the girls made up talk for dolls with names they would one day bestow on their children, their conversations were flavored with lighthearted speculation about how far the railroad would go. When one child fell out with another, it became standard to try to hurt the other with the "true fact" that the railroad was going to take his or her home. "It's a true fact, they called my daddy at his work and told him we could stay, but yall gotta go. Yall gotta." And then the tormentor would stick out his or her tongue as far as it would go.

There were only two other girls on Myrtle Street who were comfortable around pigeons, and both of them moved away within a month of each other. One, LaDeidre Gordon, was a cousin of the brothers Carlos and Carleton. LaDeidre believed that the pigeons spoke a secret language among themselves, and that if she listened long enough and hard enough she could understand what they were saying and, ultimately, could communicate with them. For this, the world lovingly nicknamed her "Coo-Coo." After LaDeidre and the second girl moved, Betsy Ann would take the long way around to avoid passing where they had lived. And in those weeks she found a comfort of sorts at Thelma and Ralph's, for their house and everything else on the other side of North Capitol Street, the rumor went, would be spared by the railroad people.

Thelma Holley, her husband, and Ralph lived in a small house on L Street, Northwest, two doors from Mt. Airy Baptist Church, just across North Capitol Street. Thelma had suffered six miscarriages before God, as she put it, "took pity on my womb" and she had Ralph. But even then, she felt God had given with one hand and taken with the other, for the boy suffered with asthma. Thelma had waited until the seventh month of her pregnancy before she felt secure enough to begin loving him. And from then on, having given her heart, she thought nothing of giving him the world after he was born.

Ralph was the first colored child anyone knew to have his own television. In his house there had been three bedrooms, but Thelma persuaded her husband that an asthmatic child needed more space. Her husband knocked down the walls between the two back bedrooms and Ralph then had a bedroom that was nearly twice as large as that of his parents. And in that enormous room, she put as much of the world as she and her husband could afford.

Aside from watching Thelma, what Betsy Ann enjoyed most in that house was the electric train set, which dominated the center of Ralph's room. Over an area of more than four square feet, running on three levels, the trains moved through a marvelous and complete world Ralph's father had constructed. In that world, there were no simple plastic figures waving beside the tracks. Rather, it was populated with such people as a hand-carved woman of wood, in a floppy hat and gardener's outfit of real cloth, a woman who had nearly microscopic beads of sweat on her brow as she knelt down with concentration in her flower garden; several inches away, hand-carved schoolchildren romped about in the playground. One group of children was playing tag, and on one boy's face was absolute surprise as he was being tagged by a girl whose cheek was lightly smudged with dirt. A foot or so away, in a small field, two hand-carved farmers of wood were arguing, one with his finger in the other's face and the other with his fist heading toward the chest of the first. The world also included a goat-populated mountain with a tunnel large enough for the trains to go through, and a stream made of light blue glass. The stream covered several tiny fish of many colors which had almost invisible pins holding them suspended from the bottom up to give the impression that the fish were swimming.

What Thelma would not put in her son's enormous room, despite years of pleadings from him, was a dog, for she had learned in childhood that all animals had the power to suck the life out of asthmatics. "What you need with some ole puppy?" she would tease sometimes when he asked. "You'll be my little puppy dog forever and forever." And then she would grab and hug him until he wiggled out of her arms.

By the time he was six, the boy had learned that he could sometimes stay all day in the room and have Thelma minister to him by pretending he could barely breathe. He hoped that over time he could get out of her a promise for a dog. But his pretending to be at death's door only made her worry more, and by the middle of 1961, she had quit her part-time, GS-4 clerk-typist position at the Interior Department, because by then he was home two or three times a week.

Gradually, as more people moved out of Myrtle Street, the room became less attractive for Betsy Ann to visit, for Ralph grew difficult and would be mean and impatient with her and other visiting children. "You stupid, thas all! You just the stupidest person in the whole wide world," he would say to anyone who did not do what he wanted as fast as he wanted. Some children cried when he lit into them, and others wanted to fight him.

In time, the boy Betsy Ann once bullied disappeared altogether, and so when she took him assignments from school, she tried to stay only the amount of time necessary to show politeness. Then, too, the girl sensed that Thelma, with her increasing coldness, felt her son's problem was partly the result of visits from children who weren't altogether clean and from a niece who lived her life in what Thelma called "pigeon air" and "pigeon dust."

When he found out, the details of it did not matter to Robert Morgan: He only knew that his daughter had been somewhere doing bad while he was out doing the best he could. It didn't matter that it was Darlene Greenley who got Betsy Ann to go far away to 7th and Massachusetts and steal candy bars from Peoples Drug, candy she didn't even like, to go away the farthest she had ever been without her father or Miss Jenny or some other adult.

She knew Darlene, fast Darlene, from going to Ralph's ("You watch and see," Darlene would whisper to her, "I'm gonna make him my boyfriend"), but they had never gone off together before the Saturday that Thelma, for the last time, expelled all the children from her house. "Got any money?" Darlene said on the sidewalk after Thelma had thrown them out. She was stretching her bubble gum between her teeth and fingers and twirling the stuff the way she would a jump rope. When Betsy Ann shook her head, Darlene said she knew this Peoples that kinda like y'know gave children candy just for stopping by, and Betsy Ann believed her.

The assistant manager caught the girls before they were out of the candy and toy aisle and right away Darlene started to cry. "That didn't work the last time I told you to stay outa here," the woman said, taking the candy out of their dress pockets, "and it ain't gonna work now." Darlene handed her candy over, and Betsy Ann did the same. Darlene continued to cry. "Oh, just shut up, you little hussy, before I give you somethin to really cry about."

The assistant manager handed the candy to a clerk and was about to drag the girls into a back room when Etta O'Connell came up the aisle. "Yo daddy know you this far from home, Betsy Ann?" Miss Etta said, tapping Betsy Ann in the chest with her walking stick. She was, at ninety-two, the oldest person on Myrtle Street. It surprised Betsy Ann that she even knew her name, because the old woman, as far as Betsy Ann could remember, had never once spoken a word to her.

"You know these criminals?" the assistant manager said.

"Knowed this one since the day she born," Miss Etta said. The top of her stick had the head of an animal that no one had been able to identify, and the animal, perched a foot or so higher than Miss Etta's head, looked down at Betsy Ann with a better-you-than-me look. The old woman uncurled the fingers of the assistant manager's hand from around Betsy Ann's arm. "Child, whatcha done in this lady's sto?"

In the end, the assistant manager accepted Miss Etta's word that Betsy Ann would never again step foot in the store, that her father would know what she had done the minute he got home. Outside, standing at the corner, Miss Etta raised her stick and pointed to K Street. "You don't go straight home with no stoppin, I'll know," she said to Betsy Ann, and the girl sprinted off, never once looking back. Miss Etta and Darlene continued standing at the corner. "I think that old lady gave me the evil eye," Darlene told Betsy Ann the next time they met. "She done took all my good luck away. Yall got ghosties and shit on yo street." And thereafter, she avoided Betsy Ann.

Robert tanned her hide, as Miss Jenny called it, and then withheld her fifty-cents-a-week allowance for two months. For some three weeks he said very little to her, and when he did, it was almost always the same words: "You should be here, takin care a them damn birds! That's where you should be, not out there robbin somebody's grocery store!" She stopped correcting him about what kind of store it was after the first few times, because each time she did he would say, "Who the grownup here? You startin to sound like you runnin the show."

The candy episode killed something between them, and more and more he began checking up on her. He would show up at the house when she thought he was out working. She would come out of the coop with a bag of feed or the broom in her hand and a bird sitting on her head and she would find him standing at the kitchen window watching her. And several times a day he would call Miss Jenny. "Yo daddy wanna know if you up there," Miss Jenny would holler out her back window. Robert called the school so much that the principal herself wrote a letter telling him to stop.

He had been seeing Janet Gordon for two years, and about three or four times a month, they would take in a movie or a show at the Howard and then spend the night at a tourist home. But after the incident at Peoples, he saw Janet only once or twice a month. Then he began taking his daughter with him in the cab on most Saturdays. He tried to make it seem as if it were a good way to see the city.

Despite his reasons for taking her along, she enjoyed riding with him at first. She asked him for one of his old maps, and, with a blue crayon, she would chart the streets of Washington she had been on. Her father spent most of his time in Southeast and in

Anacostia, but sometimes he went as far away as Virginia and Maryland, and she charted streets in those places as well. She also enjoyed watching him at work, seeing a part of him she had never known: The way he made deliberate notations in his log. Patted his thigh in time to music in his head until he noticed her looking at him. Raised his hat any time a woman entered or left the cab.

But the more she realized that being with him was just his way of keeping his eye on her, the more the travels began losing something for her. When she used the bathroom at some filling station during her travels, she found him waiting for her outside the bathroom door, his nail-bitten hands down at his sides, his hat sitting perfectly on his head, and a look on his face that said Nothin. Nothin's wrong. Before the autumn of 1961 had settled in, she only wanted to be left at home, and because the incident at Peoples was far behind them, he allowed it. But he went back to the old ways of checking up on her. "Tell him yes," she would say when Miss Jenny called out her back window. "Tell him a million times yes, I'm home."

Little by little that spring and summer of 1961 Myrtle Street emptied of people, of families who had known no other place in their lives. Robert dreaded coming home each evening and seeing the signs of still another abandoned house free to be picked clean by rogues coming in from other neighborhoods: old curtains flapping out of screenless windows, the street with every kind of litter, windows so naked he could see clean through to the backyard. For the first time since he had been knowing her, Miss Jenny did not plant her garden that year, and that small patch of ground, with alien growth tall as a man, reverted to the wild.

He vowed that until he could find a good place for himself and his child, he would try to make life as normal as possible for her. He had never stopped rising each morning before Betsy Ann and going out to the coop to see what pigeons might have died in the night. And that was what he did that last morning in midautumn. He touched down onto the roof and discovered it had snowed during the night. A light, nuisance powder, not thick enough to cover the world completely and make things beautiful the way he liked. Though there was enough sunlight, he did not at first notice the tiny tracks, with even tinier, intermittent spots of blood, leading from the coop, across his roof and over to the roof of the house next door, the schoolteacher's house that had been empty for more than four months. He did, however, hear the birds squawking before he reached the coop, but this meant nothing to him, because one pigeon sound was more or less like another to him.

The night before there had been sixteen pigeons of various ages, but when he reached the coop, five were already dead and three were in their last moments, dragging themselves crazily about the floor or from side to side in the lower cubicles. Six of them he would kill with his own hands. Though there were bodies with holes so deep he saw white flesh, essence, it was the sight of dozens of detached feathers that caused his body to shake, because the scattered feathers, more than the wrecked bodies, spoke to him of helplessness. He closed his eyes as tight as he could and began to pray, and when he opened them, the morning was even brighter.

He looked back at the window, for something had whispered that Betsy Ann was watching. But he was alone and he went into the coop. He took up one dead bird whose left wing and legs had been chewed off; he shook the bird gently, and gently he blew into its face. He prayed once more. The pigeons that were able had moved to the farthest corner of the coop and they watched him, quivering. He knew now that the squawking was the sound of pain and it drove him out of their house.

When he saw the tracks, he realized immediately that they had been made by rats. He bent down, and some logical piece of his mind was surprised that there was a kind of orderliness to the trail, even with its ragged bits of pigeon life, a fragment of feather here, a spot of blood there.

He did not knock at Walter and Miss Jenny's door and wait to go in, as he had done each morning for some thirteen years. He found them at the breakfast table, and because they had been used to thirteen years of knocking, they looked up at him, amazed. Most of his words were garbled, but they followed him back upstairs. Betsy Ann had heard the noise of her father coming through the kitchen window and bounded down the stairs. She stood barefoot in the doorway leading from the front room to the kitchen, blinking herself awake.

"Go back to bed!" Robert shouted at her.

When she asked what was the matter, the three only told her to go back to bed. From the kitchen closet, Robert took two burlap sacks. Walter followed him out onto the roof and Betsy Ann made her way around Miss Jenny to the window.

Her father shouted at her to go to her room and Miss Jenny tried to grab her, but she managed to get onto the roof, where Walter held her. From inside, she had heard the squawking, a brand new sound for her. Even with Walter holding her, she got a few feet from the coop. And when Robert told her to go back inside, she gave him the only no of their lives. He looked but once at her and then began to wring the necks of the birds injured beyond all hope. Strangely, when he reached for them, the pigeons did not peck, did not resist. He placed all of the bodies in the sacks, and when he was all done and stood covered in blood and viscera and feathers, he began to cry.

Betsy Ann and her father noticed almost simultaneously that there were two birds completely unharmed, huddled in an upper corner of the coop. After he tied the mouths of the sacks, the two birds, as if of one mind, flew together to the landing board and from there to the oak tree in Miss Jenny's yard. Then they were gone. The girl buried her face in Walter's side, and when the old man saw that she was barefoot, he picked her up.

She missed them more than she ever thought she would. In school, her mind would wander and she would doodle so many pigeons on the backs of her hands and along her arms that teachers called her

Nasty, nasty girl. In the bathtub at night, she would cry to have to wash them off. And as she slept, missing them would take shape and lean down over her bed and wake her just enough to get her to understand a whisper that told her all over again how much she missed them. And when she raged in her sleep, Robert would come in and hold her until she returned to peace. He would sit in a chair beside her bed for the rest of the night, for her rages usually came about four in the morning and with the night so near morning, he saw no use in going back to bed.

She roamed the city at will, and Robert said nothing. She came to know the city so well that had she been blindfolded and taken to practically any place in Washington, even as far away as Anacostia or Georgetown, she could have taken off the blindfold and walked home without a moment's trouble. Her favorite place became the library park at Mount Vernon Square, the same park where Miss Jenny had first seen Robert and Clara together, across the street from the Peoples where Betsy Ann had been caught stealing. And there on some warm days Robert would find her, sitting on a bench, or lying on the grass, eyes to the sky.

For many weeks, well into winter, one of the birds that had not been harmed would come to the ledge of a back window of an abandoned house that faced K Street. The bird, a typical gray, would stand on the ledge and appear to look across the backyards in the direction of Betsy Ann's roof, now an empty space because the coop had been dismantled for use as firewood in Miss Jenny's kitchen stove. When the girl first noticed him and realized who he was, she said nothing, but after a few days, she began to call to him, beseech him to come to her. She came to the very edge of the roof, for now the rope fence was gone and nothing held her back. When the bird would not come to her, she cursed him. After as much as an hour it would fly away and return the next morning.

On what turned out to be the last day, a very cold morning in February, she stepped out onto the roof to drink the last of her cocoa. At first she sipped, then she took one final swallow, and in the time it took her to raise the cup to her lips and lower it, the pigeon had taken a step and dropped from the ledge. He caught an upwind that took him nearly as high as the tops of the empty K Street houses. He flew farther into Northeast, into the colors and sounds of the city's morning. She did nothing, aside from following him, with her eyes, with her heart, as far as she could.

THE FIRST DAY

On an otherwise unremarkable September morning, long before I learned to be ashamed of my mother, she takes my hand and we set off down New Jersey Avenue to begin my very first day of school. I am wearing a checkeredlike blue-and-green cotton dress, and scattered about these colors are bits of yellow and white and brown. My mother has uncharacteristically spent nearly an hour on my hair that morning, plaiting and replaiting so that now my scalp tingles. Whenever I turn my head quickly, my nose fills with the faint smell of Dixie Peach hair grease. The smell is somehow a soothing one now and I will reach for it time and time again before the morning ends. All the plaits, each with a blue barrette near the tip and each twisted into an uncommon sturdiness, will last until I go to bed that night, something that has never happened before. My stomach is full of milk and oatmeal sweetened with brown sugar. Like everything else I have on, my pale green slip and underwear are new, the underwear having come three to a plastic package with a little girl on the front who appears to be dancing. Behind my ears, my mother, to stop my whining, has dabbed the stingiest bit of her gardenia perfume, the last present my father gave her before he disappeared into memory. Because I cannot smell it, I have only her word that the perfume is there. I am also wearing yellow socks trimmed with thin lines of black and white around the tops. My shoes are my greatest joy, black patent-leather miracles, and when one is nicked at the toe later that morning in class, my heart will break.

I am carrying a pencil, a pencil sharpener, and a small ten-cent tablet with a black-and-white speckled cover. My mother does not believe that a girl in kindergarten needs such things, so I am taking them only because of my insistent whining and because they are presents from our neighbors, Mary Keith and Blondélle Harris. Miss Mary and Miss Blondelle are watching my two younger sisters until my mother returns. The women are as precious to me as my mother and sisters. Out playing one day, I have overheard an older child, speaking to another child, call Miss Mary and Miss Blondelle a word that is brand new to me. This is my mother: When I say the word in fun to one of my sisters, my mother slaps me across the mouth and the word is lost for years and years.

All the way down New Jersey Avenue, the sidewalks are teeming with children. In my neighborhood, I have many friends, but I see none of them as my mother and I walk. We cross New York Avenue, we cross Pierce Street, and we cross L and K, and still I see no one who knows my name. At I Street, between New Jersey Avenue and Third Street, we enter Seaton Elementary School, a timeworn, sad-faced building across the street from my mother's church, Mt. Carmel Baptist.

Just inside the front door, women out of the advertisements in *Ebony* are greeting other parents and children. The woman who greets us has pearls thick as jumbo marbles that come down almost to her navel, and she acts as if she had known me all my life, touching my shoulder, cupping her hand under my chin. She is enveloped in a perfume that I only know is not gardenia. When, in answer to her question, my mother tells her that we live at 1227 New Jersey Avenue, the woman first seems to be picturing in her head where we live. Then she shakes her head and says that we are at the wrong school, that we should be at Walker-Jones.

My mother shakes her head vigorously. "I want her to go here," my mother says. "If I'da wanted her someplace else, I'da took her there." The woman continues to act as if she has known me all my life, but she tells my mother that we live beyond the area that Seaton serves. My mother is not convinced and for several more minutes she questions the woman about why I cannot attend Seaton. For as many Sundays as I can remember, perhaps even Sundays when I was in her womb, my mother has pointed across I Street to Seaton as we come and go to Mt. Carmel. "You gonna go there and learn about the whole world." But one of the guardians of that place is saying no, and no again. I am learning this about my mother: The higher up on the scale of respectability a person is—and teachers are rather high up in her eyes—the less she is liable to let them push her around. But finally, I see in her eyes the closing gate, and she takes my hand and we leave the building. On the steps, she stops as people move past us on either side.

"Mama, I can't go to school?"

She says nothing at first, then takes my hand again and we are down the steps quickly and nearing New Jersey Avenue before I can blink. This is my mother: She says, "One monkey don't stop no show."

Walker-Jones is a larger, newer school and I immediately like it because of that. But it is not across the street from my mother's church, her rock, one of her connections to God, and I sense her doubts as she absently rubs her thumb over the back of her hand. We find our way to the crowded auditorium where gray metal chairs are set up in the middle of the room. Along the wall to the left are tables and other chairs. Every chair seems occupied by a child or adult. Somewhere in the room a child is crying, a cry that rises above the buzz-talk of so many people. Strewn about the floor are dozens and dozens of pieces of white paper, and people are walking over them without any thought of picking them up. And seeing this lack of concern, I am all of a sudden afraid.

"Is this where they register for school?" my mother asks a woman at one of the tables.

The woman looks up slowly as if she has heard this question once too often. She nods. She is tiny, almost as small as the girl standing beside her. The woman's hair is set in a mass of curlers and all of those curlers are made of paper money, here a dollar bill, there a five-dollar bill. The girl's hair is arrayed in curls, but some of them are beginning to droop and this makes me happy. On the table beside the woman's pocketbook is a large notebook, worthy of someone in high school, and looking at me looking at the notebook, the girl places her hand possessively on it. In her other hand she holds several pencils with thick crowns of additional erasers.

"These the forms you gotta use?" my mother asks the woman, picking up a few pieces of the paper from the table. "Is this what you have to fill out?"

The woman tells her yes, but that she need fill out only one.

"I see," my mother says, looking about the room. Then: "Would you help me with this form? That is, if you don't mind."

The woman asks my mother what she means.

"This form. Would you mind helpin me fill it out?"

The woman still seems not to understand.

"I can't read it. I don't know how to read or write, and I'm askin you to help me." My mother looks at me, then looks away. I know almost all of her looks, but this one is brand new to me. "Would you help me, then?"

The woman says Why sure, and suddenly she appears happier, so much more satisfied with everything. She finishes the form for her daughter and my mother and I step aside to wait for her. We find two chairs nearby and sit. My mother is now diseased, according to the girl's eyes, and until the moment her mother takes her and the form to the front of the auditorium, the girl never stops looking at my mother. I stare back at her. "Don't stare," my mother says to me. "You know better than that."

Another woman out of the *Ebony* ads takes the woman's child away. Now, the woman says upon returning, let's see what we can do for you two.

My mother answers the questions the woman reads off the form. They start with my last name, and then on to the first and middle names. This is school, I think. This is going to school. My mother slowly enunciates each word of my name. This is my mother: As the questions go on, she takes from her pocketbook document after document, as if they will support my right to attend school, as if she has been saving them up for just this moment. Indeed, she takes out more papers than I have ever seen her do in other places: my birth certificate, my baptismal record, a doctor's letter concerning my bout with chicken pox, rent receipts, records of immunization, a letter about our public assistance payments, even her marriage license—every single paper that has anything even remotely to do with my five-year-old life. Few of the papers are needed here, but it does not matter and my mother continues to pull out the documents with the purposefulness of a magician pulling out a long string of scarves. She has learned that money is the beginning and end of everything in this world, and when the woman finishes, my mother offers her fifty cents, and the woman accepts it without hesitation. My mother and I are just about the last parent and child in the room.

My mother presents the form to a woman sitting in front of the stage, and the woman looks at it and writes something on a white card, which she gives to my mother. Before long, the woman who has taken the girl with the drooping curls appears from behind us, speaks to the sitting woman, and introduces herself to my mother and me. She's to be my teacher, she tells my mother. My mother stares.

We go into the hall, where my mother kneels down to me. Her lips are quivering. "I'll be back to pick you up at twelve o'clock. I don't want you to go nowhere. You just wait right here. And listen to every word she say." I touch her lips and press them together. It is an old, old game between us. She puts my hand down at my side, which is not part of the game. She stands and looks a second at the teacher, then she turns and walks away. I see where she has darned one of her socks the night before. Her shoes make loud sounds in the hall. She passes through the doors and I can still hear the loud sounds of her shoes. And even when the teacher turns me toward the classrooms and I hear what must be the singing and talking of all the children in the world, I can still hear my mother's footsteps above it all.

THE NIGHT RHONDA FERGUSON WAS KILLED

Cassandra G. Lewis, the girl the boys called Tank and Mack Truck behind her back, sat on that low brick wall outside Cardozo High School, eating two-year-old Christmas candy when she wasn't smoking Chesterfields. She'd been there since after her lunch period, and now it was nearing the end of the seventh period and the girl was getting bored because the teacher hadn't come out to get popped. At Cassandra's feet on the sidewalk was a small pile of cigarette butts and match stems, and behind her, on the grass on the other side of the wall, was a pile of candy wrappers a wind coming up 13th Street was now blowing here and there.

She had been waiting for her homeroom teacher to look out the window on the second floor and see her wasting her life away on the wall. She'd been hoping the teacher would come out and, as the woman had done that morning in the second-period English class Cassandra had with her, bark more shit in her face. Potential,

Cassandra had thought all the time she had been eating and smoking on the wall, I'll show her all the goddamn potential in the world! She had walked out before the end of the second period and come straight down to the wall, itching for the chance to knock the teacher on her bony ass. But now all the candy and cigarettes were beginning to turn her stomach and she wanted only to be somewhere else.

Parked across Clifton Street in front of her was a green 1957 Hollywood Hudson, a piece of shit that belonged to her brother-in-law, who, in his drunken moments, often called the car "my old mule." She had spent last night—and the six nights before that—in her sister and brother-in-law's apartment on Kenyon Street, the first time in a month or so she had slept a week straight in the same place. But that morning her brother-in-law had gotten up on the wrong side of the bed and picked a fight with her because she had eaten five eggs and four biscuits. After he'd gone to work and after her sister had taken the kids to the baby-sitter's before going to work herself, Cassandra had stolen the old mule to get even. She would have popped her brother-in-law before he left, as she had done a year ago, but she thought it would hurt her sister and nieces too much to see Daddy laid out cold again on the kitchen floor.

She stood up now and brushed ashes from her blouse and pants. The school bell rang, announcing the end of the seventh period. She gave one final look to the corner window on the second floor. She knew the bitch had seen her out there on the wall, but just didn't have the heart to come out. She'd made the death mistake of thinking she and Miss Bartlett were getting along fine, the way the teacher had always seemed to get along with the other girls. Miss Bartlett had even begun to include her in that small group of girls she invited to her apartment some evenings for meals and girl talk. It was there, over several weeks beginning in September, among twelve or so girls Cassandra wouldn't have given a shit about before, that she had begun to share, sitting on that brown carpet that was thicker than some beds she'd known. Among all those books and pictures of the teacher's smiling relatives, she'd said things only her sister and Rhonda Ferguson knew about.

But lately, for no reason at all, the teacher seemed to be in her face all the time, and that morning the teacher had made the death mistake of bringing up Cassandra's father and mother. Had said that her parents must be turning over in their graves to know the way their child was living, going from pillar to post with no real home. Had said all that and more in front of the dick people who couldn't stand Cassandra and were just waiting to hear some real personal shit about her life so they could talk behind her back. Then, like putting her personal business in the street wasn't enough, the teacher had gone into all that other stuff about potential and blah-blah-blah and then, after that, some more blah-blah-blah.

She had made up her mind to get in the car and take off for God knew where when someone honked and she saw Rhonda Ferguson and Rhonda's father, waiting at the light at 13th and Clifton. The car turned when the light changed and pulled up in front of her. Rhonda, in the passenger seat, waved her over. Students were coming out of school and they passed behind Cassandra leaning in the car window.

"I hope your bein out here so soon don't mean you played hooky," Rhonda said. "Hi you doin?"

"Fine. Goin to a party all dressed up like that?" Cassandra said.

Rhonda smiled and grabbed Cassandra's arm eagerly. "You haven't been around, or you'd know: I think I'm going to sign the contract today. We got a meetin downtown with the people from the record company. I think this is it," she said, crossing her fingers. "I haven't been able to think straight. I stayed home playin with Alice all day."

Rhonda's father leaned across the seat. "Hi you doin, baby girl? We looked for you last night. Been lookin for you every night this week." He had a large stomach and his stomach was touching the bottom of the steering wheel.

"I been stayin with my sister, Daddy Ferguson," she said.

Cassandra winked at Rhonda and then said, once again, "When you get out there makin all them millions, you won't forget me, willya?"

"Why do you always keep talkin that way, girl? You comin with me. Everybody's comin with me." She squeezed Cassandra's hand. "I'd sooner forget Alice or Jeffrey than you. And you know I never lie to you."

Cassandra nodded, but there was nothing behind the nod. She carried in her pocket, each wrapped in tinfoil, articles about Rhonda published in the *Afro* and the *Evening Star*. CARDOZO H.S. SINGER ON THE RISE, the *Star* headline said. FAMILY IS THE SECRET TO SINGER'S SUCCESS, the *Afro* headline said. And in the photograph accompanying that story, Cassandra was sitting on the couch beside Rhonda's youngest brother, who sat next to Rhonda. Rhonda was in the middle, holding her daughter Alice on her lap. The child was the only person in the picture who did not look directly into the camera. On the other side of Rhonda was her mother, and behind Rhonda were two older brothers and her father, who peered out through thick glasses. Beside Mr. Ferguson and directly behind Rhonda was Jeffrey Stanford, the father of Rhonda's child. His hand was resting on Rhonda's shoulder.

"But if you're gonna take care of my business for me," Rhonda said, "you're gonna to have to get a education. How will I know if they cheatin me if you don't know more than they know?"

"Thas right, baby girl," her father said to Cassandra. He was holding the steering wheel in the enthusiastic way a small child would, as if he were playing at driving the car. "We best get on now, so we won't be late. But you go on by the house. Mabel cookin up a mess of fish and waitin for you. I wanna see you at the house when I get back."

Rhonda pulled Cassandra's face down and kissed her cheek. The sidewalk was now full of kids. Rhonda and her father drove down Clifton Street, and all along the way to 11th Street, students, noticing Rhonda, would greet her. Some of them sang bits of the songs she was known for. Some of them danced.

Cassandra decided right then to make nice and return her brother-in-law's car. But after she started it up, the car would only cough and shake and didn't seem to want to move. After trying several times to get it going, she thought she'd give it time to make up its mind about going. She passed the time listening to radio music that came out mostly static because she had deliberately damaged the radio five months ago after an argument with her brother-in-law. Toward three thirty, as she was counting her cigarettes, Melanie Cartwright, on her way home, tapped on the roof. Melanie was a friendly sort who seemed to have a new boyfriend, a new "truest love," every other month. She was good for cigarettes, but she only smoked Viceroys.

"Missed you in school today," Melanie said. She had her notebook and two books in her arms and her pocketbook was hanging from her shoulder from a long strap. She was a second cousin of Cassandra's brother-in-law, and at the wedding of Cassandra's sister, Melanie and another girl had caught the bouquet together and nearly killed each other over who it belonged to.

"Wasn't up for school today," Cassandra said. She lit up a Chesterfield.

Melanie was with Anita Hughes, a quiet girl Cassandra had met at Miss Barlett's apartment. Cassandra knew next to nothing about Anita, but she would forever remember the look on Anita's face when Anita told the story one evening of how she had trembled and sung for her grandfather one final time at his funeral.

"I see you got Willie's car again," Melanie said, laughing. "I bet he don't know you got it." Melanie and Anita stood in the street at the driver's window, and whenever a car passed behind them, they leaned close to the car.

Cassandra blew out smoke and sucked her teeth. "Willie always know when I got his car."

"Listen," Melanie said, "you wanna make some money? You know Gladys Harper? She lookin for someone to take her to her father's in Anacostia."

Cassandra thought a moment. "I don't know," she said. "She gonna pay some chump change or real money?"

"I think she said her mother'll pay twenty dollars. She gotta take some things over there and they figure it's cheaper than sendin Gladys alone by cab."

Anita said that Gladys was still standing in front of Cardozo, and Melanie stepped into the middle of the street and whistled her over. Gladys explained that her mother wanted a few small boxes of stuff taken to Gladys's father in Anacostia. Cassandra didn't know Gladys at all, except to see her now and again passing in the school's halls. Taking boxes from the mother to the father all the way in Anacostia seemed strange to Cassandra, but being an orphan set adrift in the world she had learned that unless it could involve a death mistake, it was best to ask as few questions as possible. And besides, twenty bucks was twenty bucks. Anita and Melanie said they wouldn't mind coming along: Melanie's boyfriend had football practice, and Friday evenings Anita's parents allowed her a bit more leeway than they did on school nights.

"Will this thing hold up down there and back?" Gladys said of the Hudson, looking at it from front to back and up and down. "I don't want to get stuck out there with my gotdamn father and his bitch whore."

"It'll do what I tell it," Cassandra said, thinking she might get to see a fight. She and Gladys waited while Anita and Melanie took their books home, a short distance away. When they returned, Cassandra started up the car without any trouble and the four drove down Clifton Street to Gladys's house on 12th Street. The house and the yard were uncommonly immaculate. Such houses made Cassandra nervous, because she associated them with owners who, without warning, smacked the hands of visiting children reaching out with curiosity to touch something.

Mildred Harper set the four girls at her kitchen table and fed them a dinner of reheated fried chicken, string beans, potato salad, and rolls. "My husband and I," she said to Cassandra as she set out the food, "are separated. My son would take him the things, but he's out of town right now, and I can't get any of the other children to take him the stuff. He's not well enough to come get them." They sounded like words she had already said a thousand times, had learned to say to get it all out and over with. Anita and Melanie must have heard it before, because they didn't seem surprised at what the mother was saying. After she had set out the food and told them to help themselves, Mildred Harper gave Cassandra a twenty-dollar bill and three dollars for gas and disappeared into another part of the house.

It was a pleasant Friday evening in early November. The girls set off with an hour or so of the day's light remaining, and that light came through the last of the autumn leaves still clinging to the trees. The birds, somewhere among those leaves and among the nooks and crannies of buildings, were making a racket as they bedded down. Cassandra felt good, because her stomach was full and she had a little piece of change in her pocket and she had a bed waiting that night at Rhonda's. At Elson's at 11th and T she filled up the gas tank. They continued on down 11th Street. As usual when she drove, Cassandra leaned forward, her arms folded over the top of the steering wheel, the cigarette in her mouth bouncing up and down whenever she said anything. Gladys sat in the back, beside Anita, and in her lap was a small box of family photographs, the ones Mildred Harper could bear to part with. In the car's trunk were two larger boxes, containing the last of her father's stuff he had left at the house. Melanie, beside Cassandra, was trying to get a decent station on the radio.

"Why don't you leave it alone," Cassandra said to her. "You want some music, make your own damn music."

"I bet not even a hearse radio sound this bad," Melanie said, and she began to sing "My Guy."

"Sing it on. Sing it on," Cassandra said. "I remember the first time I heard Rhonda sing that."

"At that talent show, right?" Anita said.

"Right," Cassandra said. "People started standin up and shit and cheerin and everything. I felt sorry for the other people who had to come on after her, cause nobody wanted to hear em. This one girl came on and she was tryin to play the guitar and people started callin for Rhonda, and this girl just gave up and left."

"I paid my money and didn't get a good seat," Melanie said. She had turned the radio volume down, but she continued trying to get a clear station. "Yall better get all the lookin you can at Rhonda now, cause when she gets famous, you won't be able to get within a hundred feet of her. She won't even remember your name."

"You don't know what you talkin about, girl," Cassandra said. "Rhonda's gonna stay the same. I know her. You don't even know her all that well."

"They all change, and Rhonda's gonna change the most. Move out to Georgetown or Chevy Chase, if she still livin round here, and be with all them white people."

"Oh, fuck you, Melanie!" Cassandra said.

"Fuck you back, Cassandra. I gotta right to say what I think."

"Not in my car, and not when you don't know what you talkin about. And if you don't like it, you can get out and walk your sorry ass back home."

Melanie became quiet.

"Sing another song, Melanie," Anita said. "Sing 'My Guy' again."

"No, thas all right," Melanie pouted, turning off the radio and folding her arms.

"She sound like a gotdamn cat anyway," Cassandra said.

The birds in their trees continued to make a racket as they turned off 11th onto P Street. Just before 9th, they passed a group moving boxes and furniture into an apartment building across from Shiloh Baptist.

At the light at 9th, Gladys, looking back, asked if Cassandra could back up. "I think thas Joyce and Pearl," she said. Cassandra backed up until she was in front of the pickup with a used couch in it. "Hey! Hey!" Gladys shouted to a man with a load of boxes.

"That Joyce Moses in there?" The man nodded, and Cassandra parked the Hudson behind the truck.

Upstairs, in the front apartment on the second floor, they found Joyce Moses and her friend Pearl Guthrie, heads in kerchiefs, standing in the middle of a nearly empty living room lit by one naked light bulb. Practically everyone at Cardozo knew them—two pregnant girls who had dropped out of school to pool their church mice resources in an effort to make the best head start for themselves and their babies.

"Where the damn party?" Gladys asked.

"Wherever it is, you ain't invited," Pearl said, and the two embraced. Cassandra embraced Joyce, took Joyce's blouse in two fingers, shook it and wanted to know why she wasn't showing at two months "like all the other cows." Melanie, after her hellos, went snooping in all the rooms of the apartment. Anita knew only Pearl and held back, standing in the doorway.

The movers were Joyce's father and Pearl's father and their relatives and friends. They were finishing up with the couch. Pearl, still with one arm around Gladys, pointed to the place where she and Joyce wanted the couch, and the men set it in place. The room still looked empty. "We gonna make the rounds of Goodwill and Salvation Army tomorrow," Pearl said, seeing that Gladys noticed how empty the room was.

"If everything where yall want it," Joyce's father said, "I'd best be gettin back." He took his daughter in his arms and he kissed her forehead.

"Tell Mama I'll try to call her tomorrow," Joyce said. "Tell her I hope she feelin better soon."

"She'll be feelin better tomorrow just before you call. You got my word on that," her father said.

Pearl's father gave her some money and embraced her. Then, as if embarrassed with others about, he withdrew and simply held her elbow. Though the room was full of people, there were no sounds except the movement of feet and the noise from outside. The other men had already gone downstairs, and Joyce's father and Pearl's father soon followed them. Joyce and Pearl went to the curtainless window to watch them go away. For three or four minutes, as if they had completely forgotten that they had visitors, they stood watching at the window. Then Pearl began to cry and Joyce, once more, told her that it would be all right. "Hush," she said. "Hush now."

"Where the hell was them sorry men a theirs?" Cassandra wanted to know when the four were back in the car. "Where the hell was Rufus?"

"I know he was at football practice the other day, cause Dwayne told me he was," Melanie said. "And nobody in the world know where Kelvin at."

"I feel like shootin both a them," Gladys said.

"I'm all for that," Cassandra said, honking at the slow driver in front of her, "cept for that damn it-take-two-to-tango rule."

The sun had set by the time they reached 8th and H streets Northeast, and after they had crossed East Capitol Street, Cassandra pulled over to ask directions to Anacostia of a young man.

"Oh, he was sooo cute," Melanie said, when they were on their way again. "But he not as cute as Dwayne."

"Thas all you ever think about is some dick," Cassandra said. Anita and Gladys laughed.

"I'll have you know me and Dwayne are engaged," Melanie said.

"Anita knows how to sing. She got a good voice," Gladys said, wanting something to take the image of her friends standing at the window out of her mind.

"I don't sing all that well," Anita said. "I just sing in the choir."

"Oh, oh. Better cut out all that cussin, ladies," Cassandra said. "We got one of them choir girls in the car. Where your Bible, honey?"

"I just sing in the choir," Anita said again. "Nobody sings like Rhonda."

"You got that right, sugar," Cassandra said. "And for your in-

formation, Melanie, Rhonda went down to sign some contracts today and she already offered me a job with her. Any kind of job I
want. Put that in your pipe and smoke it."

"She gonna quit school?" Anita said.

"You kiddin? Her father wouldn't let her do that in a million
years, singin contract or no contract."

Despite the heavy traffic of people going home from work, they
found Gladys's father without much trouble. He lived in a small
house on Maple View Place, down the road from St. Elizabeths and
not far from Curtis Brothers furniture store. Melanie wanted to
stop at the store to see the giant chair they had in the parking lot,
but Cassandra told her to get a good look as they drove by because
that was as close as Melanie was going to get.

Gladys was out of the car as soon as they stopped and refused anyone's help with the boxes. She put the small box of pictures under her
arm as she carried the larger boxes to the front porch. The woman her
father lived with opened the door and helped her take in the boxes,
then the woman closed the door. The other girls got out of the car.
Melanie, seeing three young men harmonizing up the street, sauntered up to them, and Cassandra and Anita sat on the hood of the car,
with Cassandra smoking a Chesterfield and Anita thinking that this
was the first time in her life she was seeing Anacostia.

"My grandfather used to say people in Anacostia still lived with
chickens and cows," Anita said after a while.

"Shows you how much you know: They don't allow em to do
that anymore," Cassandra said. She flicked the cigarette butt into
Gladys's father's yard. "Even if they did, it wouldn't tell you
much—Anacostia people the best people I ever met in the whole
world, chickens or no chickens." She counted how many cigarettes
she had in the pack and decided to hold off on the next smoke. "My
mama and daddy came from Anacostia, then they had to go cross
the fuckin river to live and get killed in some car crash." She
changed her mind and lit up another Chesterfield, blew out the
match, and flicked it into the yard.

Gladys came out of the house, followed by her father. Anita was the only one of the other girls who had ever seen him, and as he walked down to the gate she could see that he was weaker and weighed less than she remembered. At the gate he took his daughter in his arms and kissed her cheek twice, then twice more. The woman he lived with stood in the doorway, her arms crossed and a sweater around her shoulders.

Glady's father was saying something to her that the two girls could not hear, then, after a few moments, his daughter told him they had to go.

"You call me now, you hear?" her father said. Gladys nodded, but Anita could see that the nod had no truth in it.

Cassandra had to go get Melanie, who was talking under a street lamp with a boy who was standing extremely close to her.

"We goin in the next gotdamn second," Cassandra said, "with or without you, Miss Engaged."

"Whew," Melanie said after everyone was in the car, "I'm glad you got me outta there. The singin was nice and he was cute, but he had the worse breath I ever smelled."

Gladys was looking back at her father, who stood holding the gate with one hand and waving with the other.

"Must be all them cows and chickens they live with, huh, Choir Girl?" Cassandra said to Anita.

"I don't know, Cassandra," Anita said. "But I do know that my name ain't Choir Girl."

"Ohhh. Ohh," Cassandra said. "Excuse me very very much."

"I felt like slappin that little bitch into next week," Gladys said. Though they were many blocks from her father, she continued looking back. "The whole time I was standin there I kept askin myself: What does this little bitch have that my mother doesn't have? And she was treatin my father like he didn't have a brain in his body. 'Honey, you chilly? Honey, you wanna put on your sweater? Honey, give her some money fore she go. Honey, make sure you give her our phone number. . . .' " She spewed out the words, as if it were a matter of talking or exploding.

"What we need is a party," Melanie said. "Help pick us up."

"Thas what you always seem to need," Cassandra said.

Melanie ignored her and turned around in the seat to speak to Anita and Gladys. "This guy told me about a party on F Street in Northeast." She looked out her window to see where they were. "Twelve oh nine F Street."

"Nine one two," Cassandra said.

"What?" Melanie said.

"You sure he didn't say nine one two F Street? Or nine oh one two? One two nine F Street? Or maybe E Street, or C Street?" Cassandra said. "You flicted bitch, you tryin to get us lost, looking for some damn party."

Melanie deflated and sat back in her seat.

"Why not?" Gladys said. "Why don't we see if it was twelve oh nine, Cassandra. We ain't got nothin else better to do. Besides, we still drivin on gas my mother paid for."

"Sure, why not?" Anita said.

Melanie perked up and Cassandra shrugged her shoulders, saying, "If we get lost, it ain't my damn fault." She patted the dashboard for good luck and turned off 8th Southeast onto C Street. But they had no sooner crossed East Capitol when Cassandra began to feel the car hesitate, and just beyond D Street it stopped after Cassandra managed to pull it to the curb. She got out, rocked the trunk a few seconds, and cursed it in a voice passersby could not hear. She was in a different country, and she thought the laws might not be the same for her here.

It was a fairly quiet street, with a few older people sitting on their porches and children playing on either side of the street. Most of the noise was coming from a house across the street where there seemed to be a party going on. A hi-fi was bouncing noise off houses. In front of the house with the hi-fi, a fellow was under the hood of a car and a small boy was beside him shining two flashlights into the maw. The fellow came out of the car, wiped his hands on a rag he pulled from his back pocket. He looked at Cassandra and her car as if deciding what to do, and then came toward her, looking back once or twice to the little boy. He was an awesomely muscled young man no more than eighteen. The muscles looked even more dramatic as the street lamp behind first silhouetted him, then gave way to the brightness of a street lamp on Cassandra's side of the street.

"Look like you got trouble," he said to Cassandra, who had opened the hood with Anita's help. He smelled like the world of dirt and oily metal and rubber Cassandra found under the hoods of all cars. The small boy had followed the guy, but he seemed interested only in shining the flashlights up and down the street, first on this house, then another.

The hi-fi music had pulled Melanie out of the car toward the house, and Gladys followed her.

"I'm Wesley," the guy said to Cassandra. "You want me to see what I can do with it?" He was country, stone Bama.

"Oh, no. Not really. We just waitin for the midnight train to come by."

"What?" Wesley said. He had a funny booklike jaw, square and unreal, and Cassandra had the urge to stroke it.

"She means we'd appreciate any help you can give us," Anita said.

The little boy stepped confidently up to the car and shone the flashlights under the hood. Wesley bent down into the car. Anita followed Melanie and Gladys into the house. Several times Wesley went back across the street to get tools, and Cassandra tried not to let him or the boy or the people on their porches see how much pleasure it gave her to see him walk. He had a very tiny behind that she felt she could cup in both her hands. He seemed entirely comfortable with himself, but was far from being a showoff, and this made him even more endearing. Is this me? she asked herself as she watched him walk. She wanted to believe that the muscles were the result of a life of hard work, not a life in a gym with dozens of other men and tons of dumbbells. "I'll hold them," she said to the little boy after a time and took the flashlights. The boy resisted until Wesley told him it was all right. Cassandra leaned into the car beside Wesley and made certain their thighs were touching.

Before long, Wesley had the car running again, and Cassandra cursed it silently.

"It'll take you home, lady," Wesley said, "but I wouldn't trust it after that. A beautiful thing if you take care of it."

"What do I owe you, Mississippi?" Cassandra said, handing the flashlights back to the boy. "I hope it ain't much, cause I'm just a poor widow woman."

Wesley raised his eyebrows, then shook his head, no charge. "No one in this city talks straight, do they?" he said. "You live round here?" The little boy had stepped into the street and was again shining the lights about the houses.

"No. I live in Northwest. Across town. That straight enough for you?"

He nodded. "Bob, get out the street." And to Cassandra, "Thas my cousin. I live with him and his family over there"—he pointed to the hosue with the music—"my uncle and everybody. Came up from South Carolina to learn some things." The boy, after a few moments, got in the back seat of Cassandra's car and at first pretended to fall asleep, then he climbed over the front seat and sat behind the wheel. "You go to movies, lady? Go to picture shows?"

"Every one I can," Cassandra said.

He took a pencil and piece of paper from his back pocket. "Well, if you give me your phone number, I'll call you sooner than you can say your name. If you don't mind. If your people don't mind."

As she wrote her sister's telephone number down, there was a scream from the house with the music. When Cassandra and Wesley reached the porch, Melanie, crying, was coming out of the house with her blouse torn, Anita and Gladys on either side of her.

"What happened!" Cassandra yelled. "What the fuck happened!"

"That guy got rough with me," Melanie managed to say.

"Who?" Cassandra said. "Who was it?"

A young man followed them out of the house. "It was all a misunderstandin," he said.

"Was it you, you sonofabitch!" Cassandra grabbed his throat and squeezed. "You try to rape my friend?" The guy was able only to shake his head before Wesley took her arm, held it. "Lady, please don't do that. He my cousin," Wesley said.

"I don't give three fucks who he is!" Cassandra said. She began to struggle, but he held both her arms and the more he held her, the calmer she became. Whatever had been in his eyes before Melanie screamed was there no more and she would have given her arms to have it back.

"It wasn't him. It was Roger," a girl said from inside. "He been drinkin too much."

"Yeah," Melanie said, "it was that Roger. He got rough. Too rough."

Wesley called for Roger to come explain himself, but someone said Roger had run out the back door. The three girls helped Melanie into the car. Wesley asked her if she needed anything and she shook her head. Then, all the while looking at Cassandra, he stood with his hands in his back pockets beside the little boy as Cassandra started up the car, which purred into life on the first try. They did not say good-bye.

"That was a close call. Another lesson learned," Melanie said after they had gone a few blocks. Anita had given her her sweater and Melanie was buttoning it. "This blouse is ruined, though. He'd be a real nice guy if he wasn't so rough. Should learn to treat a woman like a lady. But he was cute."

"You know," Cassandra said, "I'm fuckin tired of all your talk about somebody bein cute all the time. You gettin on my nerves with that shit! You sound like a damn cuckoo clock with just one tune!" For the next two blocks or so she pounded on the horn and rocked her head in exasperation. "You know how many girls pull down their panties and give up the booty just cause some boy is cute! Just cause some boy has some shitty good hair! Just cause somebody has the best rap in the whole damn world! And you, you the leader of them all, Melanie!" Melanie slumped back in her seat.

"Thas why nothin ain't right no more," Cassandra continued, "cause some dumb bitch like you think this dick-head and that dick-head is so cute! Get some brains, girl! I get so sick and tired of you!"

"I didn't mean anything by it, Cassandra."

"That's your trouble: You never mean anything by it." She turned to look at Melanie. "And if you had any sense, you'd dump that dick-head Dwayne. He's the dumbest thing in the world, but he playin you for eighty-nine kinds of fool. But you won't see that cause he's sooooo cute."

"Stop the car," Melanie said calmly. "Just stop the car right now. I wanna get out." She began jerking on the door handle. "Stop the car, I said!"

"Don't tell me what to do! Nobody tells me what to do!"

"I really wanna get out, Cassandra," Melanie said, moving the handle up and down. "Why do you hate me so much? What have I ever done to you in my whole life to make you hate me so much?" She began to cry. "What harm did I ever do you, thas what I wanna know. Why you against me just because I'm in love with Dwayne? What bad thing I ever did to you in my whole life, Cassandra?"

Melanie got the door open and Cassandra braked. Melanie stumbled out into the street and made her way to the sidewalk. Anita and Gladys followed her. Melanie, first thinking it was Cassandra, pushed Gladys when she put her arm around her shoulders. Anita walked on her other side. Cassandra followed them slowly in the car as the three went down 8th Street. She could not hear what they were saying, but she could see Melanie shaking her head no no no.

At 8th and H streets, the girls stopped and Cassandra, after waiting for the light, turned the car around and parked at the corner, ignoring the NO PARKING sign. Anita, walking backward to face Melanie, held her by the shoulders, and she and Gladys said things that made Melanie look Anita directly in the eye. Little by little Melanie calmed down and stopped crying. She nodded her head once, but Cassandra could see that it was not the yes to get back in the car. She watched them go into the Mile Long at the corner and saw them order sodas and stand at the counter and drink them.

Cassandra wanted a cigarette, but she hadn't the will to open the glove compartment and pull one from the pack. Across 8th Street a drunk was dancing with the wobbliness of a puppet. Just as he seemed about to fall, his legs collapsing, he would straighten himself and dance around the two little boys who were watching him, then his legs would give out again and the boys would reach out to catch him. The boys' mother, waiting for a bus, ignored the drunk. Cassandra watched the girls drink the sodas as if they had all the rest of their lives to do it. Gradually, Melanie began to smile, but she continued to hold her soda with both hands. Melanie did not seem to be saying anything, only listening to what the other two said. Serve the bitches right if I take off and leave them here. But Cassandra did not leave, and when the bus came and took the mother and her boys away, she began to worry that the drunk would spot her and come over and dance and make her the center of attention.

Anita was the first to return to the car. "I thought you might have left us," she said, handing Cassandra a soda.

"It never crossed my mind to do that," Cassandra said. She set the soda between her legs and did not open it.

"Sure it did," Anita said. "You were thinkin about what our faces would look like when we got out here and found we didn't have a ride back to Northwest." She sat facing Cassandra, her left arm over the back of the seat. "You sat here thinkin how good it would feel to ride off and leave us stranded. You know how I know? Cause I woulda been thinkin the same thing." She opened the glove compartment and took a cigarette from the pack, stuck it in Cassandra's mouth, and lit the cigarette. "Probably dyin for one a these, I bet." Cassandra inhaled and blew smoke out of the side of her mouth. Cassandra looked directly ahead, and then, after she had inhaled again, she closed her eyes with relief. Anita unwrapped a straw and stuck it through the plastic top of the soda cup.

In a few minutes, Melanie got in the back with Gladys. No one said anything until they were well out of Northeast. Gladys asked Melanie to sing something, but Melanie said she wasn't in the mood for no song.

"Well, what about you, Anita?" Gladys said. "What you feel like hearin, Melanie? 'My Guy'?" Melanie said nothing. "What about you, Cassandra? What happened to the party we was supposed to have? Anita, how bout 'Will You Still Love Me'?"

"It's called 'Will You Love Me Tomorrow.' " Cassandra said.

"I hear the money going down in the jukebox," Anita said. "Kerchink, ker-chink." Anita sang:

> *Tonight you're mine completely;*
> *You give your love so sweetly.*

"I'd pay a quarter for that," Gladys said.
Anita sang:

> *Tonight the light of love is in your eyes,*
> *But will you love me tomorrow?*

"I'd pay a hundred bucks," Cassandra said and honked the horn.
Anita sang:

> *Tonight with words unspoken*
> *you say that I'm the only one*
> *But will my heart be broken*
> *when the night meets the morning sun?*

That was how they went the rest of the way home.
Anita sang:

> *I'd like to know that your love*
> *Is love I can be sure of.*
> *So, tell me now and I won't ask again,*
> *Will you still love me tomorrow?*

Cassandra parked on 12th Street a few doors down from Gladys's house. She decided to leave the car there for the night and return it to her brother-in-law in the morning. Gladys went home, and the three girls went on up Clifton toward 13th Street. They were about halfway up the block when a little boy ran past them coming from 13th. "Rhonda's been shot!" he shouted to no one in particular. "Rhonda's been killed!" The three all knew the boy as the biggest liar in the world. He was followed by his mother, who carried a switch as long as the boy. "You better stop!" the mother hollered. "You just gonna make it worse when I catch you!" The girls laughed.

The chaos on 13th Street began at the corner, with dozens of people standing from the corner up to Rhonda's house in the middle of the block. The girls could see that 13th Street was blocked off from Clifton to Euclid. There were five or so police cars parked every which way about the street. One had come onto the sidewalk and was facing the low stone wall at Rhonda's place. Cassandra had begun walking faster after she turned the corner and crossed 13th Street, pushing her way violently through the crowd. Anita held on to her back, and Melanie held Anita's back. Anita's mother was standing a few feet from the front of Rhonda's house where two policemen, unsmiling, arms folded, stood as if they would never again do anything as important. One kept telling people, "Get back, get back."

"Mama, what happened?" Anita said.

"Jeffrey shot Rhonda," her mother said. "Jeffrey killed Rhonda."

"You shouldn't say that," Cassandra said. She began calling Rhonda's name. She called her friend's entire name, even the two middle ones, which Rhonda hated. There were plainclothesmen in the yard and even more in the house. All the lights in the house seemed to be on, and Cassandra could see the strange men on the first floor and in the basement walking by the windows and talking among themselves. She called Rhonda's name. Nothing seemed real, not the buzzing of the crowd, not that house lit up from top to bottom as if for a party.

"Honey, it's true," Anita's mother said to Cassandra and took the girl by the arm. Cassandra continued to call. At any moment the hated middle names would bring Rhonda, pretending to be angry, to the window.

"This is Rhonda's best friend, Mama," Anita said.

A woman next to Anita's mother said, "He just shot her for no reason at all. I was playin out there with my grandbaby and I could see her practicin in the basement." Cassandra stepped toward the policemen with the folded arms and one told her, "Get back, get back." "He shot her and then just came out here and sat down on the steps," the woman said, "like he was waitin for a ride to come pick him up."

Rhonda's father was a very thrifty man, and had he been there, Cassandra knew, had his daughter been in the basement, alive and practicing, all those lights would not have been on. Melanie took Cassandra's other arm and began to cry. They took Cassandra back through the crowd and across the street to Clifton Terrace, where Anita lived. Melanie, still crying, hugged the three women, then, as if she had forgotten what she had just done, she hugged Cassandra twice more and went home.

Anita's father and brother were playing chess at the kitchen table when they came in. Anita and her mother took Cassandra into the girl's room. Cassandra sat on the bed with her hands in her lap and looked out the window. Anita stood at the foot of the bed, one arm around the bedpost, looking down at Cassandra. An eyeless and very old teddy bear leaning back against her bed pillows had fallen over when Cassandra sat down. The ticking of the Big Ben clock Anita's grandfather had given her was the loudest sound in the room. In the kitchen, her brother was proclaiming victory over their father for only the third or fourth time in the boy's life. Beyond her window Anita could see the twinkling lights of Washington.

Anita's mother came in and gave Cassandra a cup of cocoa sitting in a saucer.

"I got to be goin . . . I got to be goin to home," Cassandra whispered, saying *bome* as if it were a foreign word. Anita told her to drink. Anita watched as her mother helped Cassandra off with her clothes and into one of her mother's nightgowns.

She made a pallet for her daughter beside the bed and turned out the light when she left the room. Occasionally, Cassandra would drift into what Anita thought was sleep. All the while Cassandra gritted her teeth. Sometime way late in the night, Cassandra spoke out, and at first Anita thought she was talking in her sleep: She asked Anita to sing that song she had sung in the car on the way home. Anita sang; long after her parents had gone to bed, long after she stopped wondering if Cassandra was listening, Anita sang. She sang on into the night for herself alone, her voice pushing back everything she did not yet understand.

YOUNG
LIONS

He stood naked before the open refrigerator in the darkened kitchen, downing the last of the milk in a half-gallon carton. Carol, once again, had taped a note to the carton. Caesar Matthews did not have to read it to know that it told him she loved him with all her heart, or that she would miss him all that day. She used to pin such notes to her pillow before she went off in the morning, leaving him still asleep. But in the night, when she brushed her hair as she prepared for bed, she would find the notes still pinned to the pillow, undisturbed and so perhaps unread. So now she taped them to milk cartons, for he could not begin his day without drinking milk, or she taped them to his gold key ring, or pinned them to the zippers of the expensive pants she knew he would wear that day. In more than two years, the wording on the notes had not changed very much. Sometimes, when he thought of it, he would fold the paper with the words and place it on the kitchen table between the salt and pepper shakers, to let her know he had come upon it before he ventured out.

This morning, after he had finished the last of the milk, without reading the words, he tossed the carton in a high arc across the room into the trash can. He pulled up the window shade and let in the morning light. He was anxious to be out in the streets; there was nothing like an empty apartment to bring down the soul.

The night before, for the fourth time in a week, he had dreamed about the retarded woman. Sherman would have told him such dreams were a good sign. Caesar was left now with only fragments of the dreams, the splintered memory that he had been roaming about in some foreign land, and the retarded woman had been standing among tall trees in that land. She never seemed to be hiding, as she should have been, but appeared to wave to him. He could not remember anything after she waved. He did remember with certainty that in all the dreams the woman was known to him not as being retarded but as being feeble-minded, which was the phrase his father had always used.

He was still naked when the telephone rang, standing at the bathroom door wondering if he wanted a shower. "These are the times," Carol would have joked, "when we miss our mothers most."

Manny, on the telephone, asked if he wanted to tend bar that evening and make some change. "I was about to hop over your place," Caesar said. He never liked Manny Soto calling his apartment, for Manny always whispered on the phone and made each word he spoke sound obscene. "He talk that way cause he's a fence and every other bad thing in the world," Sherman had said once. "He think people are listenin to everything he says, and maybe by whisperin, they'll hear a little less."

"Coincidences. Coincidences. Heh, heh," Manny said. "Good minds think a lot, they say. I was just checking to be sure, heh, heh, to see if you might be available, heh, heh." The inappropriate laughing was also why he didn't like Manny calling.

"But listen: You heard what Sherman is doing now, heh, heh, heh?" Manny said. This time he obviously felt the whole thing was funny, and he asked Caesar again.

Caesar told him no, that he had last seen Sherman in Howard Hospital. "Two, three months ago," he said.

"Well, since you last saw him, he's gone up in the world. Or gone down, whichever the case may be, heh, heh." He hung up without another word.

While dressing, Caesar found another note pinned to the collar of his shirt. He read it, crumbled it for effect, and propped it against a picture they had had taken together at a Southeast club. He would remind Carol of all the notes when he told her about the retarded woman. "Dancing with me don't end that way," were the first words she had ever spoken to him. "Try me and see." He had gone to Manny's place with Sherman Wheeler and Sherman's old lady, Sandra Wallington, and, after a good bit of coaxing by Sandra, he had asked a woman sitting alone two tables away to dance. He and the woman had slow-dragged through one record, then another, and as the woman ground her body into his, she would bite and tug at his earlobe with her lips. When the second record ended, she unwound herself and went back without a word to her table. There was now a man at her table, and the man stood and pulled the woman's chair away from the table for her. The man and the woman sat down. The woman's back was to Caesar, who stood dumbly looking at the back of her neck and at the man. The man stood again, and he looked at Caesar with the patience of someone who had nothing better to do. "No one," the man said finally, "gets more than two dances free." He sat again and Caesar, after a few moments, found his way back to Sherman and Sandra.

"Dancing with me don't end that way." He had been about to sit when Carol tugged at his shirt sleeve. He allowed her to lead him away to the dance floor. "Try me and see."

He decided that morning on the desert-brown leather jacket, a present from Carol for his twenty-second birthday two years ago. It was October, and in that month and in November before the days turned colder heading into December, he enjoyed wearing the jacket, enjoyed the opulent sound of leather with each move he made. He checked the jacket's pockets to make certain he had his address book. There was not much in the book—a few names and telephone numbers of people he knew from Manny's. But there were also the addresses and phone numbers of the three women— their names coded to read like male friends in case Carol saw them—he would go to when he and Carol argued, or when he simply wanted to spend the night with a woman whose body, whose responses, he could not easily anticipate.

He put the Beretta in one of the jacket's pockets. The moment he touched it the memory of the times he had used it came back to him. He liked remembering. The last time had been eight months ago when they crossed into Maryland and he shot the 7-Eleven clerk in the face. A few miles from the store, back in D.C., Caesar was still laughing about how the man's face had drained of blood as the gun came toward his face. A month before that he had placed the pistol beside the head of a man he and Sherman had caught far up New Hampshire Avenue near the Silver Spring line. The man had looked insulted to be robbed, and Caesar, dangling the man's watch before his eyes, had pulled the trigger to scare him into the proper frame of mind. "I wasn't gonna take this cheap-ass thing," Caesar said about the watch, "but you just ain't got the proper attitude." The bullet had nicked the man's ear, and so it didn't count the way a blast in the face counted. The nice thing about the retarded woman was that he wouldn't even have to take the pistol out of his pocket.

Sherman Wheeler had rarely carried a gun. "My daddy got his toe shot off tryin to quick-draw one a those things," he said once. "Sides, my mind is the only gun I need." Then he had made his hand into a gun, placed it against his temple, and pretended to pull a trigger. He hadn't liked Caesar carrying a gun, and in their first months together he pulled rank and told him to leave the guns at home when they weren't needed, but Caesar would sneak them out anyway. From the beginning, with the first cheap piece he had stolen during a burglary at a home in Arlington, Caesar had liked carrying a gun. And now, having to work alone without Sherman, he would not step outside the apartment without one.

In the vestibule of Manny's Haven at Georgia Avenue and Ingraham Street, there was an impressive collection of Polaroid pictures displayed behind a locked glass case. In most of the dozens of photographs, Manny, always wearing a Hawaiian shirt, stood in the center, his arms around Washington politicians, two-bit celebrities, customers for whom he had a special affection, or wild-eyed, out-of-town relatives. At the very bottom of the display, in two and a half rows, there were also photographs of men who had, as Manny put it, "made irredeemable fools of themselves in my house," as he called his bar. Most of these men, usually too drunk even to remember where they were, had refused to leave the bar when told, and Manny had had the bouncers toss them out. But throwing them out was never enough, and he would also have the bouncers beat them on the sidewalk. "Take his picture! Take his goddamn picture!" became his euphemism to the bouncers for throwing a man out and putting a hurting on him. The majority of the men were photographed leaning against the front of the bar just below the neon sign that blinked Manny's Haven. They were alone in their pictures with their bloodied faces, except, now and again, for the hand of some unseen bouncer that kept the fellow from falling over.

Manny was reading the *Post* aloud at a table near the bar when Caesar arrived that morning. Manny was alone, which didn't make Caesar happy. The whole place was dark, except for the tiny lamp on the table. Manny did not look up at first when Caesar sat down across from him and said, "Mornin."

Manny finished the page and put the newspaper aside, took off his glasses and rubbed his closed eyes with his knuckles. "Young Blood," he said, squinting. "Ain't seen you in a month of Sundays. Thought you mighta gone away on vacation." Manny dressed the way a very small child would without the help of an adult. "I always expect to look under the table and find him with his shoes on the wrong feet," Sherman had said once, "with knots and shit in the shoelaces, insteada little bows." Manny had hundreds of Hawaiian shirts, including some very expensive ones dating back to the 1920s and 1930s. He wore one every day of the year. This morning he had on a particularly loud silk and rayon thing with palm trees that looked not like trees but tiny green explosions. He was quite a thin man, and all his shirts hung loosely on him, the way they would hang on wire hangers.

"I'll need you for tonight and two three more nights this week," Manny said. "You got time for that?"

Caesar nodded. Bartending would tide him over until things were finished with the retarded woman. He could hear the rumblings of the men in the basement, sorting and cataloging the stolen stuff Manny had bought from thieves. Manny would send all of it on to an apartment on Florida Avenue where people came shopping to buy it for a little more than what Manny paid for it.

"What's this about you not hearing about Sherman?" Manny said. "Thought you two was closer than dick and his two nuts."

"We was once," Caesar said. Manny blinked, waiting for more. He undoubtedly knew everything already, but Caesar knew that having to tell him was the price of doing business with him. Besides, there was nothing to betray. He told Manny what little Sherman had told him in the hospital the last time he saw him: Sherman had ODed at the home of a woman who catered to a small group of people with "functional habits," people who could work and carry on their lives without the rest of the world knowing they needed special recreation in their off hours. A person could go to one of Regina's houses on M Street and relax in one of her small rooms, and after a few hours of traveling, get up and go home.

"I know this woman," Manny said. "Regina Carstairs. Oh, such a fine house in the Gold Coast. I went to her place for a function once, raising money for the mayor. The house where no junkie is allowed. But I didn't enjoy myself because she had somebody watch me all the time like I was going to steal something." Manny indicated with his fingers that he wanted more.

There's not much more, Caesar said. Sherman had traveled out on a far limb one night with just a one-way ticket. Regina thought he was dead or near-dead and had people dump him in a tree box on a street blocks and blocks from her house. ("Another satisfied customer," Manny interjected. "One million and counting.") Caesar did not tell Manny that in the hospital he and Sandra, Sherman's woman, had argued, with Sandra accusing him of dumping Sherman at death's door. He had looked to Sherman for support, but in the end Sherman had raised the arm without the IV and begged Caesar to go. "I'll call you," Sherman had said.

"I got some pictures here you might be interested in, heh, heh," Manny said. "Got some nice pictures. Oh, do I got the nice pictures. Bet a million you didn't know he was on that heroin shit, did you?"

Caesar said no.

"Well, I did. It's hard to tell with some fools, but I knew." He was leaning back in his chair, his arms crossed. He was thin enough for Caesar to see the edges of the chair on either side of him. "That's the thing with that heroin shit. You see, with your average crackhead, they're climbing the walls and everything. You ask them the time and they're ready to kill you cause you ain't got your own watch. But with heroin, you ask them the time, and they're ready to give you the watch. And Sherman was the mellowest man I knew." He leaned forward. "You wanna see my pictures, heh, heh? The proof from our man Polaroid that our man from Sixteenth Street has come up in the world."

Caesar was curious, but he did not want to see. It was as if someone had asked if he wanted to see pictures of his naked father. "We can take him," Caesar had said once about Manny. "We can take him. Come in wearin masks and shit. We can clean his ass out and live like kings." "And then where we gonna live?" Sherman had said. "Even if we got a million dollars from him, where in the fuckin world would we live? Stop bein such a hothead all the time, man. Manny still payin people back for some small thing they probably did to him when he was five years old."

"Come on," Manny said. "Peek on the wild side." In fall and winter, Manny's Hawaiian shirts had two pockets, and he took a set of photographs out of the left pocket.

The pictures were of a security guard standing with folded arms between two paintings in what was clearly a museum. The man seemed to stand with an air of importance and authority, but the more Caesar studied the first pictures the more he saw that the man would never be anything more than a guard whose job was simply to stand between two paintings. The man's expression changed but slightly in the series of photographs, but in the last one, as if he was finally aware that he was the photographer's real subject, he was turning his head away and the camera caught only a blur. The guard, in a dark blue uniform, wore a dark blue hat with a shiny shield in the front, and though the hat was pulled down low over his forehead, Caesar could see that the mouth and chin were Sherman's. "My father gave me my eyes and nose, but I got my mouth and chin from my old lady." Sherman had been on his own since he was ten, but he always spoke of his parents as if he had had a full life with them.

"They were taken in the Smithsonian," Manny was saying. "Not the one with that big elephant—that's my favorite—but the art museum, the one with the paintings. When I heard he was working there, I just had to see it. So I had this guy and his whore that owed me a favor: Act like tourists and go down there and pretend they were Bamas in town to see the pictures, heh, heh." Manny tapped his forehead. "Smart. Real smart."

Caesar got up. "I gotta be movin. Be back at seven, okay?"

"Seven's fine," Manny said, kissing the pictures and putting them back in his pocket. "Any later and you'll be late."

He felt suddenly exhausted and afraid and considered returning to the apartment, but Carol was not there and an empty place brought down the soul. Then he thought of the retarded woman and things brightened a bit. He took a bus downtown to see the woman for what would be the last time before Friday.

He had been following her for all of two months, since a week or so after he saw Sherman in the hospital. He had first come upon her waiting for the bus with three of her housemates. They were all adults, all at least thirty years old, but they talked as if they were new to the world and excited about being in it. The two men talked very loudly, as if they were not afraid to share whatever they were saying. Caesar figured from the beginning that the larger of the two women was the weakest, would be the easiest to pick off.

He had stood a few feet from them, pretending he too was waiting for the bus. Days later he learned that the retarded woman lived only two blocks from the bus stop in a house with perhaps six other retarded people of various ages and with a woman in her fifties. He figured the older woman was there to look after the seven. Except for the older woman, he learned, all of them worked, or at least did something that took them out of the house each morning. The retarded woman he was interested in worked in a French restaurant on Connecticut Avenue near Lafayette Park.

And so for two months he had secretly placed himself in her life, doing all the scoping out, the drudgery that had once been left up to Sherman. "You'd fuck it up," Sherman had said once. "I know you." "Have some faith in me," Caesar would laugh. "Have a little faith." "I know you, mothafucka."

Week after week, Caesar had followed the retarded woman as she made her way to work, sitting in the back of the bus so he could see when she got off. At K Street, she always walked the block and a half to the restaurant. He hung around near the restaurant, sometimes for the entire day, learning her schedule. He often saw her sweeping up the alley in the back where the employees entered and where deliveries were made. About two thirty or so most afternoons, after they had probably eaten lunch, the retarded woman and a much older woman would walk to Lafayette Park and stay for up to thirty minutes. After they went back to work, he would not see the girl again until about five, when she left work and took the bus home.

On Saturdays, she came to work at noon and stayed until eight or nine in the evening. But it was only the Fridays that concerned him now. For on Fridays, each Friday evening, she left work and walked up Connecticut Avenue to Dupont Circle, where she deposited her paycheck at American Security. He would stand beside her on most Fridays over those months as she took forever to fill out the deposit slip, making first one mistake, then another, then dropping the crossed-out slips into the wastebasket beside the table. After she got on line, he would pick up every slip she had dropped. Then he would stand behind her until she had completed things with the teller.

It was a little before two when he got to the restaurant. The retarded woman and her friend soon came out to Connecticut, heading for Lafayette Park. Not quite two thirty, but close enough to the times of other days not to worry. As the women often did, they walked holding hands. They wore green uniforms and though they seemed to polish their white shoes every day, he had noticed that they were scuffed plenty by midday. He knew their first and last names, he knew where the old woman lived, having followed her home one evening, he knew the retarded woman's favorite candy, he even knew the station the old woman had her radio tuned to.

"I can see me sometime holdin my own little baby," the retarded woman said after they sat down on a bench facing the White House, "rockin her and feedin her and doin such." The sun was warm, and Caesar sat on the grass Indian-style a few feet behind the women. He opened a newspaper he had taken from a trash can, but he watched the tourists taking photographs and the government people eating their lunches.

"Thought everything would work with Fred and me," the retarded woman said. "He like the job they got him. Me and him would sit on the stoop, makin plans bout our future."

Caesar knew about her Fred, but he had never learned if he was one of those loud talkers he had seen in the first weeks at the bus stop.

"People call us the lovebirds," the retarded woman said. " 'Look at em. Look at them lovebirds.' "

The old woman was eating orange pieces from a small plastic bag, and now and again, when the breeze shifted, the smell of oranges came to Caesar. He watched a black family come up to a very old white man at the Lafayette statue. The father gave his camera to the white man and then stood in front of the statue beside his wife and behind his three children. The oldest boy closed his eyes and would not open them again until it was all done. The old man took the family's picture, and when the mother raised one finger, the old man advanced the film and snapped again.

"Then he commence to change. He talk back to Miss Prentiss," the retarded woman was saying. "His job call Miss Prentiss and said he all the time late. Wouldn't do what they told him."

"Anna, he musta told you what was the matter," the old woman said.

"No, ma'am, Miss Elsie," the retarded woman said. "He never did. Yesday I got home, a car came with two men and they took him back to Laurel." Caesar watched as the father read what was on the side of the statue and then the father looked up at the man on the horse, shading his eyes. His little girl did the same.

The black family crossed Pennsylvania Avenue, and the father gave the oldest boy the camera so he could take pictures of the White House. Then they went down to the corner and joined the line going in.

Caesar was only half listening; there was no more that would help on Friday. The problem would be Carol. He put the newspaper aside and lay down, closing his eyes. He would not follow them back to work. On another day not long ago, he had waited for the retarded woman across the street in front of the copier business until she got off from work. He had followed her to the bus stop. She was overweight, and he saw that walking was not easy for her in the heat. For the first time since he had been following her, she was not wearing her uniform. She had on a blue skirt and a pink blouse, which she wore outside the skirt. She had on tiny, gold-plated earrings a person might not notice until he was within a foot or so of her, and that was how close he was when he walked past her. She smelled of garlic and, beneath that, of a soap that reminded him of the halls in the hospital where his mother had died.

It was a crime, Sherman had said, to fall asleep anywhere but in a safe place, and so he was up and off a few minutes after the women left. He felt he wanted to see Sherman and left the park at the corner of Pennsylvania and 16th, heading in the direction where he thought the museum was. In both his lives, he had never come down to the world below Constitution Avenue, except for those times when relatives came from out of town. His mother and father would bring everyone down to see the Washington they put on postcards and in the pages of expensive coffee-table books. He knew that his father worked in one of the government buildings, but he didn't know which one. His father was the kind of man who, if he looked out his office window and saw his son, would come down the stairs three at a time and hold him until someone called the police. "Call the law! I have a thief who robbed me! Call the law!"

At 15th and Constitution, among the tourists and office workers, he gave up the idea of seeing Sherman. It would be better to start working on Carol. He could see no problems with Anna, the retarded woman, but retarded or not, she was still a woman and there was a danger of her being skittish. He called Carol at work.

He told her that he loved her, then he told her that he missed her. In his mind, he read the words written on her notes.

"I'm glad you told me," she said. "I was beginning to wonder. You made my day."

He promised to fix her dinner before he went to Manny's and he told her once again that he loved her.

"I wish I could record that," she said, "and play it back any time I wanted."

IV

When people found out that Angelo Billings, Caesar's cousin, had in fact stolen the flowers from an I Street florist and taken them to the funeral home, they said he would never again have good luck. Never mind, they said, that he loved Caesar's mother as much as he loved anyone and that stealing the flowers was his way of showing that love. There were some things God would not tolerate, and stealing flowers for the dead was one of them.

Caesar, though, was moved, and they grew closer after his mother's funeral. Angelo introduced him to Sherman. Angelo, before Caesar gave up on school, would wait for him outside Cardozo High, and they would go to Sherman's two-bedroom apartment on 16th Street, a few blocks up from Malcolm X Park. What fascinated Caesar most about the apartment was the dominance of sound, of noise, as if Sherman were afraid of silence. In every room, there was something playing each second of the day, whether a radio or television or cassette player. In the bathroom, hanging from the shower curtain rod, there was a transistor radio that played around the clock. Sherman lived alone in the apartment, but he had two children by Sandra, who lived elsewhere in the building with the children. Most of the time when Caesar and Angelo visited, they would find Sherman wrapped in his bathrobe sitting on the couch, listening to one of dozens of cassette tapes that Sandra had recorded of the children talking and playing with each other. There were four speakers in the living room that stood three feet high, and he enjoyed playing those cassettes so loud that the noise of the children made it sound like a playground with a hundred children. Now and again, one child would hit the other or say something mean and there would be a fit of crying on the tape. Sherman would jump up and speed the tape past the crying to a place where the talking and playing resumed.

The apartment, despite the noise, became another home for Caesar and he began going there without Angelo after school. Before long, he was leaving home at least two or three days a week and going not to school but straight to Sherman's place, where he'd drop his books at the door beside the two-foot-high porcelain bulldog and make a place for himself in front of the television. In the beginning, he was able to get back home in the evening before his father arrived from work. But as the months wore away to winter, to spring, he was getting home later and later.

One night in April, Sherman dropped him off about three in the morning, and Caesar stood on the sidewalk for a long while looking up at his house. For the first time, all the lights in the house were off. When he opened the front door, his father was standing before him in the darkened hall.

"I'm just slaving away my life to raise up another Angelo," his father hissed, turning on the hall light. "A goddamn no-account." As soon as his hand was off the light switch, he slapped Caesar, knocking him back against the front door. Before Caesar could recover, his father had grabbed him by the shirt with one hand, opened the door with the other, and threw him out on the sidewalk.

"I gave you more chances than you deserved," his father said and closed the inner and outer doors to the house. Caesar, still sprawled on the ground, saw the hall light go out. Seconds later, he saw the light in the upstairs front bedroom, his father's room, go on, and a moment later, that light went out.

He got to his feet and looked up and down French Street. The new leaves rattled as if something were shaking the trees, and the sound unnerved him. He brushed off his clothes, not because of dirt or debris, but because right then he did not know what else to do. Under the street lamp, he looked at the watch Sherman had given him the week before, and it occurred to him that he had never before been awake at that hour in the morning. A cool wind sauntered up the street and chilled him, unnerving him even more, and he suppressed the urge to cry.

He considered pounding on the door, calling his father as loudly as he could and then running away. But he stood quiet. For all of his life, he had been Lemuel Matthews's son, and even now, standing in the dark outside the walls of his father's house, he was still his son and he knew he could not be a bad boy at such a place at such a time in the morning.

He saw the brighter lights at the half smoke joint at the 9th Street corner and he went toward those lights. The place was closed, but he used the outdoor telephone to call Sherman. Sandra answered, and after he had told her what happened, she told him to stay put, that Sherman would be back down to pick him up. While he waited, he called his father's house several times, stepping out of the telephone booth with the receiver as he listened to the ringing. He looked up tree-lined French Street, but there was not enough light to distinguish his house from all the others.

It was true what people said about Angelo's bad luck. He robbed the Riggs Bank on 15th Street in early May, using a gun he had rented for twenty-five dollars a day and a Safeway shopping bag. He was so curious about how much he had gotten away with that as he ran down M Street, he looked in the shopping bag, and at that moment the money, booby-trapped with a red dye packet, exploded in his face. He dropped the bag, cursing the bank teller, but he continued running, trying for the next several blocks to wipe the dye from his face and hands with the shirt he had taken off.

Sherman had thought that Angelo, eager, cocksure, had potential as a partner, but soon after the government people put Angelo away, he began to consider Caesar, who was now staying with him. Caesar knew Sherman didn't have a real job, but he didn't learn until he had been with him two months what he did for a living. He was not particularly surprised or disappointed. Caesar was seventeen, and for the first time in his life, he was living his days without the cocoon of family, and beyond that cocoon, he was learning, anything was possible.

"The first thing we do," Sherman said one day, "is get all your shit from your daddy's place. You gotta have an identity. Get you out in the world so you can stop all that mopin."

The next morning they drove down to the house on French Street and waited in the car until Caesar was certain his father had left for work and his brother and sister had gone to school. Caesar opened the front door with his key. He was surprised his father had not changed the lock, but Sherman was not surprised. "What's there to be afraid of from his own little boy?" Sherman said. Caesar stepped into the hall. Had his father suddenly appeared before him, it would have seemed the most natural thing. Indeed, he expected him, and when he stepped into the living room, he expected his father to be there as well. Sherman, silent, followed as Caesar went through the rooms on the first floor. Caesar touched nearly everything along the way—a lace piece made by his grandmother that was on the back of the easy chair in the living room; a drawing of the house signed and dated by his sister taped to the refrigerator; the kitchen curtains he had helped his mother put up. In a corner of the kitchen counter he found wrapped in a rubber band the letters he had been sending to his father; only the first one had been opened.

"Let's get your stuff," Sherman said after a bit. "Enough of this."

They went upstairs, and in the closet of his father's bedroom, Sherman found a small metal box, broke its tiny lock with his hand, and leisurely went through the papers in the box, putting aside Caesar's birth certificate and the Social Security card he had gotten the year before in hopes of finding an after-school job. Caesar watched.

"You want your mom's death certificate?" Sherman said, reaching the end of the papers in the box.

"No." He turned away and went to his sister's room, where he touched the heads of the three stuffed animals sitting on the pillows of her bed. In the room he had shared with his brother, he took as many of his clothes as he could carry, his hands shaking each time he picked up an item.

In the hall, Sherman was waiting at the head of the stairs. He took some of the clothes from Caesar. "He had a little money in the box, some cash and some gold pieces," Sherman said. "And I found a stack of pictures in a drawer. I got a few of em, mostly some with you in em. Must be your mother, too. I got a lot of em. You might want em later on when you start to forget."

Caesar nodded. In a few minutes they were on 11th Street, heading back uptown. He knew what his father would look like when he realized he had been robbed: the fist pounding the air, that pulsating vein at the left side of his head. For months and months after that, he could conjure up the image whenever he wanted and replay it. That night, they went to Manny's and Carol said what she said about dancing with her not ending that way, about trying her and seeing. She took him home that night, and when he woke up the next morning, she was lying on her side watching him. She leaned over and kissed his forehead. "It's all right," she said, "I already went and brushed my teeth." Aside from the ones in Sherman's magazines, she was the first naked woman he had ever seen. She kissed his ear. "There's a toothbrush in there with your name on it," she said. "And I bet I spelled your name right."

Two weeks after Caesar and Sherman went into Caesar's father's house, Sherman took him out for the first time, to burglarize a home in Chevy Chase. Sherman peed on the sofa in the recreation room, having taken a quick dislike to a large painting behind the sofa of a man in a tennis outfit whom he took to be the owner. The next night, in a light rain, they followed a light-skinned, well-dressed fellow from a bar on Capitol Hill to his car parked a block away. The man had tottered the whole distance, not bothering to open the umbrella he was carrying. "Not a sound," Caesar said, placing the pistol at the man's head just as he stuck his key in the car door. "Not a sound. No words. Not one word." Sherman went through the man's pockets, took his wallet and then his watch. "Please, please," the man kept saying, his arms extended high into the air. The man was balding and the hair he had left was combed perfectly to either side of a bald path that went back to the middle of his head. With the light of the street lamps, the robbers could see the beads of rain on the bald path and on his eyeglasses. "Next time," Caesar said as they stepped away from the man, "buy your shit in a liquor store and take it home to drink."

V

On the way home from following Anna that last time, Caesar bought white carnations for Carol and the ingredients for a shrimp creole dinner. He had dinner prepared when she came home, and after they had eaten, with her head swirling just a bit from the wine, he made love to her because he did not know what kind of mood he would be in when he returned from Manny's that night.

Later, as he told her about the retarded woman, he rested his hand on her bare stomach. He could feel her tensing up with each word. He massaged her stomach, then he took her belly button between two fingers and rubbed it gently.

"Don't ask me to do any of that," she said. "Don't bring me into any of that." As long as she believed it did not involve another woman, she had never wanted to know what he and Sherman did. But now she felt all of the not-wanting-to-know had come due and she pulled the sheet up to her neck against the cold.

"There's nothin to it," Caesar said. "In an out. Before you know it, we'll be back home, Carol. I promise."

"Stop. I'm not like you. I don't want to hurt anybody."

"It's just the money," he said, getting up. He began to dress.

"Don't go just yet," she said. She was naked and she got out of bed and put her arms around him. The cold came in the window and she shivered.

"I don't ask a whole fuckin lot of you," he said, "and when I do, you act like this." He left the room and she called to him as she put on her robe. He was out of the apartment before she got in the living room. He took the stairs two at a time, and she continued calling him as she leaned over the banister.

That was Monday. He did not go back home all that week. Manny told him on Friday that he was tired of Carol calling the bar. "Talk to her," Manny said. "Do something to shut that pussy up."

"Come home," Carol said when he finally called her Saturday afternoon. "Come home."

"You forgot what I asked you to do?" he said.

"No, I didn't forget," she said. "Come home."

"Then what do you have ta say bout what I asked?"

She said, "Yes. Yes. C, I can't hurt anybody. I just can't."

"Who said anything about somebody gettin hurt? Nobody'll get hurt. I already told you."

"Come home," she said.

The final days of that October were pleasant, but as the sun set, it grew cooler. There had been rain a few evenings, and when there was no rain, a wind came up that chilled as much as the rain. Caesar wore the tan Burberry Carol had bought for him. And as he sat in Dupont Circle Park watching Carol standing before American Security, there was still enough sunlight left for him to see Anna, a block or so away, make her way with the crowd up Connecticut Avenue.

Carol did not look over at him, and as she paced, she would occasionally pull from her purse the picture of a boy about three years old, study it as if trying to memorize the boy's features, and then return the picture to her purse. Caesar had taken it from Manny's wall of Polaroids, but no one at the bar, not even Manny, could remember who the child was. Carol, however, believed that Caesar knew the boy, and when Caesar laughed, she had flung the picture at him. It had taken him most of the rest of Thursday evening to calm her, convince her that, as his father would have said, he didn't know the boy from Adam.

Still, he could tell from the way she looked at the photograph that everything he had said and done that Thursday was wearing off. Carol finally looked over at him. When Anna was but several yards from her, Caesar pointed at Anna and Carol walked to her. She took Anna by the arm and gently pulled her from the flow of the crowd. "Always say nice, soothin things," he had told Carol. "Talk to her like you were longtime sisters or somethin."

The lights in the park and along the streets came on. Anna's back was to him, but he could see Carol's face. She appeared calm and this surprised him. "The makins of a pro," Sherman would have said. The boy in the picture, dressed in green swimming trunks with his back to some ocean, could well be a grown man by now, or he could be in his grave, Caesar thought, but today, on that street, his mother was saying he needed five thousand dollars for an operation or he would die as sure as anything. "Always make it seem like the choice is hers—whether he lives or whether he dies." Anna took the picture and she looked at it, holding it but a few inches from her face.

Just the way Anna was standing told him that of the million things in the world she could do, she would do the one thing he wanted. And knowing this made up for not being with Sherman. It made up for that old woman who had cut his hand two weeks before when he ran by and tried to grab her money from her coat pocket.

Anna gave back the picture. Satisfied, he took his eyes from the women and watched the passersby heading home. Somewhere, Sherman was about to do the same. He could see Sherman closing a giant museum door so people could not see his roomful of paintings. "No more. No more for the day." It did not hurt as much to think of him now. He looked back at the women in time to see them enter the bank.

When they came out, they crossed the street, and Caesar thought it a nice touch that Carol took Anna by the arm as they crossed. Anna sat on a bench across from Peoples, and for a minute or so more, Carol talked to her. Anna nodded. Everything now should be the closeout, he thought, and he felt she was taking too long. He waited until Carol walked by him and crossed the street, heading down Massachusetts Avenue. When he caught up with her, he took her by the elbow and she pulled away.

"You did good," he said, putting his arm around her. "You did real good. How much did you get?"

"Can't you wait?" she said. "Can't you even wait!" They crossed 18th Street. "Do we have to go into all this out here like this?"

"It's all right, Carol," he said. "She back there. Nothin can happen now." Midway down the block, he reached for her purse, but again she pulled away from him.

"Stop! Jesus!" She quickened her pace.

He stopped momentarily. "What's wrong with you?"

At Massachusetts and 17th, he managed to lead her into the tiny park. The place was empty except for a bum who was sleeping on a bench several yards away from them. "What the fuck's wrong with you?" He took the purse.

"Don't!" she said, taking it back. "For God sakes, don't!"

He slapped her and grabbed for the bag with the other hand. It opened and everything inside fell out. Seeing the money fall to the ground, he slapped her again, and she began to cry. Her nose bled, and her bottom lip was split in two places, and it bled as well. The bum had awakened, and seeing the woman get slapped, he asked, "What is it there with you two peoples?"

Caesar dropped the purse, and Carol knelt down and began putting things back in it. He pulled her to her feet. "What the hell's wrong with you?"

"Leave me alone. Just leave me alone."

She knelt and he pulled her up again. "I said leave me alone." He slapped her. He could now see the distance between them growing, and seeing that distance and knowing he no longer had the power to close it, he slapped her once more. The blow sent her back a few feet. She said ohh several times, but everything sounded to him like no. She put her hand to her face and trembled.

"Hey there, fella," the bum said. "We gentlemens don't—"

"You want me to come over there and kick your ass?"

The bum was silent. He knew these young lions. He eased himself off the bench and rolled under it. Better to face the rats and the filth than face a young lion in his wrath.

"Carol, get the stuff and let's go home."

She watched him. Stepping up to her, he took out the Beretta and held it to her cheek. "Did you hear what I said?" There was no surprise in her face, and there was no fear. He realized that if he beat her with the pistol, that, too, would not surprise her. And had he shot her, in the face or through the heart, she would not have been surprised at that either. He pocketed the gun and stepped back.

She walked around him and was crying softly as she gathered up the money and her belongings. It had begun to rain and she shook each thing before putting it in the bag. When she was done, she stood and looked at him. Then, as if there was all the time in the world, she walked slowly out of the park, heading down Massachusetts. He watched her until she disappeared among the lights of Dupont Circle, and then he turned away.

There was something in the air, but he could not make out what it was. He walked out of the park. He kept looking behind him, expecting something or someone, but he was alone on the street and he saw nothing but the swirling of dead leaves. He continued looking behind him as he made his way up 17th Street. He took out the address book, but found he could not read the names or the numbers under the feeble street lights. He hurried, hoping for a telephone booth where the light would be brighter. He began to run, and as he ran, he kept trying to read the names and numbers, but the rain was now turning them to blurs. He did not know what was in the air. He only knew that tonight would not be a night to be without shelter.

THE STORE

I'd been out of work three four months when I saw her ad in the *Daily News*; a few lines of nothing special, almost as if she really didn't want a response. On a different day in my life I suppose I would have passed right over it. I had managed to squirrel away a little bit of money from the first slave I had, and after that change ran out, I just bummed from friends for smokes, beer, the valuables. I lived with my mother, so rent and food weren't a problem, though my brother, when he came around with that family of his, liked to get in my shit and tell me I should be looking for another job. Usually, my mother was okay, but I could tell when my brother and his flat-butt wife had been around when I wasn't there, because for days after that my mother would talk that same shit about me getting a job, like I'd never slaved a day before in my life.

That first slave I had had just disappeared out from under me, despite my father always saying that the white people who gave me that job were the best white people he'd known in his life. My father never had a good word to say about anybody white, and I believed him when he said I could go far in that place. I started working there—the Atlas Printing Co. ("75 YEARS IN THE SAME LO-CATION")—right after I graduated from Dunbar, working in the mailroom and sometimes helping out the printers when the mail work was slow. My father had been a janitor there until he got his third heart attack, the one that would put him in the ground when I was in my sophomore year at Dunbar.

At twenty I was still in the mailroom: assistant chief mail clerk or something like that, still watching the white boys come in, work beside me, then move on. My mother always said that every bullfrog praises his own poem, but I know for a natural fact that I was an excellent worker. Never late, never talked back, always volunteering; the product of good colored parents. Still . . . In the end, one bitching cold day in January, the owner and his silly-ass wife, who seemed to be the brains of the outfit, came to me and said they could no longer afford to keep me on. Times were bad, said the old man, who was so bald you could read his thoughts. They made it sound like I was the highest-paid worker in the joint, when actually I was making so little the white guys used to joke about it.

I said nothing, just got my coat and took my last check and went home. Somewhere along K Street, I remembered I'd left some of my personal stuff back there—some rubbers I'd bought just that morning at Peoples, a picture of the girl I was going with at the time, a picture of my father, my brother, and me at four years old on one of our first fishing trips. I had the urge to go back—the girl was already beginning not to mean anything to me anymore, so I didn't care about her picture, but the fishing trip picture was special. But I didn't turn back because, first of all, my balls were beginning to freeze.

My father always said that when the world pisses on you, it then spits on you to finish the job. At New York Avenue and 5th I crossed on the red light. A white cop twirling his billy club saw me and came to spit on me to finish up what Atlas had done: He asked me if I didn't know it was against D.C. and federal law to cross on the red light. I was only a few blocks from home and maybe heat and thawing out my nuts were the only things on my mind, because I tried to be funny and told him the joke my father had always told—that I thought the green light was for white folks and the red light was for colored people. His face reddened big-time.

When my brother and I were in our early teens, my mother said this to us with the most seriousness she had ever said anything: "Never even if you become kings of the whole world, I don't want yall messin with a white cop." The worst that my mother feared didn't happen to her baby boy that day. The cop only made me cross back on the green light and go all the way back to 7th Street, then come back to 5th Street and cross again on the green light. Then go back to 7th to do it all over again. Then I had to do it twice more. I was frozen through and through when I got back to 5th the second time and as I waited for the light to change after the fourth time and he stood just behind me I became very afraid, afraid that doing all that would not be enough for him, that he would want me to do more and then even more after that and that in the end I would be shot or simply freeze to death across the street from the No. 2 police precinct. Had he told me to deny my mother and father, I think I would have done that too.

I got across the street and went on my way, waiting for him to call me back. I prayed, "Just get me back to one fifteen New York Avenue safely and I'll never come to their world again. . . . Just get me back to one fifteen New York Avenue safely. . . ." For days after that I just hung out at home. My mother believed that a day had the best foundation if you had breakfast, so after she fixed our breakfast, and went off to work, I went back to bed and slept to about noon.

When I got some heart back, I started venturing out again, but I kept to my own neighborhood, my own world. Either my ace-boon, Lonney McCrae, would come get me or I would go looking for him and we'd spend the rest of the afternoon together until our friends got off work. Then all of us would go off and fuck with the world most of the night.

Lonney was going to Howard, taking a course here and there, doing just enough to satisfy his father. I'd seen his old man maybe once or twice in all the time I knew Lonney, and I'd been knowing him since kindergarten. His father had been one of the few big-shot Negro army officers in the Korea war, and Lonney was always saying that after the war his father would be home for good. He was still saying it that January when Kennedy was inaugurated.

Lonney liked to fuck bareback and that was how he got Brenda Roper pregnant. I think he liked her, maybe not as much as she liked him, but just enough so it wasn't a total sacrifice to marry her.

I was to be his best man. One night, all of us—me and Lonney and his mother and Brenda and her parents—were sitting around his living room, talking about the wedding and everything. Someone knocked on the door and Lonney opened it. It was his old man, standing there tall and straight as a lamppost in his uniform. You know something's wrong when a man doesn't even have a key to his own house.

The soldier didn't say Hello or Good to see you, son. He just stood in the doorway and said—and I know he could see everybody else in the room—"You don't have anything better to do with your time than marrying this girl?" Lonney's mother stood up, in that eager, happy way women do when they want to greet their husbands home from a foreign land. Brenda's father stood up too, but he had this goofy look on his face like he wanted to greet his soon-to-be in-law. "I asked you something," Lonney's father said. Lonney said nothing, and his father walked by him, nodded at Mrs. McCrae, and went on upstairs with his suitcase. The next morning he was gone again.

Lonney married Brenda that March, a few weeks before I saw the ad in the *Daily News*. I think that he wanted to make things work with Brenda, if only to push the whole thing in his father's face, but the foundation, as my mother would have said, was built on shifting sand. In about a year or so he had separated from her, though he continued to be a good father to the child, a chubby little girl they named after his mother. And some two years after he married, he had joined the army and before long he himself was in a foreign land, though it was a different one from where his father was.

The day before I saw the ad I spent the evening at Lonney and Brenda's place. They fought, maybe not for the first time as newlyweds, but for the first time in front of me. I felt as if I were watching my own folks arguing, as if the world I knew and depended on was now coming apart. I slept till one the next day, then went down to Mojo's near North Capitol and Florida Avenue and hung out there for most of the day. Late in the day, someone left a *Daily News* at a table and over my second beer, with nothing better to do, I read the want ads. Her ad said:

STORE HELPER. *Good pay. Good hours.*
Good Opportunity for Advancement.

Then she had the store's location—5th and O streets Northwest. The next morning I forced myself to stay awake after my mother had left, then went off about eight o'clock to see what the place was about. I didn't want any part of a white boss and I stood outside the store, trying to see just who ran the place. Through the big windows I could see a colored woman of fifty or so in an apron, and she seemed to be working alone. Kids who attended Bundy Elementary School down the street went in and out of the store buying little treats. I walked around the block until about nine, then went in. A little bell over the door tinkled and the first thing I smelled was coal oil from the small pump just inside the door. The woman was now sitting on a tall stool behind the counter, reading the *Post*, which she had spread out over the glass counter.

She must have known I was there, but even after I was halfway to her, she just wet a finger and turned the page. I was inches from the counter, when she looked up. "Somethin you want?" she said. Oh shit, I thought, she's one of those bitches. I could feel my balls trying to retreat back up into my body.

"I come about the job in the paper," I said.

"Well, you pass the first test: At least you know how to read. What else you know how to do? You ever work in a store before? A grocery store like this?"

I gave her my work history, such as it was, and all the while she looked like she wanted to be someplace else. She kept reading and turning those pages. She seemed skeptical that the printing company had let me go without just cause.

"What you been doin since you lost that job?" she said.

"Lookin. I just never found anything I liked."

That was not the right answer, I could see that right away, but by then I didn't care. I was ready to start mouthing off like somebody was paying me to do it.

"The job pays thirty a week," she said finally. "The work is from eight in the mornin till eight in the evenin. Every day but Sunday and maybe a holiday here and there. Depends. You got questions?" But she didn't wait for me to ask, she just went on blubbering. "I'll be interviewin everybody else and then make my decision. Affix your name and phone number and if you're crowned queen of the ball, I'll let you know, sweetie." She tossed a pencil across the counter and pointed to the top of a newspaper page where she wanted me to put my telephone number. I wrote down my name and number, and just before I opened the door to leave, I heard her turn the next page.

The next day was Tuesday, and I spent most of that morning and the next few mornings cleaning up what passed for the backyard of Al's and Penny's Groceries. I had been surprised when she called me Monday night, too surprised to even tell her to go to hell. Then, after she hung up, I figured I just wouldn't show up, but on Tuesday morning, way long before dawn, I woke up and couldn't get back to sleep. And so for a change I was up when my mother rose and I fixed our breakfast. She did days work for some white people in Chevy Chase, and that morning I noticed how fast she ate, "wolfing down" her food, she would have called it.

For the first time in a long while, I stood at the window and watched her skinny legs take her down New York Avenue to hop the first of two D.C. Transits that would take her to Chevy Chase. Maybe it was watching her that sent me off that morning to the store. Or maybe it was that I came back to the table and saw that she hadn't finished all of her coffee. My mother would have sold me back into slavery for a good cup of coffee, and no one made it to her satisfaction the way she did.

"Good," the store owner said to me after she parked her lavender Cadillac and was opening the store's door. "You passed the second test: You know how to show up on time." It was about 7:30 and I'd been waiting about fifteen minutes.

She took me straight to the backyard, through the store itself, through a smaller room that served mostly as a storage area, to the back door, which took a hell of an effort for us to open. In the yard, two squirrels with something in their hands stood on their hind legs, watching us. No one had probably been in the yard for a coon's age and the squirrels stood there for the longest time, perhaps surprised to see human beings. When they realized we were for real, they scurried up the apple tree in a corner of the yard. The store owner brought out a rake, shovel, wheelbarrow, everything I needed to do to the yard what no one had done for years. I hadn't worn any good clothes and I was glad of that. Right off I took my tools and went to the far end of the yard to begin.

"By the way," she said, standing in the back door, "my name's Penelope Jenkins. Most people call me Penny. But the help call me Mrs. Jenkins, and you, buddy boy, you the help."

Beyond the high fence surrounding the yard there were the sounds of schoolchildren getting into their day. Well into the second hour of work, after I knew I was getting dirty and smelly as hell, after the children were all in school, I started throwing stones at the damn squirrels, who, jumping back and forth from tree to fence, seemed to be taunting me. Just like on the cold evening of the green light, I began to feel that I would be doing that shit forever.

The first thick layer of crap in the yard was slimy dead leaves from the autumn before, maybe even years before, and the more I disturbed the leaves the more insects and slugs crawled out from the home they had created and made a run for it under the fence and to other parts of the yard. The more spiteful and stupid bugs crawled up my pants legs. Beneath the layer of leaves there was a good amount of soda bottles, candy wrappers, the kind of shit kids might have thrown over the fence. But I didn't get to that second layer until Thursday morning, because the yard was quite large, big enough for little kids to play a decent game of kickball. Sometimes,

when I heard voices on the other side of the fence, I would pull myself up to the top and look over.

My father always told the story of working one week for an undertaker in Columbia, South Carolina, one of his first jobs. He
didn't like the undertaker and he knew the undertaker didn't like
him. But, and maybe he got this from his old man, my father figured that he would give the undertaker the best goddamn week of
work a fourteen-year-old was capable of. And that's what he did—
for seven days he worked as if that business was his own. Then he
collected his pay and never went back. The undertaker came by late
one evening and at first, thinking my father wasn't showing up because he was just lazy, the undertaker acted big and bad. Then, after my father told him he wouldn't be coming back, the undertaker
promised a raise, even praised my father's work, but my father had
already been two days at a sawmill.

I didn't think Mrs. Jenkins was the kind of woman who would
beg me to come back, but I did like imagining her sitting on her
high stool, reading her damn paper and thinking of what a good
worker she had lost. That was the image I took home each evening
that week, so sore and depressed I could not think of fucking the
world or anybody else. My mother would fix me dinner and I would
sit hunched down in my chair close to the food because I had little
strength left to make the long distance from the plate to my mouth
if I sat up straight. Then, before I could fall asleep in the chair, my
mother would run water for me to take a bath, the same thing I had
seen her do for my father so often when I was a child that I didn't
notice it anymore.

In the late mornings that week, after she thought I had done
enough in the yard, Mrs. Jenkins would have me sweep the area
around the front of the store or provide some order to the mer-
chandise in the storage room. On Tuesday she wanted the boxes of
stuff arranged just so, but then, as if she had some revelation during
the night, she wanted everything rearranged on Wednesday. Then
on Thursday I had to do things different again, and then different
still again on Friday. And because she claimed she planned to re-

paint, she also had me up on a ladder, scraping away the peeling orange paint of the store's exterior. The paint chips would fly off into my eyes and hair, and it took me until Thursday to get smart about wearing a stocking cap and the goggles my father had once used.

Saturday morning I woke up happy. Again, I was there waiting for her to open up and again I did all the shit work while she chatted and made nice-nice with all the customers. I had already planned my weekend, had, in my mind, spent every dollar I was to be paid. But I was also prepared to get cheated. Cheating folks was like some kind of religion with people like Mrs. Jenkins—they figured that if they didn't practice it they'd go to hell. Actually, I was kind of hoping she would cheat me, just so I could come back late that night and break all the fucking windows or something.

At the end of the day, after she had locked the front door to any more customers and pulled down the door's shade with the little CLOSED sign on it, she opened the cash register and counted out my money. It came to about twenty-five dollars after she took out for taxes and everything. She explained where every dollar I wasn't getting was going, then she gave me a slip with that same information on it.

"You did a good job," she said. "You surprised me, and no one in the world surprises me anymore."

The words weren't much and I had heard better in my time, but as I stood there deliberately counting every dollar a second and third time, I found I enjoyed hearing them, and it came to me why some girls will give their pussys to guys who give them lines full of baby this and baby that and I'll do this and I'll be that forever and ever until the end of time. . . .

I just said yeah and good night and thanks, because my mother had always taught me and my brother that the currency of manners didn't cost anything. Mrs. Jenkins had untied her apron, but she still had it on and it hung loosely from her neck. She followed me to the door and unlocked it. "I'll see you bright and early Monday mornin," she said, like that was the only certainty left in my whole damn life. I said yeah and went out. I didn't look back.

Despite my aches, I went dancing with Mabel Smith, a girl I had gone to Dunbar with. We stepped out with Lonney and Brenda. I didn't get any trim that night, and it didn't bother me, because there was something satisfying in just dancing. I danced just about every dance, and when Mabel said she was tired, couldn't take it anymore, I took Brenda out on the dance floor, and when I had worn her out, I danced away what was left of the night with girls at other tables.

I got home about six that Sunday morning. In the dark apartment, I could see that slice of light along the bottom of my mother's closed door.

I didn't go back to the store on Monday. In fact, I slept late and spent the rest of the day running the streets. Tuesday, I couldn't get back to sleep after my old lady left, and about ten I wandered over to the store, then wandered in. She didn't act mad and she sure didn't act like she was glad to see me. She just put me to work like the week before had been a rehearsal for the real thing. And she enjoyed every bad thing that happened to me. Tuesday I restocked the cereal section of shelves behind the counter with the cash register. As I bent down to dust the bottom shelves, a box of oatmeal fell on my head from three or four shelves up. Hit me so hard I'm sure some of my descendants will be born dumb because of it. Mrs. Jenkins went into a laugh that went on and on for minutes, and throughout the rest of the day she'd come up behind me and shout "Oatmeal!" and go into that laugh again.

"In the grocery business," she said after I replaced the box, "the first law of supply in them shelves is to supply em so that nothin falls over."

And late that Friday afternoon, as I was checking the coal oil pump to see how much was in it, a customer rushed in and the door pushed me against the pump, soiling a good shirt with oily dirt and dust. None of Mrs. Jenkins's aprons fit me and she had said she was ordering one for me. "Sorry, sport," the customer said.

"The first law of customer relations," Mrs. Jenkins said after the guy was gone, "is to provide your customers with proper egress to and from your product." Such bullshit would have been enough in itself, but then, for the rest of that day, she'd look at me and ask, "What am I thinkin?" And before I could say anything, she would say, "Wrong! Wrong! I'm thinkin oil." Then the laugh again.

That was how it was for months and months. But each Monday morning, like a whipped dog that stayed because he didn't know any other master but the one that whipped him, I was at the store's front door, waiting for her to open up. And a thousand times during the week I promised myself I would give her a week of work that only my father could surpass and then, come Saturday night, get my pay and tell her to kiss my ass. But always there was something during the week to bring me back on Monday—she allowed me, for example, to wait on customers (but didn't allow me to open the cash register and make change); and I got two new aprons with my name stitched in script over the left pocket; and I got a raise of one dollar more a week after I had been there six months; and eventually she allowed me to decide how much of what things we had to reorder. Often, at home in the evening, I would go over the day and rate it according to how many times Mrs. Jenkins had laughed at me, and it became a challenge to get through the next day and do things as perfectly as possible. By the time I got my raise I felt comfortable enough to push that laugh back in her face whenever she slipped up on something. I'd say, "The first law of bein a grocery store boss is to be perfect."

Then, too, I found that there was something irresistible to girls about a man in an apron with his name stitched on it. I had to suffer with a lot of giggly little girls from Bundy, who would hang around the store just to look at me, but there were also enough high school and older girls to make working there worth my while. Before my first year was out, I was borrowing from next week's pay to finance the good life of the current week.

The first time I waited on Kentucky Connors was just after Lonney separated from Brenda and went back to a room in his father's house. Mrs. Jenkins didn't tolerate the type of friendliness with customers that led to what she called "exploiratation," so when I wanted a date with someone who came into the store, I'd arrange to set up things after I got off. The night Kentucky came in that first time, I purposely failed to put her pack of gum in the bag and ran after her.

"Why, of all the men on this earth," she said after I caught up with her and boldly told her to clear her calendar for that Saturday night, "would I think of going out with someone like you?" You can tell when girls are just being coy and want you to lay it on just a little thicker before they say yes. But there are others who have no facade, who are not seeking to be wooed, who give out smiles like each time they do it takes them a mile farther from heaven. And after they speak you're a year older and a foot shorter. That was Kentucky.

She actually stood there for several long seconds as if waiting for me to give her some kind of fucking resume. Then she said, "I thought so," and walked away. A thousand and one comebacks came much later, when I was trying to go to sleep.

You do manage to go on with your life. Over the next weeks and months, I had to put up with her coming in a few times a week, but for her there seemed to be no memory of me asking her out and she acted as though I was no more or less than the fellow who took her money and bagged her groceries. But her you're welcome in response to my thanking her for her purchases contained no sense of triumph, of superiority, as I would have expected. I learned in bits and pieces over time that she lived in an apartment on Neal Place a few doors from 5th Street, was a year out of Dunbar, was a secretary with the government people, that her family lived in a house on N Street that her mother's parents had bought. . . .

About a fifth of Mrs. Jenkins's customers bought things on credit and each purchase was carefully noted. On a chain beside the cash register she kept an elongated accounting book for nonmeat credit purchases. The meat case, with its small array of dressed chickens and parts, wrapped hamburger and stew beef, rolls of lunch meats, pork chops, etc., was catty-corner to the counter with the register. The meats had their own credit book, and perhaps no one—except maybe Mrs. Gertrude Baxter—had a longer bill than the Turner family. I rarely ever saw the father of the two Turner children and I came to know that he worked as a night watchman. The mother seemed to live and die for her stories on television, and I rarely saw her either. The boy and girl were in and out all the time.

"My mama said gimme a small box of soap powder," one of them would say. "Gimme" meant the mother wanted it on credit. "My mama said give her a pound of baloney and a loaf a Wonda Bread." "My mama said give her two cans a spaghetti. The kind with the meatballs, not the other kind. She said you gave me the wrong kind the last time." If you got a please with any of that, it was usually from the little girl, who was about seven or so. Mrs. Jenkins had a nice way with every customer as long as they didn't fuck with her, but the Turner girl seemed to have a special place in her heart. Which is why, despite what Mrs. Baxter went about telling the whole world, I know that Penny Jenkins would have done anything to avoid killing the Turner girl.

The ten-year-old Turner boy, however, was an apprentice thug. He never missed a chance to try me, and he was particularly fond of shaking the door just to hear that tinkling bell. He never messed with Mrs. Jenkins, of course, but he seemed to think God had put me on the earth just for his amusement. He also liked to stand at the cooler with the sodas and move his hand about, knocking the bottles over and getting water on the floor. Whenever I told him to get a soda and get out of the box, he would whine, "But I want a *reeaal* cold one. . . ." He would persist at the box and I usually had to come and pull his arm out, and he'd back away to the door.

He'd poke his tongue out at me and, no matter how many old church ladies were in the store, would say in his loudest voice: "You don't tell me what to do, mothafucka!" Then he'd run out.

Just before he dashed out, his sister, Patricia, who often came with him, would say, "Ohh, Tommy. I'm gonna tell mama you been cursin." Then she would look up at me with this exasperated look as if to say, "What can you do?"

"Where me and you gonna retire to?" was the standard question Mrs. Jenkins would ask the girl after she had bagged the girl's stuff.

"To Jamaica," Patricia would say, giggling that standard little-girl giggle.

"Now don't you grow up and run off somewhere else," Mrs. Jenkins said. "There's some fine, fine men in Jamaica, and we gon get us some."

"Oh, no," Patricia said as if Mrs. Jenkins had implied that the girl was capable of doing something horrible.

"And how we gon get to Jamaica?"

"On a slow boat by way a China."

None of that meant very much to me then, of course. It was just so much bullshit heard over the hours of a long day.

By the summer of 1962 I was making forty dollars a week and that November I had enough to buy a used Ford from a longtime friend of my parents. "Always know where the seller lives in case the thing turns out to be a piece of junk," my father once said. The first long trip I took in the car was to Fort Holabird in Baltimore, where Lonney was inducted into the man's army. I came back to Washington and dropped his mother off at her house and then went back to work, though Penny had said I could take the day off. Perhaps it was the effort of trying to get through the day, of trying not to think about Lonney, that made me feel reckless enough to ask Kentucky out again.

Penny had waited on her, and I followed Kentucky out of the store. I waited until we were across O Street and asked with words that would have done my mother proud if I could take her to Howard Theater to see Dinah Washington that Saturday night.

"I'd like that," she said without much hesitation. And because she was the kind of woman she was, I knew it was the simple truth, no more, no less. She set down her bag of stuff and pulled a pen and a slip of paper from her pocketbook. She began to write. "This is my telephone number. If you're going to be late," she said, "I'd like the courtesy of knowing. And if you are late and haven't called, don't come. I love Dinah Washington, but I don't love her that much."

I found her family a cold and peculiar lot, except for her little sisters, who were as passionate about the Washington Senators as I was. A few times a month we had dinner at their place on N Street. Her father was a school principal and talked as if every morning when he got up, he memorized an awfully big word from the dictionary and forced himself to use that word in his conversations throughout the day, whether the word actually fit what he was saying or not. Kentucky's mother was the first Negro supervisor at some office in the Department of Commerce. She was a bit better to take than her husband, but she was a terrible cook and I seemed to be the only person at her dinner table who realized this.

The first time we slept together was that January. I had waited a long time, something quite unusual for me. I had started to think I would be an old man with a dick good for nothing but peeing before she would let me get beyond heavy petting. So when she turned to me as we were sitting at the counter at Mile Long one Sunday night, I didn't think anything was up.

She turned to look at me. "Listen," she said and waited until I had chewed up and swallowed the bite of steak sandwich I had in my mouth. "Listen: Thou shall have no other woman before me. I can take a lot but not that." Which didn't mean anything to me until we got back to her apartment. We had just gotten in and shut the door. She took my belt in both her hands and pulled me to her until our thighs and stomachs met. Until then I'd made all the moves, and so what she did took my breath away. She kissed me and said again, "Thou shall have no other woman before me." Then she asked if I wanted to stay the night.

A very mischievous wind came through Washington that night

and the rattling windows kept waking us, and each time we woke we would resettle into each other's arms, to drift away with sleep and return with another rattling. I can be twenty-two forever as long as I can remember that evening and that night.

When you work in a grocery store the world comes to buy: tons of penny candy and small boxes of soap powder because the next size up—only pennies more—is too expensive and rubbing alcohol and baby formula and huge sweet potatoes for pies for church socials and spray guns and My Knight and Dixie Peach hair grease and Stanback ("snap back with Stanback") headache powder and all colors of Griffin shoe polish and nylon stockings and twenty-five cents worth of hogshead cheese cut real thin to make more sandwiches and hairnets for practically bald old women trudging off to work at seventy-five and lard and Argo starch not for laundry but to satisfy a pregnant woman's craving and mousetraps and notebook paper for a boy late with his what-I-did-on-my-summer-vacation paper and Kotex and clothespins and Bat 'N' Balls and coal oil for lamps in apartments where landlords decline to provide electricity and Sneaky Pete dream books and corn flakes with the surprise in the box and light bulbs for a new place and chocolate milk and shoestrings and Wonder Bread to help "build strong bodies 12 ways" and RC Cola and Valentine's Day specials to be given with all your heart and soul and penny cookies and enough chicken wings to feed a family of ten and bottles of bluing. . . .

By the time I came on the scene, Penelope Jenkins had been selling all that and more for about fifteen years. She and her husband ("the late Mr. Al Jenkins") had bought the place from a Jewish family not long after World War II. Al had died ten years before I showed up, and Penny had had a succession of helpers, including a son who went off and died in Korea, never to come back to Al's and Penny's Groceries.

Because of my life at the store, my sense of neighborhood began to expand; then, too, it's easier to love a neighborhood when you love the girl in it. My allegiances had always been to the world around New York Avenue and 1st Street, around Dunbar, because that was Home. In fact, I hadn't much cared for the world around 5th and O; when I was still in junior high I'd gotten my ass whipped by a boy who lived around 5th and O. Lonney and I and people from our world had always associated the whole 5th and O area with punk fighters, and the boy I fought turned out to be one of the biggest punks around. From the get-go, this guy went for my privates with a hard kick and it took everything out of me; you never recover from shit like that, so even though I lost, I didn't lose fair.

The second time I realized my allegiances were expanding, that I was making room in my soul for more than one neighborhood, was when I was asked to be godfather to two babies within one month; Penny got to be the godmother and I stood beside her as the godfather. The first time, though, was the afternoon Penny gave me the combination to the safe she kept in the little room off the main room. She had me practice the combination that afternoon until I knew it by heart. After a few turns I got tired of that and ended up looking through some of what was in the safe. There was a stack of pictures Al Jenkins had taken in those early years, mostly pictures of people in the 5th and O Street neighborhood. Many of the people in the pictures still lived around there; having served them in the store for so long, I recognized them despite what time had done to them. I sat on the floor and read what Al had written on the backs of the black-and-white pictures. One picture showed Joy Lambert, the mother of Patricia and Tommy Turner. Surrounded by several girlfriends, Joy was standing on what must have been a sunny day in front of the store in her high-school graduation cap and gown. Al had written on the back of the picture, "June 1949. The world awaits." This picture, above all the others, captivated me. You could tell that they were innocents, with good hearts. And the more I looked at those smiling girls, especially Joy, the more I wanted only good things for them, the way I wanted only good things for my nieces and nephews. Perhaps it was tiredness, but I began to feel that I was looking at a picture of the dead, people who had died years and years before, and now there was nothing I could do.

"Now you know why I keep all those in the safe." Penny had come up behind me and was looking down on me and the pictures spread out before me. "Out of harm's way," she said, "way in back, behind the money."

Kentucky and I fell into an easy, pleasant relationship, which is not to say that I didn't tip out on her now and again. But it was never anything to upset what we had, and, as far as I know, she never found out about any of it. More and more I got to staying at her place, sleeping at my mother's only a few times a month. "I hope you know what you doin," my mother would say sometimes. Who knew? Who cared?

In fact, my mother said those very words that August Thursday night when I went to get clean clothes from her place. That Friday was hot, but bearably humid, and the next day would be the same. The weather would stay the same for a week or so more. After that, I remember nothing except that it stayed August until it became September. The air-conditioning unit installed over the front door, which Penny had bought second-hand, had broken down again that Wednesday, and we had managed to get the repairman, a white man with three fingers missing on one hand, to come out on Thursday and do his regular patch-up job. In the summer, we had two, sometimes three, deliveries a week of sodas and stuff like Popsicles and Creamsicles that the kids couldn't seem to do without. For years and years after that, my only dreams of the store were of a summer day and of children coming to buy those sodas and ice cream. We always ran out of the product in my dreams and the delivery men were either late or never showed up and a line of nothing but children would form at the door, wanting to buy the stuff that we didn't have, and the line would go on down 5th Street, past N, past M, past New York Avenue, past F, past Pennsylvania Avenue, all the way down into Southwest, until it went on out Washington and into another land. In the dreams I would usually be yelling at Penny that I wanted her to do something about that line of children, that we weren't in business to have a line like that, that I wanted it gone pretty damn soon. Eventually, in the dreams, she would do something to placate me—sometimes, she would disappear into the back and return with a tub of stuff that I recognized immediately as the homemade ice cream my mother said her parents always made when she was a little girl.

About a half hour or so before closing that Friday, Kentucky came by. She had bought a new stereo and all week I had been borrowing records from friends because we planned a little party, just the two of us, to break in the stereo. Penny left the locking up to me and got ready to go.

"Who's the man tonight?" Kentucky asked Penny. I think she must have had more boyfriends than Carter had liver pills. I had just finished covering the meat for the night, something Penny and I called putting the chickens to bed.

"Ask me no questions . . . ," Penny said and winked. She whispered in Kentucky's ear, and the two laughed. Then Kentucky, looking dead at me, whispered to Penny, and they laughed even louder. Finally, Penny was ready to leave.

If the sign said we closed at nine, that was precisely the time Penny wanted the store closed and I wasn't allowed to close any sooner. I could close later for a late-arriving customer, but not any sooner. And as it happened, someone did come in at the last minute and I had to pull out some pork chops. Penny said good night and left. I locked the door after the pork chop customer. I may or may not have heard the sound of a car slamming on brakes, but I certainly heard little Carl Baggot banging at the door.

"You little squirt," I said to him. "If you break that window, I'm gonna make your daddy pay for it." I'd pulled down the door shade to an inch or so of where the glass ended, and I could see the kid's eyes beaming through that inch of space. "Can't you read, you little punk. We closed. *We closed!*" and I walked away. Kentucky was standing near the door and the more the kid shouted, the closer she got to the door.

"He's hysterical, honey," she said, unlocking the door. She walked out, and I followed.

Penny's lavender Cadillac was stopped in the middle of 5th Street, one or two doors past O Street. From everywhere people were running to whatever had happened. Penny was standing in front of the car. I pushed my way through the crowd, and as I got closer I saw that her fists were up, shaking, and she was crying.

"She hit my sista," Tommy Turner was saying, pounding away at Penny's thigh. "This bitch hit my sista! This bitch hit my sista!" Some stranger picked the boy up. "All right, son," the man said, "thas anough of that."

Patricia Turner lay in the street, a small pool of blood forming around her head. She had apparently been chasing a rolling Hula Hoop, and she and the hoop, now twisted, had fallen in such a way that one of her arms was embracing the toy. Most of what light there was came from the street lamps, but there were also the Cadillac's headlights, shining out on the crowd on the other side of the girl. "You should watch where you goin with that big ole car," Mrs. Baxter said to Penny. "Oh, you know it was a accident," a man said. "I don't know no such thing," Mrs. Baxter said.

The girl's eyes were open and she was looking at me, at the people around her, at everything in the world, I suppose. The man still had hold of Tommy, but the boy was wiggling violently and still cursing Penny. Penny, crying, bent down to Patricia and I think I heard her tell the child that it would be all right. I could tell that it wouldn't be. The girl's other arm was stretched out and she had a few rubber bands around the wrist. There was something about the rubber bands on that little wrist and they, more than the blood perhaps, told me, in the end, that none of it would be all right.

Soon Joy, the girl's mother, was there. "You murderin fuckin monster!" she kept yelling at Penny, and someone held her until she said that she wanted to go to her baby. "Look what that murderin monster did to my baby!"

The police arrived, but they did not know what else to do except handcuff Penny and threaten to arrest the man who held

Tommy if he didn't control the boy. Then the ambulance arrived and in little or no time they took the girl and her mother away, the flashing light on the roof shining on all the houses as it moved down 5th Street. A neighbor woman took Tommy from the stranger and took the boy inside. Wordlessly, the crowd parted to let them by, as it had parted to let the ambulance through. The police put Penny in the back of the scout car and I followed, with Kentucky holding tight to my arm. Through the rolled down window, she said to me, "Bail me out, if they'll let me go." But most of what she said was just a bunch of mumbles, because she hadn't managed to stop crying. I reached in the window and touched her cheek.

I opened the store as usual the next day, Saturday. The child died during the night. No one, except people from out of the neighborhood, spoke when they came in the store; they merely pointed or got the items themselves and set them on the counter. I sold no meat that day. And all that day, I kept second-guessing myself about even the simplest of things and kept waiting for Penny to come and tell me what to do. Just before I closed, one girl, Snowball Patterson, told me that Mrs. Baxter was going about saying that Penny had deliberately killed Patricia.

Penny called me at Kentucky's on Sunday morning to tell me not to open the store for two weeks. "We have to consider Pat's family," she said. I had seen her late that Friday night at No. 2 police precinct, but she had said little. I would not see her again for a month. I had parked the Cadillac just in front of the store, and sometime over the next two weeks, the car disappeared, and I never found out what happened to it, whether Penny came to get it late one night or whether it was stolen. "Pay it no mind," Penny told me later.

She called me again Monday night and told me she would mail me a check for two thousand dollars, which I was to cash and take the money to Patricia's family for her funeral. The police were satisfied that it had been an accident, but on the phone Penny always talked like old lady Baxter, as if she had done it on purpose. "Her mother," Penny said, "wouldn't let me come by to apologize. Doesn't want me to call anymore." All that month, and for some months after, that was the heart of the phone conversation, that the mother wouldn't allow her to come to see her and the family.

Joy came in one day about three months after Pat died. Tommy came with her, and all the time they were in the store, the boy held his mother's hand.

"You tell her to stop callin me," Joy said to me. "You tell her I don't want her in my life. You tell her to leave me alone, or I'll put the law on her. And you"—she pointed at me—"my man say for you not to bring me no more food." Which is what Penny had been instructing me to do. The boy never said a word the whole time, just stood there close to his mother, with his thumb in his mouth and blinking very, very slowly as if he were about to fall asleep on his feet.

About once a week for the next few years, Penny would call me at Kentucky's and arrange a place and time to meet me. We always met late at night, on some fairly deserted street, like secret lovers. And we usually met in some neighborhood in far, far Northeast or across the river in Anacostia, parts of the world I wasn't familiar with. I would drive up, park, and go to her car not far away. She wanted to know less about how I was operating the store than what was going on with the people in the neighborhood. She had moved from her apartment in Southwest, and because I had no way of getting in touch with her, I always came with beaucoup questions about this and that to be done in the store. She dispensed with all the questions as quickly as possible, and not always to my satisfaction. Then she wanted to know about this one and that one, about so-and-so and whoever. Because it was late at night, I was always tired and not always very talkative. But when I began to see how important our meetings were, I found myself learning to set aside some reserve during the day for that night's meeting, and over time, the business of the store became less important in our talks than the business of the people in the neighborhood.

And over time as well, nearly all the legal crap was changed so that my name, just below hers, was on everything—invoices, the store's bank account, even the stuff on the door's window about who to call in case of emergency. After she had been gone a year or so, I timidly asked about a raise because I hadn't had one in quite a while. "Why ask me?" she said. We were someplace just off Benning Road and I didn't know where I would get the strength to drive all the way back to Kentucky's. "Why in the world are you askin me?"

I went about my days at first with tentativeness, as if Penny would show up at any moment in her dirty apron and make painful jokes about what I had done wrong. When she was there, I had, for example, always turned the bruised fruit and vegetables bad side up so people could see from jump what was what, but Penny always kept the bruised in with all the healthy pieces and sold the good and the not-so-good at the same price. Now that she was not there, I created a separate bin for the bruised and sold it at a reduced price, something she had always refused to do. But the dividing line of that separate bin was made of cardboard, something far from permanent. Every week or so the cardboard would wear out and I had to replace it.

Because there were many nights when I simply was too exhausted to walk the two blocks or so to Kentucky's, I made a pallet for myself in the back room, which would have been an abomination to Penny. "Work is work, and home is home," she always said, "and never should those trains meet."

When Mrs. Baxter came in to buy on credit, which was about twice a day, she would always ask, "How the murderer doin?" I tried to ignore it at first, but began trying to get back at her by reminding her of what her bill was. Generally, she owed about a hundred dollars; and rarely paid more than five dollars on the bill from month to month. Since Penny had told me to wipe the slate clean for Patricia's mother, Old Lady Baxter became the biggest deadbeat. Baxter always claimed that her retirement check was coming the next day. After I started pressing her about the bill, she stopped bad-mouthing Penny, but I found out that that was only in the store, where I could hear.

When I told her that I wouldn't give her any more credit until she paid up, she started crying. My mother once told me that in place of muscles God gave women the ability to cry on a moment's notice.

"I'll tell," Mrs. Baxter boo-hooed. "I'm gonna tell."

"Oh, yeah," I said, loud enough for everyone in the store to hear. "Who you gonna tell? Who you gonna go to?"

"Penny," she said. "I'll tell Penny. She oughta know how you runnin her sto into the ground. I'ma tell her you tryin to starve me to death."

Within a few weeks her account was settled down to the last penny, but I still told her never to step foot in the store again. Surprisingly, the old lady took it like a man. It was a full month before I got the courage to tell Penny what I had done. I could see that she did not approve, but she only had this look that my mother had the day my brother came home with the first piece of clothing my parents allowed him to buy on his own. A look of resignation—Thank God I don't have to live with it.

At first, with Penny's blessing, I hired my more trustworthy friends or cousins or a few people in the neighborhood, but either they could only work part time or they didn't do the job well enough to suit me. Kentucky even helped out some, but after she got into an executive training program at what she called her "real job," she didn't want to work in the store anymore.

Then, in the spring of 1965, I lucked onto a Muslim who lived on 6th Street. She was on public assistance and had three children, which made me skeptical about her working out, but I gave her a one-week tryout, then extended it another week. Then extended two weeks more, then I took her on full time, permanent, and gave her two aprons with her named stitched over the left pockets. I was always afraid that I'd find the place overrun with her kids every day, but in all the time I knew her, despite the fact that she lived only a block away, I met her kids only a few times and came to know them only by the pictures she showed me. Her name was Gloria 5X, but before she lost her slave name, the world—and she seemed to know three fourths of it—had called her Puddin. And that was what I learned to call her.

After I got where I could leave things in Puddin's hands, I was able to take off now and again and spend more time than I had been with Kentucky. We did two weeks in Atlantic City in the summer of 1965, back when the only rep the city had was what the ocean gave it, and that seemed to revive what we had had. That fall I set about redoing the store—repainting, rearranging shelves, and, at long last, getting a new meat case. The renovations left me, again, spending more and more nights on the pallet in the back. There were fewer people buying coal oil and I wanted to tear out the pump, but Penny vetoed that. "Wait," she said. "Wait till the day after the very last person comes to buy some, then you tear it out."

I passed the halfway mark in the new work before the end of winter and wanted to celebrate with a good meal and a movie. I was to meet Kentucky at her office one evening in February, but I was late getting there for a reason I don't remember, for a reason that, when it is all said and done, will not matter anyway. When I did get there, she iced me out and said she was no longer interested in going out, which pissed me off. I kept telling her we could have a good evening, but she insisted we go home.

"You know," she said as I continued trying to coax her to go, "you spend too much time at that damn store. You act like you own it or something." I was making $110 a week, had a full-time employee and one part-time worker, and I didn't particularly want to hear that shit.

"It's my job," I said. "You don't hear me complainin and everything when you come home and sit all evening with your head in those books."

"It's not every single day, not like you do. Maybe once every three weeks. You come first, and you know it."

When we got home, she began to thaw.

"Why are we letting all this come between you and me?" she said. "Between us?" She repeated that "us" three or four times and put her arms around me.

Because she was thawing, I felt I was winning. And I think I got to feeling playful, because the first thing that came to mind after all those *us*es was that joke about Tonto and the Lone Ranger looking up to see a band of Indians bearing down on them: "What they gonna do to us, Tonto?" "Whatcha mean 'us,' Kemo Sabe?"

I don't think I said that line out loud. Maybe I did. Or maybe she just read my mind. In any case, she withdrew from me, then went to the window, her arms hugging her body. "I thought so," she said after a bit. "Clean your things out of here," she said, in the same quiet way she used to tell me to remember to set the clock's alarm. "Clean everything out as soon as possible."

Despite what she had said, I left her place feeling pretty cocky and went to Mojo's. After four beers, I called Kentucky to say we should wipe the slate clean. She calmly told me not to call her again. "You fuckin bitch!" I said. "Who the fuck do you think you are!" After a while I went to my mother's place. For the most part, I had sobered up by the time I got there. I found my mother at the kitchen table, listening to gospel on the radio. I don't recall what conversation we had. I do remember noticing that she had lost, somewhere in time, three or four of her teeth, and it pained me that I did not even know when it had happened.

It took me three days to clean out my life from Kentucky's place. She stayed at work until I had finished each day. And on each of those days, I left a note telling her I wanted to stay.

I suppose any man could take rejection by any woman as long as he knew that the morning after he was cast out, the woman would be bundled up with her best memories of him and taken away to a castle in the most foreign of lands to live there forever, guarded by a million eunuchs and by old women who had spent their lives equating sex with death. No, no, the woman would have to say to the old women for the rest of her life, I remember different.

*   *   *

If you approached Al's and Penny's Groceries coming down O Street from 6th you could see the bright new orange color I myself put on, a color announcing to the world an establishment of substance, a place I tried to make as friendly as a customer's own home. Joy and Tommy and Tommy's father moved away when the paint was still fresh and bright. And it was still bright when Mrs. Baxter went on to her reward, and though she had not been in the store since the day I told her not to come back, Penny had me send flowers to the funeral home in both our names. The paint was still radiant when the babies I was godfather to learned to walk in the store on their own and beg for candy from me.

One evening—the season it was is gone from my mind now—I let Puddin go home early. Alone in the store, I sat on my high stool behind the counter, reading the *Afro*, a rare treat. At one point I stood to stretch and looked out the O Street window to see Penny, with shorter hair and in her apron, looking in at me. I smiled and waved furiously and she smiled and waved back. I started from behind the counter and happened to look out the 5th Street window and saw my father coming toward me. When I saw that he too had on an apron, I realized that my mind, exhausted from a long day, was only playing tricks.

I do not know what would have happened had Penny not decided to sell. Perhaps I would be there still, and still going home each evening with the hope that I would not see, again, Kentucky arm-in-arm with someone else. Penny and I had continued to meet in her car about once a week. The night she told me she was selling the place, we met on Q Street, between 5th and 6th. And the very last meeting was on O Street, in front of Bundy's playground. From meetings far, far from the neighborhood, we had now come to one that was just down the street from the store. I came out of the store about midnight, locked it, stepped back to take one final look at the place as I usually did, and walked only a few yards. In a few minutes, Penny drove up.

"You been a good friend to me," she said as soon as I got in the car. She handed me two envelopes—one with a month's pay for Puddin and the other with four thousand dollars for me. "Severin pay," she said. "Don't spend it on all the whores, for a man does not live on top of whores alone."

She hugged me, kissed me hard on the cheek. After a while, I got out and watched her make a U turn and go back down the way she had come. I had a feeling that that would be the last time I would ever see her and I stood there with my heart breaking, watching her until I lost her in the night.

The next week I took the G2 bus all the way down P Street, crossing 16th Street into the land of white people. I didn't drive because my father had always told me that white people did not like to see Negroes driving cars, even a dying one like my Ford. In the fall, I was sitting in classes at Georgetown with glad-handing white boys who looked as if they had been weaned only the week before. I was twenty-seven years old, the age my mother was when she married. Sometimes, blocks before my stop on my way home from Georgetown in the evening, I would get off the G2 at 5th Street. I would walk up to O and sit on the low stone wall of the apartment building across the street from what had been Al's and Penny's Groceries. The place became a television repair shop after it stopped being a store, then it became a church of Holy Rollers. But whatever it was over the years, I could, without trying very hard, see myself sitting in the window eating my lunch the way I did before I knew Kentucky, before Pat was killed. In those early days at the store, I almost always had a lunch of one half smoke heavy with mustard and a large bottle of Upper 10 and a package of Sno-Ball cupcakes. I sat on the stone wall and watched myself as I ate my lunch and checked out the fine girls parading past the store, parading as if for me and me alone.

AN ORANGE LINE TRAIN TO BALLSTON

The first time Marvella "Velle" Watkins saw the man with the dreadlocks, rain threatened and she just managed to get herself and her three children down into the subway before it began. The rain was waiting for them at the end of their trip. On the crowded Stadium-Armory subway platform, she held Avis, the baby, by the hand, lest the girl wander off, and Marvin, the oldest, stood on his mother's other side. Marvin was looking into the tunnel out of which the train would come. He held his bookbag under one arm and looked down at the lights that were flush with the floor and whose blinking would indicate the approach of the train.

"How do the lights know when the train is comin?" he asked his mother.

This was a new question. "I don't know," she said. "Avis, stop kicking like that." The girl continued to kick out at something imaginary in front of her and Marvella tugged at her arm until the girl stopped. "I guess," she said to Marvin, "that way down the line the moving train hits something on the tracks and that tells the lights ahead to start blinking."

Marvin seemed satisfied with the answer. He studied the lights and as he did they began to blink. The boy was nine. My son the engineer, his mother thought.

On the other side of Avis stood Marcus, her second son. Marvella noted out of the corner of her eye that he was yapping away, as usual, and at first Marvella thought he was talking to Avis or having another conversation with himself. "Everybody else is borin," he said to her the first time she asked why he talked to himself. He was now seven. Long before the train came into view, it sent ahead a roar, which always made Marvella look left and right to make certain her children were safe and close. And when she turned away from the coming train, she saw that Marcus had been talking to the man with the dreadlocks.

Marcus and Avis managed to find seats just in front of their mother, and she was surprised when the dreadlock man sat down beside her. Marvin found a seat on the aisle across from his siblings. Beside the boy was a woman as old as Marvella's mother, asleep, her head leaning against the window. For a few seconds Marvin looked at the old woman, then he opened his bookbag and took out a piece of paper.

The subway man running the train announced through the speakers in the ceiling that this was an orange line train to Ballston.

Marcus, after sitting for a few seconds or so, turned around and knelt in his seat, facing the man with the dreadlocks. Being so small, he hadn't been able to get a good look at the dreadlocks while he stood beside the man on the platform, but now he was closer and more or less head-to-head with the man and he planned to take advantage of the situation. I should tell him to turn around, his mother thought, but this might be one time when he's justified. Avis, a head or so shorter than Marcus, followed her brother's example and was staring at the man as well. A minute or so won't hurt, Marvella thought.

"Why you got your hair like that?" Marcus asked the man.

"You don't have no comb or nothin?" Avis asked him. "My mama wouldn't do my hair like that." Avis was four and on any given day had a different answer about whether she liked the idea of going to school next year.

"Oh, yeah," the man said, "I got all the combs and brushes I need."

"Then why you do your hair like that?" Marcus said.

The train stopped and more people entered the car. The subway man told the new people what train they had entered.

The dreadlock man said, "It's nice like this. It makes me feel good to wear it like this."

"Oh," Marcus said.

"Oh," Avis said. Then she looked the man up and down and said, "Don't you want a haircut? My mama take my brothas to the barbashop. She can take you to the barbashop too."

The man laughed. Marvella had been surprised that he did not have a West Indian accent. Each lock of his hair was at least a foot long and there were at least twenty locks with perhaps the roundness of a nickel. Around each lock, about an inch up from the end, there was a band, and each band was a different, dark color. The man smelled like the incense street vendors sold.

"No," the man said. "No barbershops for me. I like it like this."

The train stopped again. "Good mornin. This is an orange line to Ballston," the subway man said.

Now there were people standing in the aisle and Marvella could not see Marvin.

"You look like a man I saw in a scary movie one time," Marcus said.

"Marcus, turn round!"

"It's okay," the dreadlock man said, and with one finger he momentarily touched Marvella's hand. "You like scary movies?" he said to Marcus.

"Yeah," the boy said. "But my mama don't let me watch em. Me and Marvin snuck and saw one at Granny's when she was sleepin."

"They give you nightmares," the man said.

"Hey!" Marcus said, his eyes opening wide. "Thas what my granny said."

The train stopped again, and though it did not stop any more suddenly than before, Avis lost her balance and began to fall back. The man reached across and caught her arm, in a move that seemed almost as if it had been planned, as if he had known two stops or so back that the child would begin to fall at that moment. Marvella thought: If I see him tomorrow, it will be a good sign.

"Now see," she said. "Both of you turn around, and I mean it."

At the McPherson Square stop, Marvella and her children got off. Marcus and Avis told the man good-bye and he said that it was nice meeting them. It was raining when they came out of the subway. With the rain, it was hard going across 14th Street and through Franklin Square Park to 13th Street. Marvella carried Avis in one arm and held the umbrella with the other hand. She had Marcus carry her pocketbook and he and Marvin shared an umbrella. Up the street from K on 13th, they went through the wide alley leading to Thompson School on 12th Street, where she and Avis watched the boys run up the stairs and go inside. Her arms were tired and she put Avis down. She wrapped the strap of her pocketbook around her shoulder and held her daughter's hand as they made their way two blocks up 12th Street to Horizon House, where Marvella's mother lived. They took the elevator up to her mother's apartment, and in a minute or so Marvella was heading back down 12th Street to the C&P Telephone Company, where she was a service representative.

It was about eight thirty in the morning. She saw her day as blocks of time. She entered the building at 12th and H, and the second block began.

They did see the man with the dreadlocks the next day, the Friday before Washington's Birthday, but Marvella had forgotten that it was supposed to be a good sign. He sat across the aisle from the boys, and she and Avis shared the seat just in back of the one the boys were sharing. That morning, perhaps because of the holiday weekend, there were fewer people.

"You back, huh?" Marcus said to the man. "Still got the same hair, too."

"Yep, it's me," the man said. "How're you doing today?"

"Fine. No school tomorrow and we goin to the zoo if the weather good."

Avis, interested, leaned across her mother's lap. "You can't come to the zoo with us."

"Why not?" the man said.

"Cause my granny's comin and she wants to give peanuts to the monkey-see, monkey-do."

"My granny always says there ain't no good men left in the world," Marcus said.

"Marcus . . ." his mother said.

"Well, if that's so," the man said, "it wouldn't be a good thing for the world."

Marcus hunched his shoulders, as if it didn't matter to him one way or another. "You goin to work?" Marcus said to the man.

"Yep," the man said.

"They let you come to work with your hair like that?" Marcus said.

"Marcus," his mother said.

The man said to her, "You have wonderful kids." She told him thank you. Then to Marcus, the man said, "Yeah, I go to work like this. They have to let me. They have no choice. I'm the best they have."

"If they don't let you come to work, you gon beat em up?" Marcus said. Marvin had his head to the window, looking out into the darkness of the tunnel, his hands shading his eyes.

The train stopped and the subway woman announced that it was an orange line train to Ballston. Marvella and her children always got on at the Stadium-Armory stop in Southeast. It did not matter if they took the orange line, which ended at Ballston, or the blue line, which ended at National Airport, because both lines, traveling over the same tracks, went past their McPherson Square stop.

"No need to beat em up," the dreadlock man said. "You go to school?" he said to Avis.

"I ain't neva goin to school," and she shook her head vigorously. "No way. No way. No way."

"I go," Marcus said. "It ain't bad." He leaned his head out into the aisle and moved it up and down as if he were watching a bouncing ball. When he looked back up at the man, he pointed at the hair and asked, "Whatcha call that kinda hair?"

"We call them dreadlocks."

"You sure you whatn't in that movie I saw? They had this man comin out of the ground and everything. He was dead but he was still alive and nobody could kill him." He turned to his brother. "Marvin, don't he look like that man in that movie we saw at Granny's? You member?"

The train stopped again. Marvin turned from the window and considered the man for a long time. The man smiled, but Marvin did not seem impressed with him or his hair and the boy did not return the smile. "You ask people too many questions," he said to his brother and turned back to the window.

My son the old man, his mother thought. The train had just passed the Smithsonian stop and, knowing that the trip was about to end, she found that she wanted the man to ask her something, anything, before they got off. She would have settled for something as inane as what was her sign, even though she hated such questions. And though she told the world that she did not believe in it all that much, she had nevertheless learned that she was not compatible with Capricorns and Libras. Her ex-husband was a Capricorn. If she had to guess, she would have said the man with the dreadlocks was an Aries. But the last man she had slept with, three months ago, had been an Aries, a man she had met at a club she and her sister went to. The man at the club had been full of shit and she was glad that her children had never met him. "They call me Slide," the guy had introduced himself. "Short for Electric Slide."

It occurred to her as she and the children were crossing Franklin Square that the dreadlock man's finger touch the day before had been the first time a man had touched her—outside of handshakes with men at work—since the doofus she met at the club.

They did not see the man at all the next week, and she hated herself for having thought about him over the holiday weekend. Going home that Friday after not seeing him all that week, she began to think that maybe it had something to do with the fact that they had taken the blue line for at least three mornings that week. Maybe, she thought, he only went on the orange line.

The following week she managed to get the kids out the door and down to the subway platform at about the same time when she thought they had met the man the first week. On Monday and Tuesday she waited and looked about for him, then, because time was running out, she settled for a blue line.

"I thought you said it didn't matter if we took a blue or an orange line," Marvin said after they were seated.

"Well, it doesn't matter," his mother said.

"Then why we wait while all those trains went by?"

My son the lawyer. "I don't know," she said. That was the only answer in life that ever seemed to shut him up.

"Hey, it's that man with the snake hair," Marcus said, spotting the man and waving to him. It was Wednesday and they were on the subway platform. The man came over and appeared genuinely glad to see them. She was happy to see him, but she was also upset that he had not been there on the other mornings. She had in her bag a slip of paper with her name and work and home telephone numbers in case he asked.

"Mornin," the subway woman said after they entered the train.

She sounded as if the last thing in the world she wanted to do was speak. "Orange line . . . Ballston . . ."

"Where's Boston?" Avis asked the man, yawning. She was in her mother's lap and the man sat beside them. The boys were in the seat ahead of them, and again Marcus was kneeling facing them.

"It's Ballston," the man enunciated. "The end of the line. It's across the river. In a place called Virginia."

"A long way," the little girl said and yawned again. She closed her eyes and leaned back against her mother.

"Kinda. It depends," the man said.

"What's in the bag?" Marcus said to the man.

Avis's eyes popped open and she sat up straight. "What's in the bag?" she said.

"None of your business," Marvella said to both children. "And turn around in that seat, Marcus." The boy looked at the man as if for help from his mother's order. Marvin was writing a letter to his father. The movement of the subway took his words sloppily above and below the lines, but he did not seem to care.

"My lunch," the dreadlock man said. He opened the bag and took out an apple and held it before the girl. "What's that?" he asked her.

"A apple," Marcus said. "Anybody know that."

"He ast me," Avis said. "Mama, tell Marcus to stop."

"Thas all you got for lunch?" Marcus said. "Boy, you pretty cheap."

The man put the apple back. "No, I have a sandwich and a slice of cheese."

"I hate cheese," Avis said. "It taste nasty."

"Well, I love cheese," Marcus said. "I could eat it all day long."

They saw him again on Friday and he was wearing a tie without a coat, carrying the same type of lunch bag. Marvella carried the same slip of paper, but the man with the dreadlocks did nothing but banter with Marcus and Avis.

On Saturday morning, on the pretense that they would go exploring before their father picked the children up, she borrowed her nephew's car and went driving about the neighborhood. She had grown up in Southeast, but she had spent much of her married life in Northwest, where she and the children had lived before they moved that summer to Southeast to share a large house with her sister and her two children. By keeping the boys at Thompson School in Northwest two blocks from her mother, she worried less when the school day ended.

Turning on the car's engine, she realized how she must look—on a beautiful day, she was dragging her kids along to look for a man she did not know, whom she could well come across strolling hand-in-hand with some other woman, who would probably also be arrayed in dreadlocks. She drove along an area bounded by 19th Street, Potomac, Kentucky, and North Carolina avenues, a very wide area that he would surely have to live in if he got on the subway at Stadium-Armory. In case the children asked what they were doing, she made up enough lies along the way for God to send her straight to hell, but surprisingly, there was nothing said, except for Marvin's comment that being so far from home, they might miss their father when he arrived. But, as if to punish her, God did not produce the dreadlock man.

Over the next several weeks she saw the dreadlock man only four or five times, and on most mornings she simply took whatever train came first. The deeper they went into the year, the less she saw of him. But now and again, she would wake with one of the kids screaming for this or that, and she would take herself and them off to the subway determined to wait for him, for an orange line train. When she did see him, she was glad that Marcus and Avis engaged him in conversation and not once did she tell them to turn around or stop bothering the man.

"How do the lights know to turn off when the train's gone?" Marvin asked her one Thursday morning not long before Memorial Day. His father had turned down the boy's request to live with him and his girlfriend across the Maryland line in Capitol

Heights. Marvella was surprised, and relieved, that Marvin had let the matter drop the same day his father said no.

Marvella had been distracted and she asked him to repeat the question.

"None a your business," Avis said to Marvin.

"I wasn't even talkin to you," Marvin said to his sister. "You want a fat lip?"

"All right, stop it. Both of you, and I mean it!"

Marvin asked her again.

She tried to think of something that would satisfy him. "I guess the last car of the train hits a switch that tells the lights it's gone and the lights turn themselves off."

The lights blinked, and a blue line train came without them getting on. Marvin wanted to know why and Marvella told him to be quiet, for a few people were staring at them. Marvin quieted after they got on the next train, an orange line. The subway was packed and at their stop they had to fight their way to the exit. "Hey! Hey!" Marcus hollered. "Lettus outta this joint!"

As they went up the first set of escalators at McPherson Square, Marvin began asking again why they had to all the time wait when the blue train was like the orange. Just in front of the farecard machines, Marvella put down Avis and grabbed Marvin by the arm. She pulled him along to a corner, away from the passing people. Marcus and Avis followed silently.

"I'm the boss around here, and you seem to be forgetting that," she said to him. He was utterly surprised and began to shake. "Who's the boss around here, you or me? Who? Who? Who's the mama in charge around here?"

His eyes filled with tears. "You are," he said, but not loud enough for her.

She did not like scenes like this, particularly around white people, who believed that nothing good ever happened between black people and their children, but she could not stop herself. "Who's the mama in charge around here, I said?" she kept asking the boy.

"You are," he said louder, crying. "You the mama. You the mama. You the mama in charge."

"Mama's the one in charge. Mama's the one in charge," Marcus chanted as they made their way across Franklin Square Park.

"Marcus, shut up!" his mother said just as Avis was about to take up the chant.

After that, she did not ever again see the man with the dreadlocks and she did not look for him anymore. But for some time, as she went about her days with their blocks of time, she would find herself comparing his hair with other dreadlocks she saw. By then the subway people had extended the orange line all the way to Vienna.

THE SUNDAY
FOLLOWING
MOTHER'S
DAY

When Madeleine Williams was four years old and her brother Sam was ten, their father killed their mother one night in early April. If their mother sent forth to her children a cry of help, or of good-bye, they did not hear it, at least not on any conscious level, and they slept clear through to morning. About six thirty that morning, their father, Samuel, called his sister Maddie to tell her what he had done, how he had done it. "I stabbed her a lot," Samuel said, and though Maddie was still rising up from sleep as he talked, those words were forever imprinted on her mind. He told her to come get his babies, that soon they would be up and ready to eat. As far as anyone could ever tell, the two-minute-or-so conversation he had with Maddie was all he would ever say in life about the murder of a woman the whole world believed he loved— give or take this or that—more than anything. After that, the most Samuel would ever say to anyone about it, including his own attorney, was that he was the one.

"Mr. Carlson, it's obvious you cannot structure a defense for a man who does not want to be defended," the judge assigned to the case of the *District of Columbia* vs. *Samuel Lamont Williams* said at one point to the attorney assigned to defend Samuel. That was but one of the sentences in the transcript of the trial that Madeleine Williams would come to memorize.

When Maddie arrived at the apartment that morning, she found her brother sitting in near-darkness on the floor near the couch, the telephone resting like a black pet on his lap. Still not quite fully awake, Maddie had traveled the three blocks to the M Street apartment only partially aware of what she was doing. Samuel was dressed only in his underwear; there was no sign of trouble about him that she could see, and for a bit this gave her comfort, and this was what she told the courtroom one sweltering day in July.

But in his bedroom she found her sister-in-law, dead, head down, sitting on the floor with one leg under her in a giant pool of drying blood. In her left hand, the greatest friend of Maddie's life gripped a hairbrush, and her right hand was open, also resting on the floor, palm up, as if expecting a small surprise to be dropped into it. It seemed to Maddie right then that all the innocence and joy and kindness had seeped out of Agnes Marie Williams and had become the pool of blood about her. The floor tilted, and so the blood had flowed through the night in several thin lines from the dead woman, and one line had been heading directly toward where Maddie was standing in the doorway. The front of Agnes's nightgown was soaked through with blood. "He said to me on the phone, 'I stabbed her a lot.' " These words her niece, Madeleine, would find on page twenty-eight of her $75.86 copy of the trial transcript. The day she bought it—some twenty years after that morning—Madeleine made it all the way home before she discovered that her copy was missing pages forty-five through fifty-two. It would be three weeks before the court clerk could produce the missing pages, and on those pages there were no sentences that Madeleine would come to memorize.

In the next room, Maddie found the children, still asleep, and it was only then that she began to cry. She backed out of the room, went to her brother, and stood over him. "Say somethin to me," she hissed. She waited, and then she kicked him as hard as she could in his side, and the force of the kick sent the telephone sliding off his lap. It was the last time in their lives she would ever touch him. Samuel raised his fist to her and kept it raised until she backed off.

"Say somethin, gotdamnit! Say somethin, you sonofabitch!" She was reliving a spot or two in the last year, the times when Agnes had said it would be all right and Maddie said No and Agnes said Yes it would and then Maddie said Yes because she wanted to believe too.

Maddie called the police. She went back to close the door of the adults' bedroom and went to the children's room. It took her a few minutes to wake the children and help them dress. As usual, Pookie, as Sam Williams was then called, acted as if he were older than his ten years and dressed without much fuss. But Madeleine was a problem. She complained that she was hungry, and her aunt told her she would get all the food she wanted at her place. Then Madeleine could not find her doll, and it took the three of them several minutes of hunting about the room to find it. Finally, before their aunt opened the door, Pookie said he had to pee. Maddie told him to hold it and Pookie quietly told her that maybe he couldn't, that he might pee on himself. "I told him we were in a hurry," Maddie would tell Madeleine years later, "and that if he did pee on hisself, it wouldn't be the worse thing in the world for a boy to do."

Madeleine, as she was used to doing, tweaked her father's nose as Maddie was ushering the children to the front door. This was how her years of nightmares would begin, the nightmares that would keep her sleeping in Maddie's bed until she was eleven.

Outside, Maddie found two white policemen getting out of their patrol car. "Go up to the second floor," she said with authority. "The door's open. I'll be back soon as I can." One, the older, the larger, did not look up when she spoke and seemed preoccupied with fixing something on his hat. The other kept blinking as if he too had come directly from his bed; Maddie, pestered by Madeleine years later, would remember that the new day's sun flowed in on the street and bits of the sun were caught on the blinking man's badge, his brass buttons, the plastic over the brim of his hat.

"Come," she said to the children, and she took Madeleine's hand.

"Aunt Maddie, we ain't even washed our faces," Madeleine said, holding her doll by the back of the neck. "We ain't even brushed our teef yet." "It's okay," Pookie said, patting his sister's head. The woman and the children headed down M Street toward 5th, and so the sun was at their backs.

Judge John Tellingford chose to sentence Samuel Williams to twenty-five years at Lorton and, Madeleine found on page 164 of the transcript, the judge noted that for whatever demented reason the father had stabbed to death the mother of his children, he had seen fit to spare his children an equally horrendous fate. "You are lucky, Larry, your wife wasn't white," he said. "Or the full force of the people would have come down on that head of yours." In *A Pictorial History of the Judicial System in the District of Columbia*, Madeleine would find a picture of Judge Tellingford. He had had a huge forehead many inches high and he had been a very small white man ("a towering figure on the bench," a *Washington Post* obituary would say), much smaller than any of the other judges in the book, and Madeleine could tell this even though Judge Tellingford had been photographed, like the others, in his judicial robe.

Of the newspapers, only the tabloid-sized *Washington Daily News* reported what had happened. In a drafty room at the Library of Congress, with the light on her microfilm-reading machine flickering the whole time, a pregnant Madeleine would find the headline, at the bottom of page thirteen, accompanied by about an inch and a half of print: NEGRO CHEF KILLS WIFE.

Madeleine and Pookie never saw the apartment again, and until she was about six, when Pookie told her to stop saying it or he would knock her in the mouth, she would pass the apartment building at 427 M Street, Northwest, and tell whomever she was with that up there on the second floor was where her daddy had stabbed her mama to death.

By default, Maddie Williams became their guardian. Maddie, who had lived with few cares, with neither child nor chick, as she told the world, had long before made peace with herself about never marrying, about never wanting a family. And so for weeks and weeks after the murder she beseeched Agnes's family to take Madeleine and Pookie. The idea of being responsible for them for years and years terrified her. But each time she called on the telephone or knocked on their door at the fine house on New Jersey Avenue, someone in Agnes's family would remind her that they had never wanted their daughter, their sister, their Aggie, to marry that man. "We knew he wasn't any good," they would say, and Maddie would go away knowing that what they really meant was that her brother had always been too dark for them.

She herself was a very dark skinned woman with long hair she usually wore in a bun propped in all its abundance with hairpins on the back of her head, like a picture hanging on a wall. She loved men, men who would have killed for her, and it frightened her that she would have to give up all the colored men in the world for two children. Sometimes, for years after she took the children into her life, as she lay on that freed hair in the arms of some man after they both had come and come again and the man was no longer drowning her with such foolishness about baby this and baby that, she would find herself beginning to fall asleep. Then, ever so slowly, her eyes would begin to open as she tried to remember if she had left the children with someone. And if she hadn't, the man, in the dark, would reach across the bed to her as Maddie dressed.

"Oh, baby," the man would say. "Oh, baby, I thought we'd have another go-round."

"Next time, sweetie. I promise. The next time."

Most of Maddie's male friends had cars and they were all too happy to give her and the children a ride down to Lorton to visit Samuel. In the beginning, despite Madeleine's nightmares and despite

Pookie's questions to Maddie, the children would go up to him willingly in the crowded visiting room and play the games, like tweaking his nose, that they had played once upon a time. But gradually Pookie retreated to a corner of the waiting room and would not move until it was time to go. "I won't force him to do anything! Not a single gotdamn thing!" Maddie told Samuel once when he called from Lorton to ask her to get Pookie to be more affectionate. "You lucky they even come see you a tall. You gettin more than you deserve and don't forget that." And it wasn't a matter of Pookie being moody, she told her brother. "You gotta have a lotta moods to be moody," she said. "And he ain't got but that one mood."

Madeleine, torn between wanting to be loyal and stand beside Pookie in the visiting room and wanting to be with her father, nevertheless opted to sit in her father's lap and they would share whatever snacks Maddie had brought. Samuel had begun to smoke, and when Madeleine left him, she and her clothes smelled powerfully of smoke. "You smell like Daddy," Pookie would say to her during the ride back home. "Get away from me."

Maddie would sit throughout the visit across the table from Samuel and Madeleine, talking to whatever man had brought them to Lorton. And if the man stayed in his car, she would sit reading a magazine. The only word she ever spoke to her brother during the visit was good-bye, never hello and never anything in between. "I wouldn't have taken you if it was up to me," Maddie would one day tell her niece. "But you and him was tied to each other by blood and there was nothin I could do about that."

At thriteen, Pookie said he would not ever go back to Lorton. "Daddy won't like that," Madeleine said, waving her finger in her brother's face. "I don't care what Daddy don't like," he said. And to Maddie, Pookie said that if Jesus could throw the men out the temple at twelve, he could go down to Lorton or not go down to Lorton. "Pookie actin up," Madeleine told her father during the next visit. "What did he say to that?" Madeleine asked her aunt years later as she held her sleeping son on her lap. "I don't remember," Maddie said.

*   *   *

The children in the realm made up these words and they would chant, particularly when Pookie was around:

> *Yo daddy killed yo mama*
> *And soon he'll get yo sista*
> *Then you'll be next, brotha, brotha.*

After weeks of the chanting, he went after the biggest of the boys who teased him and worked his way down to the smallest, to the ones his own size. Even if it took weeks of picking a fight with one of them, he would persist until he had finally whipped the kid decisively, whether with just his fists, or the help of a brick, dirt in the face, the limb of a tree. And when he was all done, when it seemed that all the boys in Washington, D.C., knew not to mess with Pookie Williams, he would, from time to time, go after someone he had already whipped. "Sing that song," he would say before the first punch. "Sing that song you useta sing."

When Pookie was fifteen, he stayed all night at a friend's house on Ridge Street. It was the first time he had stayed away all night without Maddie knowing where he was. In the morning, he dressed while all in the house were still asleep and went to the kitchen. He had not eaten since lunch the day before and hunger gnawed at his insides. But he found nothing to eat. On the table, he saw a pocketbook with twenty-eight dollars and he pocketed twenty-one. Then, before leaving, he poured salt in the palm of his hand and licked his hand clean and convinced himself that that was enough to fortify him for the time being.

He sat on the corner at New York and New Jersey avenues and waited for the rest of the world to wake up, for Madeleine as she made her way to Walker-Jones.

"Aunt Maddie called the police and had everybody lookin for you," Madeleine said when she saw him.

"It's all right. I done talked to her," he lied. "It's gonna be all right." He gave her twenty dollars. What had worried him most about the hunger he felt before the salt was that his sister would somehow suffer the same, and he could not abide that. "I'm gonna be goin, so you do everything Aunt Maddie tell you."

"Where you goin, Pookie?"

"To the navy."

"What navy?"

"The navy navy."

"Where you get this money?"

"I took it," he said.

"Aunt Maddie won't let me have no stolen money."

"Hide it away," he said. "You can do that. And don't spend it on somethin stupid. Use it for a mergency."

For a moment, he touched her cheek with the back of his hand, then she watched him walk away, and watching him, she was reminded of a short poem a teacher had made them memorize about a hungry man who went down to the river one day to fish for his supper. "Bye, Pookie," she said, but if he heard, he did not acknowledge. "Bye, Pookie," she said again. She noticed that already he was getting too big for the pants Maddie had purchased only the month before. In her child's mind, he was doing no more than playing hooky for the day and she thought they would see him that evening, but in fact he was gone fifteen years and eight months.

Madeleine never gave Maddie a moment's trouble, her aunt was proud of telling her customers at Cleopatra's Hair Emporium, a small beauty shop of five chairs at 9th and P streets Northwest. At the shop, at the bottom of the mirror at her station, Maddie taped her two favorite photographs, one of herself and the children taken at Sparrow's Beach one day not long after they came to live with her. The man she was seeing at the time had captured the three with their backs to the ocean. She treasured the picture because her nephew and niece were smiling. Above that picture, she had taped a photograph of her and Agnes in their late teens. They were sitting with crossed ankles on the hood of an automobile with an ornament of some being preparing to take flight. There was, on both their faces, a look of boredom, and there was, as well, a hint of don't-fuck-with-me.

Madeleine took copies of these photographs when she went off to Columbia University, which, she had decided, was far enough away to feel she was setting off on her own and still close enough to get back to Maddie in less than a day.

From Columbia, she wrote to Maddie and Sam, wherever he happened to be, at least three times a week. Aside from a postcard now and again, she stopped writing to Samuel after she was fifteen, for no other reason than that she simply had little to say to him. Way before this, she had stopped going to Lorton to see him, but it was for the reason young people usually stop doing things—there were a thousand other things to do in an ever-expanding world. Her father became little more than a man in prison who, she remembered, smelled of cigarette smoke and who would beg for some sugar when she visited him. But when depression hobbled her and gave her new eyes with which to see the world, she began to imagine that she had seen what her father had done, to imagine that she, standing in the doorway, had been a witness, powerless, but somehow nevertheless culpable. "I told him to just stop writin you when you left for New York," Maddie told her after Madeleine returned for good to Washington. "I told him, 'New York City's bad anough as it is.' "

In her sophomore year, she began to do volunteer work at a preschool for Harlem children. All of the children at the center took to her and she to them, but she was particularly fond of a precocious three-year-old girl, Clarine, who, having learned where Madeleine was from, insisted on calling her Miss Washton. Somewhere in her life, the child had been told that she was adorable, and she enjoyed standing before Madeleine and the other adults and slowly turning around so that they could get a good look at her in her dress. "See, see, see," she would say as she turned, the hem of the dress in both her outstretched hands.

In that second year as well, she began seeing Curtis Wallace, an energetic junior from Norfolk. "They all act like they're God's gifts to the world, running around with their giant Afros and talking that trash about treating us like black queens, like the queens we used to be in Africa," she once wrote Maddie. "How many damn queens could there be in one African village anyway? At least he has some humility and feels that he is just one among billions on this planet. . . . If and when we taste the 'forbidden fruit,' as they say around here, I'll let you know. So far, though, he's been hands off."

They would walk the girl Clarine home in the evenings because often no one came for her. The child lived in a crowded two-bedroom apartment with at least a dozen other people, including some five or six other children. In all the times she and Curtis took the girl home, she had seen the mother only a few times, and each time the mother had stood in her bathrobe in the entrance to the kitchen smoking a cigarette and watching as Madeleine said good-bye to the girl. "Whatcha takin up?" the mother asked each time. "What's your major?"

In Madeleine's junior year, Clarine's father killed the mother with four pistol shots into the heart. Madeleine could not remember what the mother looked like, and even when she looked down at the woman in her coffin, she could not connect the dead woman with the woman standing in her bathrobe. The girl, along with the other children, had seen her father shoot her mother. She never returned to the preschool, but Madeleine would go to the girl's apartment each day after she had worked at the preschool. They would sit on the couch together, with Madeleine doing all the talking and the girl following the movement of Madeleine's lips as if that were the only way she could understand what was being said. At first, she brought the child small gifts: barrettes, slippers, coloring books. But when she returned, the things would have disappeared, so she took to bringing only snacks, whatever Clarine could eat right there in her presence.

"Why did he do it?" Madeleine asked her aunt one night after she had returned from Clarine's apartment and found everyone and everything in the apartment gone. Some in the building said the girl's people had come from the South and taken her there, and others said the city government people had put all the children in a house for orphans on Staten Island.

"I don't know," Maddie said. "I only wanted her back, and knowin the why of it didn't have the power to bring her back." She had waited all Madeleine's life for her to ask, had kept that nonanswer poised, and though she had been dozing beside the telephone watching the eleven o'clock television news, the nonanswer sprang from her as if she had been asked her name. "I don't know," Maddie said again. "You alone there?"

"No. Curtis is here. I've been drinking, and please don't tell me I shouldn't have," Madeleine said.

"I've had my share. Why should I tell you different?"

"Why would he shoot her in front of the kids?" Madeleine said.

Maddie said, "He didn't shoot her. He stabbed her. If you say the word, I'll have Bo drive us up there tonight."

"No," Madeleine said.

"Then put Curtis on the phone. And put him on now."

She struggled on at Columbia, spending much of her time in an unsuccessful effort to find Clarine. After graduation, she returned to Washington, where Curtis was finishing his first year in law school at Georgetown. He wanted to get married, or, at least, begin living together, but Madeleine said no, and she continued saying no even after she found she was pregnant.

She named the child Sam, after the brother she now knew only from pictures and telephone calls. She was not superstitious, but when she learned her son was retarded, she felt it some trick of God's for giving the child a name that had originated with a man who had killed his wife. Against everyone's wishes, she had the child put in the Children's Center, the D.C. government's Laurel, Maryland, facility for its retarded citizens.

Once or twice a month, Madeleine and Maddie and Curtis and

Bo Cromwell, the man Maddie had settled down with, would drive out on Sunday to the center to see Sam Wallace. The government people had put him in the Martha Eliot Infirmary, for Sam could not walk, and, they would find later, he could not talk. They brought him ice cream or Nilla Wafers or some other treat. Maddie would set him on her lap and coo at him, while Madeleine or Curtis fed him. If he enjoyed what they gave him, there was never any indication from him. And had they brought him nothing, but simply kept him in his wheelchair and watched him the whole visit, he would have responded the same way.

Sunday became the only day off from researching the Why, and after visiting their son, Madeleine and Curtis would spend the rest of the day at Maddie's or go off to a play or movie and restaurant. She had found work as a cataloguer at the Library of Congress, and every day after work she would walk the stacks of that library or of the Martin Luther King, Jr. Memorial Library for an answer to something Maddie had said did not matter because it would not have brought Agnes back. Everything she found about the Why, however remotely relevant, ended up at her apartment far up Connecticut Avenue. She taped thirty cassettes with Maddie alone, and then searched out people who had lived in the M Street neighborhood when the murder had occurred. Most of them did not remember her or the killing, but she taped them anyway.

By the time her son was one year old, her father had begun writing to her again. Ten- and twenty-page letters in the most beautiful handwriting of anyone she had ever seen, about nothing more than what his days were like and who were the men he spent his days with. And he'd send newspaper and magazine articles he himself had found of interest, each article neatly cut out and pasted on a piece of ruled notebook paper. And he'd send poems—"On Missing a Daughter's 25th Birthday," "The Rage of Being Caged," "On Becoming a Grandfather," "The Light Through the Barred Window." She was, simply, captivated, and it was a very long time before she told anyone what he was doing. He spoke of everything in the world except the Why, and over time she lost the courage to ask. "I am thinking of you this day and all days . . . ," he began his letters.

A month after he left the sea for good and returned to Washington, Sam Williams found a wreck of a place on Martin Luther King, Jr., Avenue in Anacostia that had been a trophy shop, a place he thought would be perfect for a bakery. In a few months of working alone, he had the place gutted, renovated, equipped, and opened for business. The children in the neighborhood began calling him the donut man. He hired a young man and woman from the neighborhood and trained them in what he called the life wonders of baking. He named the place after his mother and aunt. *The House of Agnes and Maddie. Fine Baked Goods.*

Among the regular customers were some of the parishioners from the Cleansing Waters Baptist Church two blocks away, including the pastor's daughter, Hazel Watts. She was one of the few people who never asked who Agnes and Maddie were. She came in one Saturday to pick up a cake she had ordered for a birthday party for the oldest member of the Usher's Board, and, as had become his custom, Sam waited on her himself. He carried the cake—an orangeicing thing of one layer, two by three feet—to her station wagon.

"Miss Watts," he said, after he had set the cake in and shut the car's back door, "we'd like to see you sometime." He had developed the habit of often speaking about himself in the first person plural. "Maybe dinner, a movie. Something like that. That is, if you aren't married or keepin company with someone." He did not falter.

"I'm a free woman in that way, Mr. Williams," she said. "Dinner or whatever would be nice."

He walked with her to the driver's side of the car. "Miss Watts, I hope you're not the kind of woman who likes a man to sit around and talk a lotta of sweet nothins to a woman, cause we ain't it."

"That's all right, Mr. Williams," she said, looking for her keys in her pocketbook. "I've had my fill of sweet nothings." She opened the door. "And Mr. Williams, I hope you're not the kind of man who likes a woman to swoon every time she's within a mile of him, cause I ain't it." She got into her car and handed him a card from the glove compartment.

Having known only prostitutes throughout his time in the world, he was surprised by candor coming from a church woman, and she liked the fact that he was surprised. She said, "I guess this means I don't have to tip you."

In the most luxurious hotel in the Bahamas, with the smell of the ocean thick throughout their room, Sam would say that first day, standing in the night dark at the window, "We're never gonna believe in anything but right now. Not very much of tomorrow. Maybe a little of the tomorrow mornin but no farther than that."

"A bride doesn't want to hear that on her wedding night," Hazel said, coming up to his back and putting her arms around him. She massaged a scar about his stomach, the result of a knife fight with a man in a bar in the Philippines. The keloid scar covered the place where his navel had been. "A bride wants to hear that there will be a million tomorrows. She wants to hear that there will be an always."

"I know," he said. "But I could be dead tomorrow, and then what would you do with all them words?"

That afternoon, on the beach, she had drawn a tiny football field in the sand to begin to teach him the game. He had never had any patience with games beyond a bit of poker here and there. But she had a passion for football. It was one of the few sins she had allowed herself, she said, "and I want you to taste it so I don't go to hell alone." When the lesson for that day was done, she threw the stick into the ocean. "Now," she said, "you teach me something." The sun was at his back and she looked at him with her hand shading her eyes.

"We don't think we have anything like all them quarterback people," he said.

"It don't matter. Anything will do. It don't matter," she said, for she had been a bride less than twenty-four hours. "Some trick with a string will do."

He moved so that his body was enough shade for her and in moving he covered the football field. "We can teach you to defend yourself if two guys come at you at once," and he held up his fists, ready, coiled, forgetting where he was and to whom he was talking. "I can teach you to put em down flat."

She laughed. She liked it. She reached over and patted his stomach where the scar was. "Can you teach me how to defend against someone who wants to do that to me?" she said, thinking of the Philippines fight.

"That's a lesson for another day," he said, thinking of something else.

That night, in their hotel room, her arms around him as he stood at the window, she said of his words about having only right now, "All right, just don't talk about it anymore."

"We won't," he said. "We won't say a word as long as you know that's what we're thinkin." From the day he arrived back in Washington to the night of the conception of his first son, it was ten months and three days.

Not long after Sam and Hazel returned from their honeymoon, the prison people released Samuel Williams. He made his way alone from Lorton Prison to Washington, a city he had not seen for twenty years. He found a room at Hartnett Hall on 21st Street Northwest, and a few days later, with the help of an ex-offenders' group, he got a job as a short-order cook in a diner on E Street downtown.

Except for a movie now and again and a visit every two weeks or so to see his sister ("I'll give you one hour on Tuesday," she told him, "from six to seven. No more, and it might be less, cordin on how I feel"), the job was about all he had of life. He refused to become friends with any of the people he worked with or with the men who roomed in his building. Once or twice a month he paid for a whore, but he never brought her back to his room, choosing instead to pay for a two-hour room at the Buckingham, a place at L and 14th that catered to prostitutes and their johns. "Sheets Changed With Regularly," a hand-written sign at the desk said.

Once released, Samuel began writing to his son and received no reply for three months. "20 years of happy living isn't long enough for a motherfucker like you," Sam finally wrote his father. "Get back to us after you spend 10,000 years in hell."

Samuel bought a fireproof box for the letters he received from Madeleine. Though he wrote her at least five times a week, she wrote back only once or twice a week. The most current letter from her he always kept on the top of his room's chest of drawers, dead center, the way some people keep a vase of flowers.

Sam was furious when he learned from Maddie that Madeleine had not only not told Samuel where to go, but that she was writing back to him. And for weeks he refused to talk to her. A reconciliation was arranged by Hazel and Maddie on the Sunday before Mother's Day, which happened to be Maddie's birthday. They held a small party for her at Sam and Hazel's house in Anacostia. Late in the day, Sam stopped Madeleine in the kitchen. She was refilling the pitcher of lemonade and he took the pitcher from her.

"Why would anyone in the world write to the man who killed their own mother?" he said, sliding the pitcher far back on the counter.

"Let's not get into all this," she said. "I'm just here to have a good time and to give Maddie a good day."

Despite something in him that abhorred backing down from any position, he had been eager to reconcile because each and every day since his return he was aware of how much he and Madeleine had lost by not being together. So many years, important years, he had told his wife, they had known each other only through hurried, of-ten dutiful, letters and through telephone calls with horrible con-nections and photographs that often arrived folded despite the "Do Not Fold" instructions written on envelopes. Sometimes, in addi-

tion to the times they had on weekends, Sam would pick her up after work and they would eat at some restaurant near her apartment.
It had taken them several months before they could speak to each
other without considering each and every word, before they could
even comfortably hug hello and good-bye.

"I just wish you'd explain to me this need to write to that guy. I
mean, this ain't some kinda fuckin pen pal."

"I know what he is, Sam." The others—Maddie, Hazel, Curtis,
Bo, and Sam's new baby—were in the backyard, and Sam and
Madeleine could see them through the kitchen window's curtains.
The baby, newly weaned from Hazel's breast, had just been bottle-
fed, and the adults were taking turns trying to get him to burp.

"I don't think he has anyone else. There's Maddie, but she
could take or leave him, and she usually leaves him," Madeleine
said. With two fingers she wiped condensation from the pitcher.
"It's not like I don't think about what he did. I just think I remember this father man and some good things he did. Maybe I write because blood is thicker than water."

"So's goddamn cookie batter. So what?" Sam said.

"You act as if it's easy for me to write him. It's not. Sometimes
I'm afraid, but he keeps writing me, and he sends me things, be-
comes a father. He sends me things for my son. I want to write
'Why?' but all I can manage to ask is, 'How was your day?' He
scares me sometimes, because it's overwhelming, so it's not as if I
look forward to hearing from him. He wants to see me, but I always
tell him no. Give me credit for that."

He took her arm and squeezed it. "You give us the word," he
said. "Just give us the word and we'll break his neck in a thousand
places. Break his hands so he can't ever write again." In a few seconds he had become something else.

"No," and she pulled away, looking at him in that "Who are
you?" way she did before she became comfortable with him again.
"Is that what you think I want?"

"Who the hell knows what you want."

Outside, Maddie, in a chair under the peach tree, had the baby with his head resting on her shoulder and, with two more pats on the back, the baby finally rewarded her with a loud burp that even Sam and Madeleine could hear. The adults in the backyard shouted "Hooray!" which frightened the child and he began to cry.

"You should talk to him or something," Madeleine said. "He's your son's grandfather."

Sam pulled the pitcher forward and wrapped her fingers around the handle. "You listen to me good: I been all over the damn world," he said, "so when I came back here I knew what I wanted to put in my own world, and he'll never be in it. He's the only black person who can never be in it. We have our wife and child, and you and Maddie and Hazel's family. And there're new friends all over Anacostia I've made, and people who come in the bakery, and people at that church Hazel drags me to." He parted Hazel's lace curtains to get a better look at those in the backyard. "Now and again we meet a complete stranger we like a whole lot and I include that person in." He released the curtains, then straightened them. "But no matter how big we make that world, it'll never be big enough to include him. And he's very lucky, cause we could have killed him a long time ago. I've driven over there a hundred times to do it—that's how much I hate him. But I won't. We won't unless you and Maddie told us that's what yall want. Every day he wakes up he should feel lucky."

He took the pitcher from her. "Your trouble's that you live up there among all them white people. With the ghost people. They believe in that all forgivin shit, in all that stuff that cripples the soul. You should move out to Anacostia to be with real people, the people who know what day and night is like and never get the two confused." Then he put his hands at the corners of her mouth and tried to fashion a smile. She hugged him, clung to him, and for those moments they were no more or less than a boy and girl without a mother and father.

Madeleine and Curtis had planned to spend Mother's Day at the Children's Center with their child, but Curtis's father became ill during the week and Curtis went to Norfolk. Madeleine would have waited until he returned to visit the center, but she did not want too much time to pass after Mother's Day before she saw her son.

On the Sunday morning following Mother's Day, she was ready to leave her apartment when the chime on her door rang. She opened the door without looking through the peephole. Samuel stood before her, holding a paper bag with one hand and removing his hat with the other. What she saw was not the man in the letters with the beautiful handwriting, not the man of the poems.

"I'm your father," he said. He smiled and looked momentarily down at his shoes. At five, she stopped counting his missing teeth.

"How did you get in here?" she asked, looking to either side of him into the hall. "The front door is always locked."

He stopped smiling. "Somebody was comin in and I got to the door fore it closed. I know this ain't spected. I wanted to wish you a happy Mother's Day." He sounded like every black country person she had ever heard, those people who talked of fetchin this and wearin britches and someone commencin to do such and such.

"Mother's Day was last Sunday. It's past," she said.

"I know," he said. "I started up here last Sunday, but I left your address at home and when I tried to go by memory, I got lost. Never get lost in white folks' neighborhood. The first law a the land." He smiled again. His suit coat and pants had been stylish a generation ago. They did not match, though they were both a dark blue that might appear similar at a glance. His dark gray fedora was now so old that it had the look of something abandoned, something a child pretending to be an adult might wear at Halloween.

"Well, I'm on my way out. I'm afraid I've no time for a visit."

"I can take you," he said. "I can take you wherever you wanna go. I got a car and I can take you wherever you need to go."

"I have my own car. Thanks," she said.

"But I can save you wear and tear on yours," he said. "Save you gas, too. Sides"—and he reached into the paper bag and pulled out a red, drug-store box of chocolates—"I brought you this. Happy Mother's Day. You can eat em on the way to where you goin."

She told him thanks and placed the box on the table by the door. She did not tell him that she had once, before age twelve, been able to eat all the chocolate she wanted, but now all chocolate made her ill.

With her directions, Samuel drove out of Washington and found the Baltimore-Washington Parkway, heading to Laurel and the center. He and his car smelled heavily of cigarette smoke. All that May the days had been wonderful gifts, and that day was no exception. After they had crossed into Maryland, after there was enough fresh air blowing through the car to force out the smoky air, she relaxed somewhat and lay back in her seat.

"I been tryin to get up the nerve to come see you for a long time," he said at one point, "but I guess it took spring to give me the nerve I needed." He drove with his hat cocked back on his head. It was a sight she remembered from somewhere, but she did not know if it was a memory of him from before they had stopped being a family or from some movie she had seen with Curtis. "It ain't like goin to the store and buyin a loaf of bread, I know that."

Before long, she directed him onto the center's grounds and he parked in front of the infirmary. The infirmary was a one-story brick building of offices and wards where the city people kept the most severely retarded residents, those children and adults who could not talk or walk or feed themselves or communicate. There, too, were the patients from other buildings who had been beaten by the staff or other residents or who had been injured accidentally or neglected to the point where they could no longer care for themselves.

On the lawn there was a family fussing over a fellow who could have been five or in his teens or a man of thirty or so, and who was sitting in the lap of a woman who may have been his mother. Two cars down from where Samuel parked, a man was working deep under the hood of an ancient car. The woman raised her arm and gave an uncomfortably loud hello to Madeleine and Samuel.

Inside the building, they saw no one until they had walked far down the hall to D Ward. All the way down they could hear the crying and cackling and laughing and shouting of those in other wards. Madeleine realized that she had come without some treat—pieces of fruit or a small box of cookies, something that Curtis usually remembered to bring. At D Ward, after the attendant had wheeled the child Sam out of his ward and left without having spoken one word, Samuel bent down and kissed the boy on the cheek, which embarrassed Madeleine. Sam blinked once and then after a few seconds he blinked again. In the ward, those patients not in their beds were in wheelchairs, gathered around a very loud television set propped up on a dull blue bureau that had no drawers. The only person in the room who seemed interested in the television was an attendant painting her fingernails.

Samuel took the handles of the wheelchair and they went outside. Madeleine had never come there without Curtis or Maddie and she would have preferred going into one of the unoccupied offices in the front and shutting the door.

The woman on the lawn waved them over. "Yall set a spell with us," she said, then began to introduce those in her family. "And this here is Clement," she said of the retarded boy in her lap. "The baby a the family. Six years old."

"That's the biggest baby I ever saw," said the woman's daughter, who stood beside an older brother, just behind their mother. The brother whispered something in the girl's ear and the two laughed.

"All right now," their mother said, "Thas anough a that." The woman, Arnisa Isaacs, gave Samuel a blanket and indicated that he should spread it on the grass for him and Madeleine and Sam to sit down on.

"We'll just move around a bit," Madeleine said. She resented Curtis for not being with her, for not protecting her from all this.

"Oh, there's time for that," Arnisa said. "The day is long. Sit a spell." She pointed to the blanket in Samuel's hand and he and Arnisa's son opened it and spread it in front of the woman and her retarded boy.

Sam, freed from the makeshift straps of cloth that had bound him to the wheelchair and placed beside Madeleine on the blanket, began to look about for the first time. Noticing an empty carton of ice cream, Samuel asked if there was a store nearby. "Like to get my grandson somethin," he said.

"No," Arnisa said. "There used to be a canteen, but all that's gone. This place is goin to hell. The closest place is that place out on the road you came in on."

"Oh, he doesn't need anything," Madeleine said, tying one of the laces on Sam's tennis shoes. "He's probably just eaten lunch. It's not necessary to get him anything."

Samuel did not remember the place on the road and asked Arnisa for directions. She called to her oldest boy, who was helping the man working under the hood of the car. "He'll show you where it is," and before Madeleine could think of something to say, Samuel and the boy were in his car and heading back up the lane. The girl and her brother began helping the retarded brother into his wheelchair and they maneuvered the wobbly chair through the grass onto a paved, stone-littered area that had once been a playground.

"Yall be careful now," Arnisa said. She reached across and took Sam's chin in her hand. "And how old's this precious thing?" she said. "Oh, oh, ain't he just the most precious thing in the whole world!" She took Sam onto her lap. "Come here, sugar."

Sam began to drool almost immediately. Madeleine recoiled, and Arnisa leaned around to see what Sam had done. "Oh, honey," Arnisa said, wiping Sam's mouth with a paper towel, "it's only spit. It ain't lye." Then she began telling Madeleine about her life, sparing nothing, it seemed to Madeleine, as if the two women had known each other from day one. The man working on the car was not the children's father, wasn't even her legal husband. "I lucked out when I found him," Arnisa said, looking lovingly at the man still deep in the car. "A good man is hard to find, they say, and that's the eternal truth. And then you throw in a kid—three kids!—not countin the one out here, and you talkin bout a hello and good-bye all in the same day."

Madeleine felt she knew this woman, knew her children, who

were destined for nowhere, knew her common-law husband with his unreliable trash-heap of a car, knew this woman and her wig of "real human hair!" as the television ads proclaimed. Knew their tabloid lives. It occurred to her that they were a part of the same tribe as the nearly toothless man who had come to her door that morning, saying he was her father. The more Arnisa talked, the more she was aware of how much time was going by and kept looking up the lane for the car that would take her back to Washington. Sam leaned his back against the woman's breasts and fell asleep.

Nearly an hour later, Samuel and the boy returned, but they were walking, with the boy trying to balance on the narrow strip of yellow-painted concrete dividing the grass from the lane.

"Where have you been?" Madeleine shouted to Samuel when he was still yards away. "What have you been doing to leave me like this?"

Samuel was surprised at the outburst, but the boy began to explain that the car had died just before they left the center. Samuel had insisted on going on to the store, and he was now holding a bag of something as his daughter raised her finger and berated him. Arnisa stood with Sam in her arms.

"Help me get Sam into the wheelchair so we can get him back," Madeleine said to Samuel. "How in the world are we going to get back home?"

"Oh, honey, Bill can probably fix that car," Arnisa said. "He can fix anything."

They put Sam in his wheelchair, and as Samuel wheeled the boy up the ramp, Madeleine looked her father up and down. "Don't you even know how to dress? Can't you see that that tie doesn't go with that suit—if you can call it a suit—with those shoes. Don't you even know how to match colors?" Samuel said nothing. After they had returned Sam to the ward, Madeleine waited in the infirmary lobby while Arnisa's husband drove Samuel to where his car was. In very little time, they returned with Samuel driving his own car.

Madeleine said nothing more to Arnisa, and she and Samuel drove silently back to Washington. At her apartment, she got out without a word and did not hear Samuel say he was sorry. She opened the building's front door and made sure it locked behind her. When she was back in her apartment, she looked out the window and found that the car had died on him once again. The car was parked in a space near the entrance to the parking lot with its hood up and Samuel was leaning into the car, a man being swallowed up. She lived on the second floor, facing the parking lot, and she could hear him and what he was doing. White people passed and paid no attention to him.

He worked late into the afternoon, now and again stopping to try to start the car or to step back and stare at it as if some solution might rise up from the roof and announce itself. The day was completely ruined for Madeleine, and throughout the afternoon as her father worked she sat angry in the chair with its back to the window. That morning she had looked forward to going to the deli down the street where she and Curtis sometimes bought sandwiches and pastries. But she knew she could not go out with Samuel blocking the path to the deli and the deli would soon be closed. There were few cars or people passing, and most of the world was quiet. The loudest sounds were those of her father's muttering and of his tools against the car's metal, all of it reminding her, first before anything else, that the day was forever wearing itself away.

LOST
IN THE
CITY

When the telephone rang about three o'clock that morning, she sat bolt upright in her bed, as if a giant hand had reached through the ceiling and snatched her up. The man sleeping beside her did not stir until the seventh ring, and then only to ask "What? What?" of nothing in particular before returning to sleep. She first sat on the side of the bed and began to hope: a wrong number, or Gail, drunk, in from an evening of bar-hopping, calling to talk about a man. She then sat in the dark on the floor in front of the nightstand. If it was true what her mother had once told her, then nothing rang the telephone like death in the middle of the night.

On the fifteenth ring, she picked up the telephone and said nothing.

"Ms. Walsh? Ms. Lydia Walsh?" a woman said.

"Yes."

"We are very sorry to call at such a time, but your mother died twenty minutes ago." The woman was waiting. "Ms. Walsh?"

"Yes. I'll be there soon as I can," Lydia said.

"Very well. We, the entire staff here at George Washington, are very sorry. Your mother was an exemplary patient," the woman said. "We will expect you very soon."

"Listen," Lydia said. "Don't . . . don't put that sheet over her face until I get there, okay? I don't want to walk in and see that sheet over her."

"Very well," the woman said. "We will expect you soon. And again, we at George Washington are very sorry."

Lydia hung up the telephone. She continued sitting on the floor and watched the clock that could tell her the time in the dark. The minute numbers on the clock moved ahead one, two, and then three more minutes. Twenty minutes ago, what had she been dreaming? Try to remember, she told herself, for all of it must go in the diary: On the night of June 29th, I was dreaming such-and-such and such-and-such when my mother passed away. Try to remember where you were.

She tapped the base of the brass lamp once and the bulb's lowest setting came on. The man in the bed was naked, as was she. There was a foreign smell about herself and she realized that it was his cologne, a popular and very expensive concoction that many of the men she knew wore because someone in their world had decided that the smell conveyed power and success. She thought she had been dreaming of Antibes and the naked Texan on the beach when her mother died, but the more she thought the more it seemed that Antibes had actually been on her mind when she came the first time hours ago.

What is his name? she asked herself of the sleeping man. From a nightstand drawer she took one of the three appointment books she kept in the town house. On the June 29 page there were the initials JL scrawled across all the hours after eight in the evening. She remembered they had met at Trader Vic's for dinner after she had come from the hospital, and then they had come to her place. But what had she called him all those hours? She flipped back through the pages: "Gyn-nw dia" on the 22nd morning; "B Kaufman—Sen Fin" lunch on the 20th; "Taylor—Amer. Con Life Bst" at two on the 19th afternoon. Finally, on the evening of the 15th, she found "Dinner and ?????? with Jack Lawrence, Amer. Bankers. . . ."

"He's pretty light-skinned, ain't he?" her mother had said of the first boy she had ever slept with, though all her mother knew at that time was that the boy had taken her to a movie and Mile Long for a steak sandwich. "Does he come from a sickly family?" her mother had asked. She told her diary about the evening the boy busted her cherry: "The movie was *Who's Afraid of Virginia Woolf?* He told me that I was the most beautiful girl at Dunbar, but when he walked me back home after the 'dirty deed' was done, he acted like he didn't know me anymore."

She shook Jack Lawrence from Amer. Bankers, who was not light-skinned but the color of dark honey. He grabbed her hand and squeezed it so hard she thought she heard her bones cracking—in his sleep he had perceived some threat to himself. She screamed and he woke up, his hand still holding hers and his head turning about to find out where in the world he was. He released her and she rubbed her hand. "What the hell's wrong with you?" she said.

"Sorry . . . sorry," he said. "I must have been dreaming." The way he said "dreaming" prompted more details about him: Something he called fate had plucked him from the streets of Harlem and sent him to Horace Mann prep, then sent him to Dartmouth, then sent him to Harvard Law. At their first dinner, he had said of the place where she had gone, "I would have gone to Yale Law, but there was something I didn't like about the white guy that interviewed me." "You okay?" he said now. He was still lying down.

"I'll be all right. I have to go," Lydia said. "My mother has died and I have to go to her."

"Oh, Cynthia, I'm very sorry."

My name is Cynthia and I come from Washington, she chanted in her head. What was that from? Jumping rope or playing hopscotch? He does not even know my name on the very night my mother has died, she thought, wanting him out of her bed and out of her house. "You can get some sleep," she said. "Make sure the door is locked when you leave."

He yawned. "Yeah, I'm beat," he said. The way he said "beat" brought more details about him. He turned over and pulled the sheet up to his shoulders. Even now, she thought that they were nice shoulders.

"I can't believe I'm walkin the same paths that my Lord walked," her mother had said that second day in Israel, standing at the Church of Gethsemane. Lydia had presented the trip to her mother on her sixty-fifth birthday and had even paid the way for Georgia Evans, her mother's best friend. Lydia had not wanted to go, but her mother had insisted. "Oh, Lydia," her mother had said, "what would the Holy Land mean to me without you bein there with me?"

Georgia, lazy, far less religious that her mother, had complained about all the hills. "How did Jesus get any preachin done goin up and down these hills?" she said the second day. Georgia would drink all the water she carried, then want more from Lydia and her mother. "I never done so much walkin in all my life. Never drunk so much water either." On the third day, after the Via Dolorosa, Georgia was unable to go on and spent the next days moping about the hotel. "I never thought all I'd get to see of the Holy Land was a big old hotel. Must be a sin in that somewhere."

My mother lies moldering . . .

She tapped the base of the lamp three times and the bulb went through the rest of the settings, then the room went dark. In the living room, she knew she needed some coke. One line, she said to herself, one line and no more. This fur and no further. With the gold razor blade, she spread out the cocaine on the black marble tray, then inhaled a line of two inches or so through the crystal straw Gail Saunders had brought back from Bonn. "I hereby make this oath, this pledge, this whatever," Gail said the night of her return. "I'll sleep with no more white men. They make you feel like you should be grateful."

In the shower, Lydia held her face as close as she could to the nozzle. After she had finished, she soaped herself again. "Best get his smell off me," she said to the water. "Or else when I walk in there, they'll know I've been fucking. The nurses and doctors will look at me and they'll say, 'Why, Ms. Walsh, your mother lies moldering and you've been fucking.'"

"Forgive me, Father, for I have been fucking," she said to the mirror as she toweled off. The exhaust fan made a low humming sound, barely audible even in the quiet of the night. But though the repair people had been there four times, it was still too loud for her. "No sound," she had said to the second repairman. "Absolutely no sound whatsoever. Can you manage that?" She did not want to go back to her bedroom, to her closet, so she dressed in the clothes she had returned home in the evening before. They, the clothes, were scattered about the living room, where Amer. Bankers had taken her the first time and where Antibes had entered her head. That first Sunday in Antibes, she had done as the natives did and gone naked on the beach, and a stranger, the naked Texan reading Ayn Rand, had said in the most exquisite French that her breasts were perfect. *Je m'appelle Lydia et j'habite a Washington.*

She called a Capitol cab, because that was the company her mother had always used. "Trust Capitol to get you there and back in one piece," her mother had said. "Don't trust D.C. National or Empire." Lydia opened the front door and listened to the night sounds. She felt the coke was wearing off. Way off to the left, through the thick leaves of June, she thought she saw the sun inching up, but she knew how deceptive the light in Washington could be. Once, as a girl, she had traveled with her mother's church through most of the night to an edge-of-the-world mountain town in Virginia, where the church members had held Easter sunrise services as the sun came up over the mountains. "We proclaim," the preacher had said, "that Jesus has risen." "We proclaim it so," the congregation had said, huddled in blankets and covered with dew. "We proclaim it so."

She did another line of cocaine. Her town house was in an enclosed area in Southwest protected by a guard in his tiny house at the entrance. Generally, the guard would call to tell her that a cab was coming to her door, but she felt she might want to go out to the entrance and meet the cab. But then, as the coke flowed through her, she relaxed and thought it best for him to come and get her. "Ten dollar tip," she said to the marble tray and raised her eyebrows up and down several times. Before closing the crystal canister that contained the drug, she put some in a plastic packet with the small gold spoon she kept in the canister. "Who knows what evil lurks in a hospital," she said, laughing.

On that sixth morning in Israel, Georgia had gone back to her bed after breakfast and seemed unable to move, but she had insisted that Lydia and her mother go on without her. When mother and daughter returned from floating on the Dead Sea, they found Georgia in a lounge chair at the swimming pool, descending into drunkenness, not quite certain who they were or where she was. When Lydia's mother told her that she was in the Holy Land, the land of Jesus, Georgia said, "Yes. Yes. I been to that place." Then, after Lydia's mother slapped her, Georgia asked her friend for forgiveness.

Back in the room the two older women shared, Lydia had tried to reassure a sobbing Georgia. Her mother refused to say anything more to Georgia. "It's all right," Lydia said to Georgia as she put her to bed. The old woman kept saying that she was going to die in the Holy Land and Lydia kept telling her that she wouldn't. They left her and had dinner in the hotel dining room, but her mother only picked at her food.

Georgia was contrite throughout the last six days, and though it was clear to Lydia that the woman's legs and feet could not manage it, Georgia, uncomplaining, went out each day for the rest of the tour. Each place along the way, in Jericho, in Bethany, in Nazareth, she stayed close to Lydia's mother, but Cornelia paid her no mind, and it showed on Georgia's face.

On the living-room wall in Lydia's town house, among the photographs of places she had visited around the world, between the pictures of her standing before the Kremlin on a winter day and of her in a cavernous room in a Danish castle the guide said was haunted, there was the picture of Lydia and Cornelia and Georgia standing where the tourist bureau said Joseph's carpentry shop had been, Georgia in her hideous wig standing on one side and her mother in the middle. It was the tenth day of the trip.

She did two more lines of cocaine. "Just a shorty shorty this time, girl," she said as she spread out the drug. All of this and more I offer to you if you would but bow down and worship me. . . .

She did not know how long the cab driver had been standing in the doorway when he said, "Lady, you call for a cab?" He was an old man who had probably done nothing but work all his life. Father, may I? . . . What would that old man have said to see her perfect breasts adorning the beach at Antibes? Have you seen the Egyptian pyramids? the naked Texan asked, fingering the pages of Ayn Rand.

"Yes," she said to the old man, sounding as if there had been a death in the family. "It's for me. My mother has died." Immediately, he took off his hat and made the sign of the cross. She stood and put her things, including the packet of cocaine, into the Fendi bag.

"My heart goes out to you, lady," the cab driver said. "It really does. I know what it's like to lose a mother. And a father too." Through the screen door, he looked about the room as if there might be others to whom he should express condolences.

At the door, she could see that he was not just an old man, but an extremely old man. Her father, had he lived, would have been such a man. She closed the door and locked it. The sounds of birds were louder, and she knew the sun was not far off. The old man helped her down the three brick stairs and held the cab door for her. She had wanted to buy a second town house in the area as another investment and have her mother and Georgia live there, but her mother told her that she did not know if she could live among so many white people. "I'm not used to their ways and such like you are, Lydia," and Lydia had been offended.

The old man drove out of the compound and turned right on G Street. He was looking at her in the rearview mirror. She smelled dead fish from the wharf. At 7th the man turned right again. "I knew folks who lived in Southwest before they threw the colored out and made it for the wealthy," her mother had said when Lydia told her she had bought a town house there.

"Ma'am, maybe you should tell me where you goin?" the cab driver said.

"Just get me lost in the city," she said.

"What, ma'am?"

"Just keep on driving and get us lost in the city. I'll pay you. I have the money."

"No, ma'am, it ain't a matter of money. I just thought. . . . You know, your mother. . . . And besides, ma'am, I'm a Capitol cab driver and I ain't allowed to get lost."

"Try," she said. "Try ever so hard." She took two twenty-dollar bills from her bag, leaned forward and placed them on the seat beside him. "And the more lost you get us, the more you get paid. Or is it, the more loster, or the most lost? There are, you know, Mr. Cab Driver, so many grammatical rules that the grammar people say we must not break."

"Yes, ma'am, I know. I've heard it said."

He did not know what else to do, so he continued driving. He passed the federal buildings along 7th, then the mall and its museums. In one of the museums white men had allowed her father to make a living pushing a broom, and now she was paid in one year more than her parents had earned in both their lifetimes. Soon, she would pass a point in her life where she would have earned more than all her ancestors put together, all of them, all the way back to Eve.

At New York Avenue, he turned right, then left on 5th Street. He thought that maybe she had been born elsewhere, that she did not know Washington, would not know the streets beyond what the white people called the federal enclave. But in fact, the farther north he went, the more she knew about where they were going. My name is Lydia. . . . Say it loud. . . .

"You gettin us lost?"

"Yes, ma'am, I'm tryin."

"All right. Try very hard." She placed another twenty beside the other two.

They passed where the K Street market once had been. Two pounds of chicken wings for twenty cents. Had she remembered to finally write down her mother's recipe for that wondrous beef stew somewhere in one of the appointment books? They continued on up 5th Street. Her father had died at 1122 5th Street in a back room on the top floor where they had lived when she was four. It occurred to Lydia that in the world there was now no one from whom she could get that full medical history she had always planned to get. Who now could tell her if there was a history of breast cancer among the women in her family?

"I'm sorry for all this," her father had said on his death bed to her mother. "I'm very sorry for all this, Cornelia." They had not known that she was standing in the doorway watching them.

"For what?" her mother said to her father. "What's there to be sorry about? You do know that I love you. You do know that, don't you? If you go away with nothin else, go away with that."

At 5th and Ridge streets, she asked the cab driver, "Hi you doin up there, buddy? You doin okay?"

"Yes, ma'am, just fine, thank you."

While living at 457 Ridge Street, in the downstairs apartment, they had come to know Georgia, who lived in the upstairs apartment. Georgia would never have children of her own and, except for Lydia, was uncomfortable around other people's children. Until Lydia, was fourteen, she gave her a doll every Christmas. "Now see, if you pull the string Chatty Cathy will talk to you, honey. Tell Chatty Cathy your name, honey." "My name is Lydia Walsh and I live in Washington."

The sun was even higher when he turned right at O Street. In one of the houses on that street her mother lived until Lydia's last year of law school. She had once brought down from New Haven a professor of linguistics who thought the sun rose and set on her. He had had a kind heart, the professor had, but his love for her had shown through all too clearly, and that was his downfall. For thirty days during the month of her birthday he had sent her the reddest roses she had seen up to then: one on the first day, two on the second day, three on the third, and so on. "How much do professors of linguistics make?" she asked a friend on the twentieth day, looking down at his name on the card that came with the roses. "Does he come from a sickly family?" her mother had asked while the man was in the bathroom.

She wanted more coke and she began to cry. "And first prize, for her particularly beautiful enunciation, goes to. . . ." John Brown lies molderin where my mother lies molderin. . . . The cab driver thought that her crying meant that maybe it had finally hit her that her mother had died and that soon his passenger would be coming to herself.

At New Jersey Avenue, the cab driver turned left, then right at Rhode Island down past Frazier's Funeral Home. At a large apartment building on Rhode Island where the Safeway now stood, they had lived on the same floor as a woman who was terrified that her husband would leave her. "So all the time bein scared of him leavin," her mother told Lydia years later when she thought her daughter was old enough to understand, "she just became his slave. He was a night foreman at a bakery way out in Northeast. I guess some thought he was a handsome man, but I never cared for him. Had what they call that good hair. Night and day she worried that he'd leave her. She begged me and all the other women not to take him from her. She wouldn't believe that I whatn't studyin bout him. She worried herself sick and they came and took her away to St. Lizabeths one day. In those days, they gave you twenty-five dollars if you turned in a crazy person. Twenty-five dollars and a pat on the back. Somebody turned her in, but it whatn't me."

HIS MOTHER'S HOUSE

When his mother moved into that 10th Street house Santiago Moses bought for her, one of the few things she brought from the place she left behind was the coffee table made of see-through glass and false wood. And once in the house he bought, in the renovated house, one of her pleasures in the first weeks was watching the neighbors watch as the trucks came to deliver furniture, some of it still in sealed boxes and crates, brand new furniture and appliances that no other woman in the world had lived with. In the midst of all the new that her son bought for her—the living room couch itself cost as much as all the furniture in the place she left behind—she put the coffee table that had been owned by God knows how many people before she herself bought it in that second-hand store on H Street in Northeast and had her man rope it to the roof of his eleven-year-old Chevy.

Her whole life, in dozens of pictures, could be seen through the glass top of that old coffee table, and that was what she told her son.

"Oh, don't give me that stuff, Mama," Santiago told her two months or so after she had moved in, "go back to Levitt's. Go back to Woodie's. You can find somethin somewhere that'll be better than this piece of shit." He was sitting on the leather couch beside Rickey Madison and her son leaned forward and knocked twice on the top of the table. It was along about midnight.

"Stop," Joyce Moses said, "you'll break the glass." But her words lacked the scolding force of the old days, and she giggled and put both hands to her mouth and shook herself: She was still exhilarated by the new world her son had bought for her, and, in any case, one more crack in the top wouldn't have been the end. Her two younger children were upstairs, asleep in oaken beds, safer than they had ever been in their lives. Santiago Moses watched his mother, then he gave the table another playful tap. He was twenty years old.

"Nope nope nope," Joyce said. "Don't want another table." She had been drinking, but "only a teensy-weensy bit a wine," as she told Rickey after he arrived with Santiago. The carpet was down, having been installed throughout the house before she and Rickey and her two younger children moved in, but much of the new furniture had yet to be arranged in the rooms just as she wanted. There was no hurry. She sat on the floor, leaning back on her arms, her toes disappearing into the carpet. "With all this other stuff, don't you think if I'da wanted another coffee table, I woulda gone out and ordered it?"

"It's a gotdamn shame to buy the best and then have this shit sittin in the middle of all the good stuff," Santiago said. He laughed. "We can give this old one to the poor," and he laughed again. His feet were propped on the edge of the coffee table, and as he laughed he stretched his legs out over the table and shook them up and down.

"He's right, honey," Rickey said. He had been her common-law husband for six years. "Better find somethin new. We can look next week."

Santiago stopped laughing and turned to Rickey. "My mother's old anough to know what she want. She ain't nobody's child, Rickey. She don't need nobody tellin her what to do."

"I didn't mean anything by it, Sandy. Why you gettin all upset again? Sides, I think I should be able to tell my own woman somethin."

"Rickey, you can't tell nobody shit! Just do what I tell you and keep your mouth shut."

"All right now, you two," Joyce said. "I don't want yall startin nothin." She stood up quickly, for this was how the last fight started. "All right. All right. This conversation's closed far as I'm concerned, cause I'm keepin this table and thas all there is to it. Why yall wanna go and spoil a good time?"

"We gotta be goin anyway," Santiago said.

She walked them to the door, and Santiago kissed her cheek, the same kind of peck he had been giving her since he was months old. He turned up his jacket collar and went out the wooden and iron-bar doors and down the steps to his Range Rover. Rickey kissed her mouth. "See you later, baby," he said. He whispered that she should get a new table and she gave him a playful push.

"C'mon," Santiago said, "You know what she taste like by now. I ain't got all night."

The layered curtains were now up, and she parted them and watched her son and husband ride away down 10th Street. She continued to stand by at the window. She loved this time most, the hours when her house and all that was in it seemed to conspire with the quiet and envelop her. She had, while still in the old place, passed this house a million times, when it had contained a horrible family of loud people. Back then, she would have bet the souls of her children if someone had told her that one day the house would be made over and then hold her and her family.

She turned out the lamp beside her, and by and by she saw a form across the street peel away from a huge shadow, take the shape of a man, and walk toward the house. Before the man was midway across the street, she could see, in the walk without purpose, in the thinness, that it was Humphrey, her godson. For a minute or so, he stood in the middle of the empty street and looked up and down, his hand shading his eyes as if it were the middle of a very sunny day.

"Mama Joyce, it's so good to see you," Humphrey said, holding on to the banister with both hands as he made his way up the stairs. She opened the wooden door wider. "Sandy here?" He smiled through the iron-bar door, then he began to laugh, and she saw that he was out of his head again.

"Sandy just left," she said and opened the iron-bar door. "He might be back fore long. Come on in, sweetie." She did not bother to ask why he was across the street, as if he had been waiting, because she knew she would not have received an answer that meant anything.

"Mama Joyce, I can't stay." He laughed. "Could I just leave some money here for you to give him?" He stepped into her house.

"Now, honey, you know I don't handle any money for Sandy. You gotta take that up with him."

He blinked uncontrollably, then turned his head and looked at something invisible beside him. He laughed again, then he turned back to Joyce. "It's all right, Mama Joyce. I told him . . . I said, I said, 'I'm gonna leave it with her just this one time.' "

"You sure bout that?"

"Please, Mama Joyce. Please please. Pretty please with sugar on top." He giggled.

"All right, you crazy thing. Just this once." She shut the iron-bar door, listening for the click that told her it was secured, and then locked the wooden door. The world was not a safe place, Rickey kept telling her. Humphrey handed her a folded lump of bills. "Wow," she said, "nough to choke a horse."

He looked intently at the money. "It's never enough," he said, and for a second or so he straightened himself up. "But you tell him, Mama Joyce, you tell him I'll get the rest to him as soon as I can. Sooner than soon."

"You hungry?" She took off his baseball cap and ran her hand through his hair, something Santiago would no longer let her do. "You need a haircut. You want somethin to eat?"

He shook his head and then stared at her as if he were trying to remember something. "I ain't hungry, Mama Joyce. Thanks all the same." He continued to stare. "Gettin in shape. Gettin in shipshape." He began to box with the invisible something beside him. "We gettin in shape, ain't we?" he said to the thing. "Ain't we gettin in shape?"

Finally, he sat on the couch. Joyce put the money on the coffee table and the wad began to unfold. In little or no time, Humphrey had tumbled over and was asleep. A few tiny, clear packets fell out of his jacket pocket onto the floor. She picked up the packets and placed them on the coffee table. She could have counted on one hand the times she had seen the stuff, but each time she did, the cream-colored nuggets always reminded her of small chunks of white Argo starch she had eaten when she was pregnant.

From the hall closet, she took new sheets from their wrappings and covered him, then put a couch pillow under his head. In his sleep, he was laughing again. "He uses more of the stuff than he sells," she had once overheard Santiago tell Rickey.

She unlaced Humphrey's tennis shoes and discovered that they were the same pump kind Santiago had bought for her other son. She pushed the air-release button and thought she could hear the hissing of the escaping air. She set the shoes under the couch.

"Two-hundred-dollar shoes," she said, "and holes in his socks." She and Humphrey's mother, Pearl Malone, had been like sisters since they were ten years old. They had, at seventeen, given birth to their oldest sons, Santiago and Humphrey, within three weeks of each other.

Joyce sat across from Humphrey in what the store salesman had called a Queen Anne chair. One of her legs was resting across a chair arm, an old habit she was trying to break in the new house. She watched the sleeping boy and listened to the grandfather clock in the hall. Before Santiago and Humphrey were born, Joyce and Pearl had decided to share an apartment to save on the money they would get from public assistance. They discovered, a week or so after Humphrey was born, that Pearl's milk had mysteriously dried up, and Pearl became convinced that without her milk, her son would grow up without immunity.

"Oh, girl, you worry too much" Joyce told her one morning in a splendid June. "They makin formula and stuff thas just as good as breast milk."

"Joyce, I don't wanna feed my baby outa no box." They were in their kitchen and Pearl, standing at the stove, was reading aloud every word on the box of formula. Then she held it to her ear and shook it, as if just the sound of the contents was evidence of a lack of something vital. "He'll get all those diseases. I read about it." The babies were in plastic carriers, setting on the table. Santiago was asleep and Humphrey was watching Joyce, who sat playing with his hair.

In the end, Joyce offered to feed Humphrey from her own breasts. And for the six months or so Pearl felt it took to give Humphrey protection against the world's diseases, Joyce would take him up and put him to her breast. "I'm gonna teach him to call you Mama Joyce," Pearl said, wiping sweat from her brow one day in the crushing humidity of August.

In the very center of Joyce's coffee table, under the see-through glass, were pictures of her children and Pearl's as babies. Chubby-cheeked beings looking off to the side uninterestedly, or looking dead at the camera eye as if to challenge. Surrounding those pictures were photographs of the children in later years, and surrounding those were pictures of Joyce's parents and aunts and uncles and the children of her friends. There were pictures of her and Rickey together, arms around each other, and there were pictures of her alone, at the beach, at parties, sitting with crossed legs on the hoods of boyfriends' cars. In the top left-hand corner of the glass, there were cracks of one or two inches, radiating out, like the sun's rays in a child's drawing. Santiago, not long after they bought the table, had promised that if the cracks got any longer he would use his summer job money to replace the entire glass.

About two that morning Santiago called. The telephone sounded with the most unobtrusive chime she had been able to find. She was on the second floor, in the room she had furnished with such care and set aside for her mother, who would not ever step foot in her daughter's house. When she told Santiago that Humphrey was there, he told her not to let Humphrey leave. "I been lookin for his bony ass for two whole days," he said.

"He downstairs sleepin," Joyce said, "and I don't think he goin anywhere." She wanted to know where Rickey was, why he wasn't home yet, and Santiago told her that he would send Rickey home soon and that he himself would be staying at his Capitol Heights apartment if she needed him.

She had little use for sleep anymore, and after the call, she roamed the house with all the lights turned out, something she often did, even when Rickey was home. She and Pearl had shared poor-women dreams of living in a place like this, with furniture no one else in the whole world had ever used. As she walked about the dark house, she liked to remember what she and Pearl had said once upon a time, remember how painful it could be just to dream. Then, her mind would leap to now and she would touch something, the grandfather clock, the shelves of food in the pantry, the drawer of brassieres still with their price tags, the silver racing bicycle her youngest son was too small to ride.

About three that morning, while Joyce stood looking out the third-floor hall window, Humphrey got up and stumbled out. She got downstairs and found the iron-bar and wooden doors open to the world. She discovered later that he had taken the money. Toward three thirty, Rickey, nearly dead on his feet, finally came home. She fixed him a sandwich with thick slices of ham and then sat across the kitchen table from him, sipping a beer. "What a way to pay the rent," he kept saying between bites. She helped him upstairs and into bed. Then she roamed the house some more until about four thirty, when she came to bed and curled up close to him. But she could not sleep because she kept thinking she had not locked all the windows and doors.

The pictures of her mother started in the center of the coffee table display. Her mother rarely smiled in the photographs and she often looked into the camera as if the eye had caught her doing something God would not approve of. "I just don't take the good pictures," her mother had said when she saw the display at the apartment Joyce had left behind.

The pictures of Rickey began under the see-through glass more or less where the photographs of Santiago at ten began. Rickey did not like having his picture taken, and so most of the photos were of him in unguarded moments. One was taken at somebody's house during Christmas. The camera had caught him with his mouth parted in a small O and the camera had given him red eyes. Rickey's pictures had replaced those of the two men who had fathered her three children. He was the first man in her life who had never beaten her. And for a long time she thought that because he did not beat her, he did not care for her as much and that one morning she would wake up and, like the others, he would be gone.

Before Rickey Madison became a driver and bodyguard for Santiago Moses, he worked construction. The work was steady enough so that at least once a week he could take Joyce and her children to the Flagship on the wharf. One evening two years or so before, they came out of the restaurant and found that Rickey's Chevy wouldn't start. Rickey, after spending more than half an hour under the hood, stepped away from the car with resignation and spat into the gutter. Joyce watched him. He was the kind of man who had nightmares about not getting to work on time. Santiago, laughing, made the sign of the cross over the car.

"What the hell you laughin at, boy?" Rickey said. Clovis, Joyce's little girl, came up to him and put her hand in his.

"You," Santiago said. "You look like you don't know whether to shoot that thing or beg it for another chance." He put his arm around Rickey's shoulder, for by then Santiago was a head taller than the man.

"You think this so damn funny, huh?" Rickey said. "If I can't get to work in the mornin, you may not eat next week." Joyce worked as a home care aide, but it was Rickey's money that kept the family going.

"Oh, I'll eat all right," Santiago said. He took several new bills from his pocket. "Next week, and the week after that, and the one after that, and all the ones after that too." He stuck some of the money in Rickey's pocket. "Take a cab to work tomorrow."

"It probably some play money," Clovis said.

"Play money my ass," Santiago said. He had not come to the restaurant that evening with the rest of the family. And when he did arrive, he was accompanied by a woman who must have been at least ten years older than he. The woman had brought along her son, about three or four years old. "Play money my ass," the woman said.

Rickey counted the money, then he counted it twice more, spread it fanlike and turned to show it to Joyce. "Look," he said to her. "Look at this." He said to Santiago, "You hit the number or somethin, boy?"

"God provides," Santiago said. "God is good." He said to the woman, "Ain't that right, baby?" She sidled up to Santiago and began to giggle. The woman wore a low-cut blue dress and a gold crucifix on a gold chain around her neck, and all through dinner Joyce had looked at the cross resting between the woman's breasts. "God is everything," Santiago said. "God is good."

The moment Joyce had seen the woman walk into the restaurant, she knew she would not like her, knew the woman had been doing things with her son. Santiago continued on about God and goodness, and the woman leaned herself and her breasts against him. "Now why don't you go find a cab so you can take the family home," Santiago told Rickey. Rickey, without words, went off to look for a cab. "Me and Tamara gon take her car." The woman's little boy, looking at Rickey walk away, sat down on the sidewalk with a very loud sigh, as if he thought there would be much more talking and he may as well wait until it was all over.

In the cab, Joyce, seeing how happy Rickey was, told the cab driver to take the long way back to their apartment.

The next time Joyce saw the boy and his mother, it was the day after they had delivered the pool table for the basement in the new house. The woman had reached through the iron-bar door and knocked at the wooden door, and she was about to knock again when Joyce opened the door.

"You tell Sandy he can have him," the woman said to Joyce. She took one of the boy's hands and wrapped his fingers around one of the bars. "This is my settlement for all the money I owe him." In his other hand, the boy was holding a little car, and leaning against his leg was a small suitcase held together with rope. "You tell him he can stop buggin me now bout what I owe him. Mark me down paid in full. And tell him to send me a receipt care of General Delivery." She went clackety-clack down the stairs in her high heels, wobbling the way Joyce had seen Humphrey wobble, and the boy began to cry. "Shut up, gotdamnit! Shut up, I said!" She was down the street before Joyce could collect herself to say anything.

"Hey! Hey! Wait a minute! Whas goin on here!" Joyce opened the iron-bar door, nearly knocking the boy down the steps. "Come back here!" The woman was nearing O Street. "Sweet Jesus," Joyce said to herself. Had she not been in her bathrobe she would have run after the woman. "What are you doin?"

The boy was still crying. "Well, I don't love you neither!" he yelled to his mother as she turned the corner, and then he threw the car in her direction. "And I never even did."

When Santiago called that afternoon, he told his mother it would be all right, that the boy would be gone by the evening. "The dopey bitch just made a mistake, thas all," he said. But the boy, Adam, stayed three weeks, and no one ever again saw his mother. He was a silent presence in the house and never caused Joyce a moment's problem. Whatever Joyce told him to do, he did without question or sass. He had retrieved the car the first day, and for all those three weeks, he mostly sat out of the way in a corner of the living room, rolling the car back and forth. The carpet was too thick for the car to move very far on its own, and the boy usually pushed it all the way. Unlike other boys she had known, he did not make car sounds as he moved it. By the time the city government woman had come to get him, Joyce had given him a piece of her heart. The city government woman, who quickly produced a large red sucker as if she expected trouble from Adam, spoke college-people English and double-parked in front of the house. The city government woman took him by the hand, and the boy did not say good-bye and he did not cry. Quite often after that, after Santiago had released Rickey for the night and Joyce had curled up beside him in their bed, she would see Adam in her dreams. But in the dreams he was always a grown man and he would somehow come through the iron bars of one of the basement windows in the dead of night, and when, in the dark, they came upon each other, in the kitchen, on the stairs, in one of the children's rooms, she did not understand why she was not afraid of him.

"I guess he must get that kinda need from you, cause he done gone and bought a house in Fort Washington," Rickey said to Joyce one evening, nearly a year after they had moved into the house. They were in their second-floor bedroom, in their pajamas on the bed, the way Joyce liked to relax with Rickey after her two youngest children were asleep in their beds on the third floor. For a change, Santiago had let him go early. Rickey was leaning back against the headboard and Joyce was lying across the foot of the bed, and in front of her were a beer and her cigarettes and an ashtray on a bamboo tray that could not be tipped over. "I guess he'll be invitin you and the kids out to see it soon." This was how she received most of the news about Santiago, in bits and chunks from Rickey when the day was all but over.

"You look so tired, baby," she said. "Why don't you lay down and let me give you one of my special back rubs?"

"I don't want nobody's gotdamn back rub!"

"Well, you sure look like you could use one." When he moved his head, she could see that it was making a greasy spot on the white headboard. She considered what it would take to remove the spot. The day before, he had accidentally dropped a lighted cigarette on the carpet in the hall and she had cursed him for being careless.

"You know what I saw last week?" he said. He took a swig from his own beer on the nightstand.

"No, baby, what did you see last week?"

He did not like the way she said that, and at first he thought he would just shut her out and turn over and go to sleep. But soon he said, "I saw the most money I ever seen in my whole life." He suppressed a belch. He squinted, gazed at the bedspread as if the memory of the money were now a scene unfolding in the spread's pattern of palm trees and sand and birds in flight. "And it was in a room with a few kids that couldn't a been no more than thirteen, fourteen years old. They was playin this big radio that was sittin in the windowsill and they all knew the songs that was playin on the radio, and every time a song came on they would sing along, like they was at camp or somethin. They were at this big round table, countin that money and laughin and havin all the fun in the world like they were just countin so many leaves and it wouldn't be anything if it all blew away." He yawned. "So much money that it musta been some kinda sin just to have it at one time in a place that wasn't a bank. Some house in Northeast, maybe it was Southwest. One place is gettin to be like another now. 'Drive me here, Rickey.' 'Drive me there, Rickey.' "

Joyce took a sip of beer and lit another cigarette.

"I thought you was gonna quit them things," Rickey said. She could tell one of his drunk spells was coming on.

"You member: I told you the first of the month. Don't you remember? I promise." She could tell he didn't believe her.

Rickey said: "All the men there ever was in my family, that'll ever be in my family, each one could work day and night for a thousand years, and all the money they would make would never come close to what I saw in that room. I can still hear some a those songs that was on the radio, and I can tell you some a the words." He sang one of the songs.

"You ready for that back rub now, sugar?"

He yawned again, then inspected his fingernails and slid farther down in the bed. "I forgot to tell you that day fore yesterday I finally got a look at this Smokey Peebles. Himself. *The* William 'Smokey' Peebles everybody talks about. After all this time, I guess Sandy trust me enough." Despite Joyce's pleadings, he refused to wear the silk pajamas she bought for him. The cotton and synthetic ones, he told her, didn't let him slide off the bed as the silk ones did. "Gimme a sip." He reached for Joyce's beer.

"You got your own." She lit another cigarette. "Rickey, why you gotta always bring that stuff home? Those people don't interest me in the least. I thought we was gonna have a nice evenin, just me and you, baby." She was afraid he might start pouting, as he now did more and more when he was drunk, and to head him off, she pushed the tray out of the way and crawled up the bed and put her arms around him. "All right," she said. "I'm sorry. So this was the one himself, huh?"

He was silent for a long time and she reached into his underwear and stroked him.

"Not right now," he said, taking her hand out. "Besides it don't seem to be doin the job anyway."

"You gotta be patient," Joyce said. "Thas the thing bout makin babies. It helps if thas the last thing on your mind. Makin em. Then they come one two just like that."

Rickey said, "Sandy had me drive him to this place off Florida Avenue, to some kinda old-fashioned drug store. But they didn't have a pharmacy or nothin like that. It was mostly just a soda fountain and some booths. A few tables and chairs, just like in those old black-and-white movies." She put her hand inside the shirt of his pajamas and stroked his chest; sometimes there was nothing to do but ride the whole thing out.

"I could tell that Sandy'd been there before, just from the way he gave me directions," Rickey said. "When they let us in, Sandy goes to the counter and sits down beside this little boy, who was drinkin a milkshake all slurpy-loud and everything. I stood near the big front window, just like he told me to. There was two men I'd seen someplace else before standin near the front door, and there was a large man in one of the booths sittin across from this very pretty woman who was drinkin a big milkshake just like the little boy. This big fella had on the best-lookin suit I'd ever seen, the kinda suit I want you to bury me in when I pop off. Sandy was steady-talkin to this little boy and I just kept lookin at Smokey, at that big back a his. It made me nervous at first to be near somebody they say had killed three men. The woman he was talkin to had on a lot of makeup and she was more interested in the milkshake than whatever it was Smokey was sayin to her."

Joyce continued to stroke his chest and threw her leg over his thighs. "Shoulda went up and introduced yourself," she said. " 'I heard so much about you, Mr. Peebles. Can I call you Smokey?' "

Rickey smiled. He said, "There was an old white man in a nice clean apron behind the fountain and he had one a those old-timey soda jerk hats on. He held up one a those metal glasses they useta make milkshakes in and he shook it at me, wantin to know if I wanted one. I shook my head. There wasn't nobody else in the place but these people, and no aisles with soap and toothpaste and aspirin and whatnot, and I gradually got the feelin that this white man's one job in life was to make milkshakes and banana splits and everything for whoever big Smokey told him to."

The grandfather clock in the hall downstairs struck ten, and Joyce lifted her head momentarily from Rickey's chest to listen for Clovis getting up and going to the bathroom.

"At the last, this little boy Sandy had been talkin to turned in his seat and hopped away from the stool. He twisted his body around without movin his feet to see how far he'd hopped away from the seat. Then he wiped his mouth with the back of his hand. He came toward the door and everybody jumped up, includin Sandy. One a those guys opened the door. The boy stuck out his hand to me, and I could see that he wasn't a boy atall. 'You Rickey, huh?' he said. 'I'm Smokey. Smokey Peebles. You keep watchin out for my boy there. There's some bad shit in the world, y'know, and I don't want my boy hurt.' He pointed over his shoulder to Sandy. 'He my righthand man.' I just shook his hand, cause I didn't know what to say. 'How you like my tennis shoes,' he said. 'They Chuck Taylors. Converse. Thas all I wear is Chuck Taylors.' He just went on like me and him was old walk partners and like the only important thing in the world to him was what kinda tennis shoes he wore. The fella who'd opened the door closed it, seein that Smokey wasn't headin out. I could see some children gatherin at the door. 'When I was a little boy,' Smokey was sayin, 'Chuck Taylor was the thing. Every boy had to have Chuck Taylors. They were like ten dollars or somethin back then, but that was a whole lotta money. My mama—I'll never forget this—my mama got me these cheap-ass three-dollar tennis shoes from Becker's on 7th Street. You know how mamas can be. If you saw those tennis shoes like from a mile away you'd think they were Chuck Taylors, but up close, even a blind man could tell you they was just imitation. And people, my own friends now, got on my shit about it too, stomped all over my feelins. Every time I wore them they'd like come up to me, bend down, and point real close at these imitation Chuck Taylors.' "

Rickey reached over and drank the last of his beer in one swig. "I think he musta been twenty-five or somethin like that, and all he was talkin about was those damn tennis shoes. This woman at the booth came out and zipped up his jacket. Then I saw that she wasn't really a woman but a girl, maybe eight, nine years old, and I thought I was gonna be sick. She had on high heels and big earrings and a short dress and a painted face that made you wanna cry. She moved like every move she had learned by practicin, like maybe she'd studied how to move like a real woman while standin in front a some big mirror. She put her arm through Smokey's, just like they was man and wife or somethin. Smokey was steady talkin. 'Now all I wear is Chuck Taylor tennis shoes. High-tops, low-tops, red, yellow, gold, green, purple. All colors. Even the regular white or the black ones. Guys all over the world wearing hundred-dollar, two-hundred-dollar, three-hundred-dollar tennis shoes and me—I'm happy with some of the cheapest on the market. No pump, no flyin; just me and Chuck.'

"The guy opened the door again, and everybody followed him on out. The big man who'd been in the booth started to open the back door of this Mercedes for him, but Smokey said, 'Oh, no. I feel like tryin out my drivin muscles.' And he raised his arms and flexed his muscles. One man took this thick pad of foam and put it in the driver's seat. All these kids was crowdin round Smokey, and one of the fellas with Smokey started throwin change in the air and the shit came down on some a their heads, but the kids didn't care cause it was money. 'Yall stay off dope, you hear me?' Smokey told em. 'Yall stay off dope. Stay away from that mess. And stay in school. Stay in school.' All the kids knew his name and they started singin what he'd just said. Made up a little song right there on the spot. The white man in that apron came to the window and started wavin to nobody in particular. Then I heard him lock the door and I could see the shades comin down."

When the telephone chimed, Joyce was dozing. Rickey picked up the entire telephone and handed it to her. She sat up and blinked herself wide awake. "Pearl? Pearl, what is it?" she said after a bit. "Stop cryin now, honey, and tell me whas wrong."

Rickey went downstairs to get more beer because the tiny refrigerator in their bedroom had conked out the day before. When he returned, Joyce was wetting her finger and rubbing it on the greasy spot on the headboard.

"What Pearl squawkin about?"

"Somethin about Humphrey owin Sandy money," Joyce said. "She want me to talk to Sandy, have him let up on Humphrey."

"He ain't gonna do it," Rickey said, sitting on the side of the bed and kicking off his slippers. "He done give the Hump too many breaks already. Pearl sound like all this stuff is somethin logical, like some Riggs Bank loan. She should bring her ass out of Potomac once and a while and see what it's like in the real world. What can she know bout what Humphrey's up to if all they do is talk on the phone?"

Three years before, Pearl had married what she told Joyce was her "dream man," a much older man who owned four restaurants scattered throughout Northeast and Anacostia. They moved to Potomac, but while her new husband had accepted her second child, he told Pearl that he would have nothing to do with Humphrey until the boy "straightened himself out." The result, essentially, was that home for Humphrey became just about anywhere he happened to be. He had declined to come and live with Joyce.

"I'll talk to Sandy," Joyce sighed.

"Talk to the Hump while you at it."

The telephone chimed again. Joyce answered, said, "Yes, mama, tomorrow," a few times and then hung up. "She sounded very calm," she said to Rickey. "But the calmer she sounds, the madder she is about somethin. Problems, problems. Ain't I got problems." She took Rickey's beer from him and placed it on the nightstand. "If Daddy want a baby, Daddy gotta work for it."

The next day was Friday, and she put off going to see her mother because it was too nice an April day not to begin preparations for her backyard garden. Santiago called twice during the day and he assured her that his Mama Pearl was exaggerating about what Humphrey owed him.

"Then what's this she talkin about?" Joyce said to him Sunday morning. Sundays were the only days he would agree to come over early so she could have everyone together for breakfast.

"I don't know," Santiago said. He was sitting across the table from his brother, Taylor. "Think fast!" he told the boy before tossing a biscuit at him. "You know how Mama Pearl can be." Taylor ran around the table and grabbed Santiago's ear. He feigned pain and then pretended to choke Taylor.

"Then you won't mind talkin to Humphrey when he get here. I made him promise to come over."

Santiago stopped playing with Taylor. He shrugged. "I don't mind. I told you it was cool."

Taylor continued to play with Santiago. "All right," Joyce said. "Thas anough of that. Get upstairs and clean your damn room! You know I'm still hot about that bike, so you better stay outa my sight today." She said to Santiago, "After I told him again not to take the bike, he took it out last night and busted the front wheel."

"What's the use of havin some toy if you can't play with it," Taylor said. Joyce had promised that he could begin riding it on his next birthday, when she thought he would be tall enough to reach the pedals.

"When the toy cost three hundred dollars, it ain't no toy no more," she said. "And listen here: I'm gettin tired of all this mouth you been givin me lately. Les not forget who runs things around here. You keep it up and you'll be missin some teeth."

"Oh, it's all right, Mama," Santiago said. "I'll just have Rickey take it next week to get fixed." Rickey, sitting next to Santiago, said nothing. He was reading the newspaper and he turned the page.

Joyce came in from her garden when Humphrey arrived and had him and Santiago go into the living room. "I don't want yall to come out till this whole thing is straightened out," she said and reminded them of the way she and Pearl used to do it when they quarreled as boys. Then she returned to her garden. A half hour or so later, Rickey came out and stood on the steps watching her. "I'm gonna put some corn over there," she said when she noticed him. "I'm gonna put the tomatoes right there. Might even try some peppers. You know how you like peppers. How's it goin in there?" She had a transistor radio playing on the last step and he had not heard most of what she said.

Rickey turned off the radio. "I wasn't in there, but when I went by I heard em talking like the old days."

"Well, thank the Lord Jesus," she said, taking off her gloves. "Whew. No wonder my mama and daddy left the farm for the city."

"You takin the pill or somethin?"

"What?"

"It's takin you longer to get pregnant than it took em to make Frankenstein," Rickey said.

"Well, I hope we aimin for somethin far better than that," she said. She was standing before him now and she reached around him and began kneading his behind. "It's discouragin," he said. She said, "I know, baby. Just hang in there."

Inside, she pinched the cheeks of Santiago and Humphrey and told them she was proud of them. She offered to make a celebratory dinner that evening. But the dinner did not come off as planned. Humphrey did not show up, and Rickey called about eight to say he and Santiago would be out late.

A year or so after she moved into the house, she began searching for another coffee table similar to the old one. The old table was running out of room for new photographs, and whenever she added new pictures, she was forced to overlap everything. In some cases, a face was hidden by the picture above it or next to it; in others, these were missing limbs, and in still others, entire bodies were gone, except for a sleeve or shoe here and there. There was always an empty space she saved for some especially wonderful picture that might come along. That space shifted about, according to how she arranged things. On the day Rickey asked her about the pill, the space happened to be next to a picture of her in a white-and-green cotton print dress, and she was standing beside the man who was Clovis's father. The photograph had been taken a year or so before she met Rickey, and a month after her tubes were tied. "I hope he tied the knot tight enough," Joyce said to one of the hospital nurses who had befriended her." "A pretty bow," the nurse said. "It's one of the few things they get right in this joint."

Three weeks after she had promised to come by the next day, Joyce finally got up the courage to visit her mother. She waited until one o'clock, hoping the washer and dryer repairman would show up before she left. Her mother had not called back to remind her of the promise, which was her mother's way. As always, Joyce tried to anticipate all that her mother would throw at her and spent the walk down to her mother's thinking of ways to counter it. She would not have noticed the woman and the three children walking down the other side of 5th Street had the little girl with the woman not cried out to one of the boys, "Stop, you hurtin my sore!" When Joyce looked over, she saw the woman scolding the youngest of the boys, shaking her finger in his face. Joyce saw immediately that the other boy, standing off to the side of the others, was Adam. She uttered an oh loud enough for the man passing by her to ask if she might be ill.

She crossed the street and touched Adam's shoulder, saying, "I know you remember who I am, your Aunt Joycie." The boy looked up at her and blinked twice, then looked at the woman he was with as if she might have the proper response.

"Thas my child, lady, leave him be," the woman said.

"It's all right," Joyce said. "Me and Adam know each other from way back, don't we, Adam?" The boy shook his head. "Sure you do," Joyce said. "Come on now, think. Remember how I useta to fix you all them banana splits piled up this high?" There seemed to be no memory at all in the boy's face, and for several seconds he looked out into the street as if Joyce were a bother. "Remember all them baths with the soap bubbles? Bubble time?"

"Listen, you can see he don't even know you," the woman said.

"It was a long time ago," Joyce said. She took money from her purse and gave Adam five dollars. Then, seeing the other two children look hungrily at the bill, she gave them five dollars as well.

"I don't let my children take money from strangers off the street," the woman said.

"She useta to be my mama," Adam said, inspecting the back of the bill.

"You can't have him back," the woman said, grabbing each bill and throwing them at Joyce. "I got him fair and square. I got the papers on him to show it. You can't have him." She gathered the children by the hands and hurried them against the light across H

Street. She continued to watch the woman and the children go down 5th Street, and when they were nearing F Street, Adam turned to look back, as if to confirm the feeling she had that the initial denial was part of some game.

Her mother lived in the Judiciary House, an H Street apartment building for senior citizens and the disabled. Joyce let herself into the apartment with her own key and found her mother in the living room. The small black-and-white television Joyce's father had bought on credit twelve years ago was on, but her mother was reading a paperback book and paid no attention to the television. Her mother, who did not look up when her daughter entered, was wearing, as usual when she was inside, one of her dead husband's shirts and a pair of his checkered socks. And as Joyce bent down to give her mother the kind of kiss on the cheek that Santiago would give Joyce, she smelled her father's cheap musky aftershave.

"I want you to give Sandy a message," her mother said, taking off the eyeglasses she kept on a string around her neck. "And if you want I'll tell it to you slow so you can get every word down."

"I'm fine, Mama," Joyce said. "Thank you very much. And how you doin?" Her resolve to do battle had dissipated in the street with the woman and Adam. In that second-floor bedroom in her 10th Street house she had set aside for her mother, there was a telephone with giant numbers so her mother would not have trouble dialing her friends. And there was a picture over the poster bed of Jesus Christ, blonde hair down to his shoulders, praying in the garden at Gethsemane.

"Santiago been comin by some nights and sleepin sida my bed like he did when he was young," her mother said.

"That sounds like good news to me, Mama. I'm glad you two friends again. You coulda told me this on the phone." She sat across from her mother in a cheap metal chair that was part of the dinette set. "I would think you'd be glad to see your grandkids, since you don't want to come to my house."

"It ain't the comin and stayin and what not. He stayed here the other night. Got up early when that beep-beep thing went off and let hisself out. And when I got in here I found a hundred-dollar bill on the table layin under the sugar dish. One hundred dollars. It's on the table there and you take it outa my house when you go. I ain't some sportin woman in the street. I told him never to bring a thing in this house but hisself and the clothes on his back. Well, maybe he'll listen if the words come from his own mother." She had been reading a romance novel and now she inserted a funeral-home bookmark in her place and closed the book.

Joyce said, "He just wants to make you happy, Mama. You know how he likes to be generous with his family."

"I just this moment changed my mind," her mother said. She never once looked at her daughter, only watched the people on the television. "Since all this givin is in his blood that way, then tell him not to come to my house again. And if he comes I'll have him locked up."

"That'll break his heart, Mama."

"Tell him not to worry: God don't put no more on us than we can bear." Her mother put on her glasses and opened the book.

Joyce stood and went to the door, and her mother told her not to forget the money.

She took the long way back home, lest she bring bad feelings back to her house. She walked downtown along F Street and looked in the store windows. At a shop at 12th Street, she bought a doughnut and several large cookies with the hundred-dollar bill and ate them unselfconsciously as she walked along, the way a child would. At a shoe store near 13th Street, she abandoned once and for all any hope she ever had that her mother would come to live with her and spend the rest of her life in the room on the second floor. And at Garfinkel's she wondered if that doctor could go back inside her and pull one end of that pretty bow so that it would come untied and she might make Rickey, with all his whininess, happy.

There had been, along the false-wood part of the coffee table, a few cigarette burns when she bought the table. Rickey had somehow managed to make the burns disappear and the table looked almost new. The burns had been near some pictures taken at various Christmases. In one, taken months after his mother married, Humphrey was sleeping in a chair by a window. In his lap was a knit cap Clovis had given him. When they woke him for dinner, he was angry, as if he had been arguing in his dreams and did not know he was now awake. "I got my pride, you know," he shouted. "I still got a whole lotta pride people don't even know about."

In another picture, taken during a Christmas when he was still courting her, Rickey had allowed Joyce to set Clovis in his lap, arrange the boys on either side of him, and photograph the four of them in front of the Christmas tree. "I'm a family man without a family," he'd told her not long after they had met at a cabaret in Southeast. And those words were in her mind when she knelt on the linoleum floor and took their picture. Three times. "I can give you all you want," she had said before he moved in with them. "I can give you all the kids you can afford." "I can afford a hundred," he said. "Then that's how many I can give you."

The garden came up beautifully, despite a week or so of bad weather. It had rained hard three days straight, and on the second morning they had awakened to find the basement floor covered with three inches of water. All the rain in the basement was gone now, but it had left some seed, some indestructible life form, that threatened to turn the basement into something prehistoric. Despite a virtual army of men hired by Santiago to disinfect the basement periodically, Joyce would come down some mornings and find green, furlike mold growing along the paneled walls, sprouting in corners, sharing space with the mousetraps.

But the garden thrived, and a summer came on, Joyce spent more and more of her days there. She was there, bent down in a row of tomatoes, when Clovis ran out to her and told her that Sandy was picking on Humphrey again down at the corner. Calmly, and with an exasperated sigh, she took off her hat and gloves and told Clovis to stay in the house.

She would not ever remember if she heard the two *pops* before she got to the corner at O Street. When she turned the corner, she saw a crowd, but between her and Humphrey there was no one. He was backing toward her, and he would have reached her, but Santiago shot him again and he fell. She thought that he had only stumbled, and when she saw Rickey out of the corner of her eye standing in the street watching them, she was somehow nearly reassured that Humphrey had only misstepped.

She shouted to Santiago. "Stop it fore you hit somebody!" When she got to Humphrey, he was sitting, and when he began to lie back, she reached down to help him, took him by the front of the dark jacket with one hand and the back of his head with the other. When he was down all the way, he shook his head as if to say, "Clumsy me." There was wetness on the hand that had taken the jacket, but she was concentrating on Santiago too much to take note of it. She continued on toward him and he lowered the gun and did not move.

"You stay outta this, Mama. This ain't got nothin to do with you."

"What you been doin?" she asked him.

She slapped him twice, and when she saw the blood on his cheek and then on her hand, her heart sank because she thought she had injured him.

"All right now, Mama, I'm warnin you." He pointed the gun between her eyes, then he backed away. "This ain't none a your business." He pushed back against the people behind him, and they made room for him, then he ran to the Range Rover that was double parked. In seconds he was gone.

She called to Rickey, who was now standing on the sidewalk across O Street, and then she began to scream his name. He ran away. She went back to Humphrey, whose front was now completely bloodied. She asked someone to call for help. Joyce sat down and cradled Humphrey's head in her lap. She thought that he was already dead, but he opened his eyes and said, "Please don't tell my mama." He said it again and would have gone on saying it, but she covered his mouth with her hand.

It was well after dark when the police left her house, and when they had all gone, she called Pearl. She stayed on the telephone for several hours, until Pearl's husband got home from work. Pearl said that she forgave Santiago, but Joyce knew that that would never be true in this life. After she hung up the telephone, she sat on the floor in the living room until the grandfather clock told her it was ten. In a small cabinet near the couch was a fifth of vodka, which she drank in less than an hour. Then, beginning in the basement, she went about the house undoing the locks on all the doors and windows, for Santiago had no key to her house. And outside that house there was a very cruel world and she did not like to think that her child was out there without a place to come to.

A BUTTERFLY ON F STREET

The man Mildred Harper was legally married to for twenty-seven years had been dead and buried five months when, standing on an F Street traffic median, she came upon the woman her husband had lived with for the last two years of his life. Mildred had crossed to the island from Morton's, going to Woolworth's, her eyes fixed upon a golden-yellow butterfly that fluttered about the median. A child swatted half-heartedly at the butterfly, which rose as high as seven or so feet at moments, zigzagging back and forth over people's heads and around an advertising kiosk and around the small, lifeless trees. Then the butterfly set off into the traffic heading toward 13th Street. It astonished her to see such a thing, wild, utterly fragile, in the midst of the buildings, the noise, the cars and buses, and she figured the thing must have lost its way. Before long, the butterfly was consumed in the colors of 13th Street.

When Mildred turned back toward Woolworth's, she came face to face with the woman her husband had left her for, whose leaving had picked Mildred up by the hair and dropped her down at the doorstep of insanity. She had seen the woman four or five times before, always from the back seat of her son's car. But to see her now so close was like finding that a being from a recurring dream had stepped out into her life.

"Mildred," the woman said, "I'm real sorry for your loss."

Two months before, the woman had turned over to Mildred's son all the belongings of Mansfield Harper, including dozens of pictures of his family. "She didn't say nothing much, Mama," her son kept telling Mildred. Then he said, "She just said, 'I'm real sorry for your loss.' "

The woman stood but a few feet from her on the median. Perhaps if she had said something else, Mildred might have walked away. But she was surprised by the note of sincerity in the woman's words. "Thank you," Mildred said.

He had not, this man she was married to for twenty-seven years, told her he was leaving. One day his things were in their 12th Street home ("God Bless This House"), and the next day when she came home from work, many of those things were gone. The imported Swiss razor. Mildred had put his note in her Bible. ("Place your hopes among the Psalms; the Psalms is good luck.")

"The doctors," the woman was now saying, "had given him all this medicine, so he didn't suffer any. Cancer, you know, can kill you twice. Once with all that sufferin, then with the final dyin itself. But he passed on peacefully into the next world." She was a rather plain woman, Mildred decided, but only because she did not fix herself up. Her hair was combed back with the ends captured in a red barette at the nape of her neck. She wore no makeup and her thick eyebrows grew together, meeting in a neat line over the bridge of her nose that would have been becoming on a woman who fixed herself up.

They had lived, this woman and the father of Mildred's four children, in a small house on Maple View in Anacostia, where Mildred had forced her son to take her. "I live in Northeast, Mama. I don't know one thing about Anacostia." "Buy a map. Get a map. I want to see where they live, where him and her live together." "You just actin crazy." "Do what I say."

"I haven't been downtown in so long," the woman was saying.

"They sure have built it up." Mildred's oldest son had forgiven his father almost from the first day, but their only daughter, Gladys, Mansfield's favorite, could not forgive. And on those days when Mildred managed to get far enough away from insanity's doorstep to see hope, she would come upon her daughter tearing up still one more treasure Mansfield had given her. This little piggy had roast beef. . . . This little piggy stayed home. . . .

"I hadn't been down here in a long time either," Mildred said.

"I really miss the way we used to be able to cross right in the middle of the street when all the lights changed," the woman said. "You know, the lights would change and the people on the four corners could just walk right out in the middle of the street to the other side. I miss that."

"I remember," Mildred said. She wanted to go now. The pain was coming back, day by hour by minute by second. She wanted to go on across the street to the things of Woolworth's. ("If it ain't at Woolworth's," Mansfield had said once, "they ain't makin it.") The woman's plainness continued on down her body, with a gray sweater and a blue blouse, both of which had had all the life washed out of them. Her skirt, a darker blue, was pleated, but it had been ironed by someone who had not quite lined up the pleats correctly, so in some places there was the definite line of the original pleat only a fraction of an inch from the less pronounced line made by the iron.

"Mildred, I hope you didn't mind that I didn't make it to the funeral," the woman said. She expected the woman to say that it would not have been proper for her to be there, but instead she said, "I was not well and couldn't make it."

Mildred began to feel she was back in that chair in front of her television, talking back to the people on the television. She thought what an easy thing it would have been to strike the woman. But she looked away, up 13th Street, at the sign at Kitt's music store, at people looking in the store window. Then she looked down. The woman's shoes were loafers, black and shiny. They appeared new and there was a dime in each one. It was something her husband had always done, and something her daughter did as well, following her father. ("No pennies in penny loafers for me. Put in a dime, and if a quarter would fit in there, I'd put in a damn quarter.")

The dimes were very shiny, too, and it slowly came to Mildred that perhaps all the woman had was now in Harmony Cemetery, six feet under, returning to ashes and dust. It came to her, too, that the woman must have been in a kind of mourning, and she began to feel like something of an intruder, as if she had come into that woman's house and disturbed the woman, kneeling in prayer.

"It's all right," Mildred said about the funeral. "His own brother didn't make it in from California."

"He ain't gonna die, Mama," her son had said the first time they waited in his car for Mildred to get a look at them. They were across the street from the house in the twilight of the day, and Mildred sat in the back. "I see him a lot, and I should know. He ain't gonna die no more than you or me." It was about then that her husband and the woman had come up the street, his strong arm around her, lovers, whispering into the woman's ear every sweet word that had ever been invented. She had expected it, but it still surprised her. ("Say you want me. Say you can't do without me. Say you can't live without me. Say you want me day and night, and all the time in between. Say it. Say it now.")

"Don't start anything out here, Mama. You just stay put, y'hear? Don't get out a this car." But they were not walking that way at all: The woman was actually holding Mansfield's elbow. And when they got to the house, she opened the gate and led him up the few steps, and they stood on the porch as moths circled the overhead bulb that offered next to no light. Mansfield waited patiently while she unlocked the front door, then she guided him into a dark room.

"Well, I'd best get along," the woman said now. "I been huntin a winter coat, but I ain't seen nothin I like. And the prices so high, it make you wanna cry. I'm gonna try Morton's, then go home."

"I just come from there," Mildred said.

She had, toward the end, sent her daughter down there to

Anacostia under the pretense of taking some of his things to him. She had hoped that Gladys, after seeing her father, would come back home with some love restored. But Gladys had come back cursing him, and she had cursed him all that night, and all the next day, and well into the next, a Sunday.

The woman extended her hand. "My name's Elizabeth Ann Coleman, but all my friends call me Lady," the woman said, shaking Mildred's hand. "God is with you." But Mildred knew that that had not been true for a long time, and that it would never be true again. The woman walked across F Street against the light and entered Morton's. Mildred did not turn to look at her. She went to the corner of the traffic median and waited for the light to turn green. People on either side of her crossed against the light. But she stood waiting as if she had the whole day and a good part of the next.

GOSPEL

As the House of the Solitary Savior Baptist Church burned to the ground one December Sunday morning, Vivian L. Slater was in her bath, arranging a program of gospel songs her group was to sing at the church. A Sunday morning bath was just about the only constant in her life, and every Sunday God sent she stretched out in a fragrant mixture of baby oil and water and the most expensive bubble bath she could find. On a stool beside the tub, she always placed a huge glass of soda, grape or some kind of cola. She chilled the drink with several small plastic balls containing water that had been frozen. And beside the glass was a large transistor radio tuned to WYCB or to some station broadcasting church services that offered more spirituals and gospel songs than preaching.

If someone telephoned for her while she was in the tub, her husband, Ralph, would answer and tell the caller that Mrs. Slater was indisposed for the time being. From time to time, without her even calling to him, Ralph would get up from reading the Sunday newspaper and come in without knocking and refilled her glass and replace the colored balls of ice. He was seven years older than she and a man of extreme handsomeness, with no sign of sickness, and when she accompanied him to D.C. General every week for his treatments, men and women of all ages would stare at him, pitying a man who was saddled with a cancer woman perhaps not long for this world. It bothered her that the world did not know which of them was sick. As Ralph refilled her glass and dropped in fresh balls of ice, he never once would look at her nakedness.

As the House of the Solitary Savior burned down, she was also arranging a program for the Holy Tabernacle AME Zion, a magnificent church of three thousand members where her group, the

Gospelteers, was to sing later in the day. She knew it was the sin of pride, but Vivian no longer got any pleasure from singing at the House, as the members called it; it was something she did only because she knew that for singing there, God would make some small, positive notation beside her name in that book of His.

The House of the Solitary Savior had had but one pastor in its thirty years—a tall, gaunt man who made his living as a plumber's helper. His wife, an elementary school teacher, was as tall and gaunt as her husband, so that anyone seeing the couple would have mistaken them for brother and sister. In all the time that Vivian had known the Reverend Wesley Saunders, the church had never had more than fifty members, despite the reverend's boast that he preached more of God's truth than any pastor in Washington.

About eleven o'clock she was dressed and ready to go. Ralph was in the easy chair in the living room, and that was undoubtedly where she would find him, drunk, combative, that night when she came home.

He said, "Paper say maybe some snow tonight, sugar." He was a man who loved profoundly and he had not stopped looking at her since she came into the room. He watched her now as she put on her coat and considered herself in the mirror on the back of the hall closet door. She said, "If it does snow, them new snow tires'll get a workout." She turned to the side and considered herself in the mirror that way. He said, "You look real good today, sugar." From the closet she took the slippers and gown she wore when singing. She turned her other side to the mirror. Finally, she leaned over him, put her finger an inch from her lightly rouged lips and touched it to his cheek. She said, "I'll see you when I get back." He said, "Okay, sugar. Be careful."

To get to Diane McCollough, her best friend and the first member she had recruited for the Gospelteers, she came down Martin Luther King, Jr., Avenue and crossed the bridge over the Anacostia River. Generally, she did not like driving, particularly not over the bridge, for having so many cars around her made her feel as if she were a part of some uncontrollable tide and could only be helplessly swept along. But on a Sunday morning the traffic was tolerable, and after she had crossed the river, she relaxed and reviewed the day's programs in her head. Now and again, she looked at herself in the rearview mirror.

Diane lived in a house half the size of Vivian's on 9th Street Southeast, not far from Lincoln Park. Vivian let herself into the house with her own key. Diane lived with her second husband, Harry, and her youngest daughter from her first marriage, along with her daughter's only child, an overweight boy of four who had been spoiled beyond redemption. Two of Diane's sons were in Lorton for selling cocaine. "She ain't had a happy life, I can tell you that," Vivian would say in defending her friend to people who thought she had raised her children wrong. "Have a little sympathy."

Diane, dressed and made up, was at the kitchen sink, drinking the last of her coffee. Everyone said good morning except for the little boy, who sat beside his mother at the table, playing with a truck that was as big as his head. Vivian sat down across from the boy, as far away from him as she could get. The boy would have thought nothing of touching her with his greasy hands. The odor of coffee and bacon had settled about the room, and Vivian counted off the weeks she had been on her diet.

"Vi, don't get comfortable, cause I'm all ready," Diane said.

"We got plenty of time," Vivian said. "A minute or two won't hurt."

"Who yall got today?" Cherry, Diane's daughter, asked. She was, like her mother, a very plain and charming woman who could immediately put the world at ease. She had waited until she was thirty-one to marry, but it was to a man she now fought with night and day. And usually after the worst fights, she ran away to stay with Diane, until her husband came and knocked contritely at his mother-in-law's door. "And think of that poor ugly daughter of hers," Vivian would say to people as she defended her friend.

"The House first, ain't it, Vi?" Diane said, coming up behind her grandson. "The Hoouuse . . ." She dragged the word out as if the sound of it could frighten the boy, and then she tickled his sides. "The House gonna get you." The boy, moving the truck along the edge of the table, ignored her.

"The House in the early afternoon," Vivian said, "then Holy Tabernacle in the evening."

Diane's husband said, "That House got that Reverend Saunders, ain't it? God's gift to the world, ain't he?"

"So he think," Vivian said. In the world of Washington gospel, Vivian's Gospelteers, a group of four women and a piano player, had a respectable reputation that she felt had outgrown a storefront like the House. But twenty-five years before, just after the group's birth, Reverend Saunders was the first to say, "Come and sing before my people." She felt she owed him. It was an obligation he could remind her of on the phone with no more than a "God bless you and a good evenin to you, Sister Slater." Reverend Saunders, even with a flock that could fit into one Metrobus, was a proud man, and though Vivian always told him the church owed them nothing, he would have the Gospelteers wait at the end of the program while he and his wife went about the church collecting what the members could contribute to the group. At the large churches built to last until kingdom come, payment came in a check with the church's name in bold, unflinching letters at the top center.

"Yall gonna sing, 'I'm a Pilgrim'?" Diane's husband said. "I do like that song. Reminds me of what they used to sing back home. I could listen to it all day long."

Vivian said, "We'll do it at the House, but not at Holy Tabernacle. Reminds you of bein back in your mama's arms, huh?" She reached across to pinch his cheek. He was a large light-skinned man and he blushed.

She began to sing to him, and for the first and only time the boy raised his head and looked at her.

> *I have trouble on ev'ry hand*
> *But I've started for the city . . .*
> *I'm goin down to the river Jordan*
> *I'm gonna bathe my weary soul.*

LOST IN THE CITY

"Oh, get outta here," he said, and she sang on because she liked seeing that she had pleased. When she had finished, he asked, "You think your no-count piano player'll show up this time?"

"He'd better," Diane said.

"You got that right," Vivian said. "Just thinkin about last Sunday sets my teeth on edge."

Despite being a young man who spent most of his Sundays in churches hitting the ivory keys for God, the piano player, Counsel Smith, lived a fast life, much of it packed into Friday and Saturday nights. So it was often difficult for him to collect himself on Sunday morning, to pull himself away from a willing woman and clear his head of alcohol, and to go off to be with four other women, one of whom was old enough to be his grandmother, two of whom were old enough to be his mother, and one of whom had a ring through her nose about another man.

"We already told him if he miss one more time or be late one more time, he's finished," Diane said. She set her cup in the sink, then looked sternly at her daughter and pointed into the sink full of dirty dishes. "There ain't nothin worse in the world than gettin up at some church and havin to make up excuses about why you didn't bring your piano player."

"Yall should be able to sing without a piano player by now," her husband said.

"Ain't that much singin in the world," Vivian said. The adults laughed, and then the boy, as if afraid he was being left out, laughed as well.

"You ready?" Vivian said to Diane.

"As ready as I'll ever be." She gave her husband a passionate kiss on the lips, a kiss that Vivian thought was too much for a Sunday morning at the kitchen table. Diane then pinched the boy's cheeks. "Ooh, ooh," she said. "Ooh, my little butterball." The boy wiggled away.

In the car, going to pick up the other two women, Diane inspected her face in a palm-sized mirror she took from her pocketbook. Vivian drove down to Massachusetts Avenue.

"How long Cherry gonna be with you this time?" Vivian said.

"Can't tell," Diane said. "Can't ever tell. Just have to wait till they both come to their senses, and lately it's takin em longer and longer. Soon they won't have any sense at all. I'm just thankful for a understandin husband."

Vivian watched her friend out of the corner of her eye. She noted that Diane was putting on more weight. The two women were both fifty-seven years old, though Vivian would have been quick to tell anyone that she was younger by seven months.

Diane sighed and grew quiet. She put the mirror back in her pocketbook and studied the road before them. Her singing voice was no longer what it had been once upon a time and she knew this, but she and Vivian went back a long way. Then, too, in most of the churches of Washington, the people who heard the Gospelteers were generally more concerned about the message than the messenger's delivery.

Vivian laughed, shaking her friends's arm. "Oh, come on now," she said. "Snap out of it. Pull up them droopy lips."

"Lord, yes," Diane said. "It's gonna be a wonderful day. And"— she drummed her fingers on the pocketbook—"there is a bright spot there out on the horizon." She shook her head with delight.

"Oh," Vivian said, "what is this bright spot?"

"Later, I'll tell you later, when there's time," Diane said, and she shook herself some more.

The woman who was old enough to be Counsel Smith's grandmother was Maude Townsend, a blind woman who lived at Claridge Towers on M Street Northwest, an apartment house for old people and the disabled. On the day the House of the Solitary Savior burned to the ground, Maude was waiting outside Claridge Towers with Anita Hughes, the newest and youngest member of the group.

After Maude and Anita were in the car, Vivian said, "Standin out there like that yall looked like two sportin ladies on the corner waitin for some gentlemen. I had to look twice to make sure I was at the right address." The four laughed.

"I ain't lookin for no man," Maude said after they were on 11th

Street. "Thas all finished. All I want is some more Jesus." Maude, too, was one of the original members of the Gospelteers. She was seventy-eight, and of the dozens and dozens of her people who had been alive when the group sang that very first Sunday at the House, not one was now alive.

"But you sho right about that sportin stuff," Maude said. "You wouldn't believe what that place done turned into. Claridge was such a nice place when I first moved in." She leaned back in her seat and crossed her ankles.

"I keep telling her that she should move out, find someplace else," Anita said. As she often did the night before the group sang, she stayed with Maude. "John and I will help her find a place." John was the man with whom she lived, a gentle country man who was in his last year of medical residency at Howard University Hospital. Anita was twenty-five, in the second year of studying for a biology doctorate. She sang gospel because she felt that was the only way she could speak to God.

"Every senior citizen buildin in this city done turned bad," Maude said. "The only thing to do is to just pick up and move back down South. I got two friends that done that and they say they shoulda done it long ago."

"Oh, Maude," Diane said, "I been back South and you ain't gonna find it no different."

"She right," Vivian said.

Maude said nothing. Her head was turned to the window. In one hand she carried her tambourine. On the wrist of the other arm she wore a watch, but it was the type for sighted people, and aside from being a pretty thing on her wrist, it was not any good to her unless someone with eyes looked at it and told her what time it was.

Vivian found a parking space on S Street, between 10th and 11th. Maude walked with her arm through Vivian's, and Diane and Anita walked behind them. Not until they had reached the corner of 10th Street did the three sighted women notice that a policeman was not allowing traffic to continue on down 10th. Once on 10th Street, they could see a crowd of people on both sides of the street and the fire trucks about midway up the block. And when they got closer, they could see Reverend Saunders and his wife, their heads high above all the others, even the firemen who hurried about them. Counsel, for once, had been early and he stood beside the couple.

Counsel told them what had happened, and the three women could see that not one part of the small building had been saved. As he spoke, a mood of utter sadness swept over the four women. They did not think very much of Reverend Saunders's work, but they did not believe that anything bad should ever happen to any of God's houses.

"Well," Counsel said in a voice only Vivian could hear, "that's one excuse for a piano I have won't have to coax some life into again."

Vivian watched the reverend's wife clinging to her husband, her face buried in the shoulder of his coat. There was a general stench of burnt wood, and above the murmurs of the crowds on both sides of the street, Vivian could hear the water falling through the charred skeleton of what was left of the church. She watched the water rain down and flow with black debris over the sidewalk into the gutter and the street. People stepped back from it. She could see clear through the church now into what had passed for a back-yard. Now and then, a small burst of dark smoke would escape from the structure and dissipate a few feet above it. The busy fire-men spoke to each other as if they had all been raised together from birth.

Reverend Saunders turned around and took note of the four women. He shook their hands and he thanked them for coming. And then the members of his church came up to the women and they, too, thanked them for coming. Most of the members were women who were nearly as old as Maude. Vivian could see that most of the women had been crying and it tore into her heart. From program to program, she never remembered any of them ex-cept in some vague way, and whenever she happened to meet one of them in any other place on any other day she was never able to re-call from where she knew them.

The firemen were now packing up to leave, rolling up the fire hoses and taking off their suits. The fireman who seemed to be in charge came to Reverend Saunders and said a few final words to him, then he went back to helping his men. The sun was at the top of the sky. In a voice loud and undeniable, Reverend Saunders asked his people to pray and everyone on both sides of the street fell silent. Some of the firemen would occasionally stop what they were doing for a second or two, but for the most part, they contin-ued on.

When the prayers were done, Reverend Saunders asked the Gospelteers to sing one song.

"Vi, I feel 'Amazin Grace' in my heart right now," Maude said. The four women locked their arms and began to sing, and again the people fell silent. And though he did not usually sing, Counsel joined the four women.

"We gonna build us another one, Sister Slater," Reverend Saunders said when the hymn was over. "And I hope yall will come to sing at the dedication." His words still had a touch of that boast-ful quality. He turned back and took a few steps toward what was left of the church, and his wife, her arm still in his, followed. "Everything is a sign from the Master," he said to no one in partic-ular. Vivian could see, for the first time ever, that he was no longer a young man. "And maybe tomorrow or the next day, I'll figure out what it is." His wife had not said a word the whole time.

The group now had a few hours before the program at Holy Tabernacle. Counsel had parked near Vivian's Cadillac and he walked the four women to the car. Though none of them was very hungry, they decided to go to the Florida Avenue Grill, because Anita's aunt was a waitress there. Counsel told the women he would meet them at the church. Vivian warned him not to be late and Maude, teasing, told him not to bring one of his women along.

*   *   *

The second assistant pastor and a deacon at Holy Tabernacle greeted the Gospelteers just outside one of the dressing rooms in the basement just off 14th Street. The hall was crowded with groups going in and out of other dressing rooms and offices being used as dressing rooms. Vivian could see Counsel at the end of the hall, where he was conversing with a young woman in the corner.

That Sunday was the last day of a month of festivities inaugurating the new head pastor, Reverend Melvin Ritter, the son of the last pastor, Reverend Louis Ritter. The older man had turned over most of his duties to his son a year before, and he began spending most of his time at a home he and his wife had bought in North Carolina, where he had been born and raised and where God had called him. Six months before he had gone for a walk in the dark and drowned in the river that bordered their property.

Upstairs, the old man's son was speaking to those assembled in the church, and he was telling them about his father and the river. There were speakers installed in just about every ceiling corner of the building and the son's words rained down on the people in the basement hall and in the rooms.

As the Gospelteers got ready in their dressing room (they were to be the third group to sing, after the Watchers, and Jesse Mae Carson and the Heavenly Choir), they remembered the day a year before when the old man had been preaching and had seemed to lose his way. The women and Counsel and members of a few other groups had been waiting in one of the back halls that led to the church when they heard the old man grow silent. At first they thought the speakers had malfunctioned, but they heard him breathing loudly. Then he said, "Mother," which was what he called his wife.

Vivian had gone to the hall door leading into the church and had seen the old man absently flipping the pages of his Bible. He said "Mother" once more, took up the Bible, walked to the edge of the pulpit, and extended his hand, as if for help, to his wife. Only those near him could hear him say "Mother" yet again. She got up from her place in the Amen Corner, came to him, and led him back to a seat behind the lectern and just in front of the church's choir. Eventually, the second assistant pastor, a deacon, and his wife helped the old man out of the church. The old man's son had come to help his father as well, but his mother shook her head and pointed to the pulpit. The old man and his wife and one of the pastors and the deacon passed by Vivian. The old man's eyes gave her nothing, and though they were leading him, she could see that his legs were still strong. His son, who was then the first assistant pastor, went to the pulpit.

"Did you see what Jesse Mae was wearing?" Diane said now. The room was not very big but it was large enough to accommodate two dressing tables, a lounge chair, and a settee. "I tell you: If Jesus gave out seats in heaven accordin to how good a dresser you are, she'd go straight to hell." She sat at one of the tables and Anita was at the other. Vivian was helping Maude button her gown.

"What did she have on?" Maude asked. "Somebody tell me what that little hussy had on."

The words of the old man's son came out of the speaker. He said that the river where his father had died was the same one he had swum in as a boy, and it was the same one where he had been baptized.

"Fur," Diane said.

"Fur?" said Maude. "You mean a fur coat?"

"No, fur trim, Maude. Fur for her collar. Fur round the sleeves. Fur round the hem a that gown a hers."

"Everybody in the group wearin gowns like that?" Maude asked.

"You kiddin?" Vivian said. "She wouldn't be the Queen of Sheba if she let everybody wear what she has on."

Jesse Mae Carson and her Heavenly Choir had the greatest reputation of any gospel group in Washington. They were wealthy enough to have paid to cut three record albums with a D.C. company. To sell the records Jesse Mae's great-grandson would set up a table in the lobbies of the churches where they were singing and offer as a bonus a photograph of the group that had been autographed by Jesse Mae herself. Jesse Mae was eighty-eight years old and stood four feet and some inches high. A person had to stand very close and look real hard to find even one line on her face. She hadn't sung with the group for more than fifteen years, but would stand before the group and, like a conductor, guide the Heavenly Choir through their numbers. She had had eight husbands. "All of them legitimate," she had told a radio interviewer once. "God," she said, "don't mind you havin a vice. He just don't want you to abuse it."

"What color is the gowns they wearin?" Maude wanted to know of the Heavenly Choir.

"Blue, I think. Some kinda blue," Vivian said. When they wanted to tease her, Vivian's friends would call her Little Jesse Mae or Jesse Mae, Jr., because she had had five husbands, three "legitimate" and two common-law.

Upstairs, Reverend Ritter had finished his remarks and was introducing the Watchers, a group of five men, all over sixty, who had been his father's favorite. The Watchers set into "Oh, What a Friend We Have in Jesus." As the group went into "Deep River," Anita suggested that she and Maude go on out and catch up on the gossip as they made their way upstairs. "If we see that hussy," Maude said to Anita, "just turn me loose. Don't try to hold me back, child."

Deep River, my home is over Jordan—

"Ain't nobody in the world can sing that like them," Diane said of the Watchers. "I musta heard a hundred people sing that spiritual over the years. And they the only ones to give me the goose bumps."

"Know what you mean," Vivian said. She rarely had anything to say about any other group, but the Watchers, being older and male, were not in competition with the Gospelteers. "Me and you might as well make our way too. You got the key?" Diane nodded and locked the door after them. In the hall, Jesse Mae was talking to Anita.

The Watchers sang:

Oh, chillun, oh don't you want to go to that gospel feast
That promised land, that land where all is peace?

"I know, I know," Anita was saying. "It does sound nice, but I keep telling you I'm happy where I am."

Vivian came up and put her arm around Anita's shoulder. "Still trying to steal you away, huh?" she said to Anita.

"Not steal, Vi," Jesse Mae said. "Just . . . how do I say it? Just . . . entice. Ain't that right, baby?" and she winked at Anita. It was said that Anita had a voice beautiful enough to lure the angels down from heaven. Gospel groups up and down the East Coast envied Vivian for having her in the Gospelteers, and for more than a year Jessie Mae had been trying to get Anita to come over to the Heavenly Choir. She had sent her copies of her group's record albums, lists of the churches along the East Coast where they had sung in recent years, and pictures of the group posed before landmarks in other cities and standing with well-known politicians and soul singers and athletes. And with all she sent, there was always a note that ended, "I look forward to seeing you the next time. Forever Yours in the Lord. . . ."

But Anita had never once wavered in her desire to stay with the Gospelteers, and Vivian took heart from this. Some days, as she sat in her office at the Agriculture Department, she would think of Anita arrayed in the pasture-green gown the Gospelteers wore on the fourth Sunday. She would be solo, standing just in front of the other women acting as chorus, and Anita's voice would take hold of the church and all the people in the church would be telling her to bring it on home, bring it on home, child.

"Oh, Jessie Mae, why don't you just give it up," Diane said. "You just gonna have to face the fact that Vivian got you beat on this one." It sometimes irritated Vivian that Diane, of all people, came to her defense.

Jessie Mae offered each of the four women a practiced smile, a patient smile a tired adult gives a small child who has said one too many absurd things.

"And how is Ralph?" Jessie Mae asked Vivian. "Still handsome as ever? My my my."

"Yes," Vivian said. "Still the most handsome in the world. Still the best in the world." She had told no one that Ralph was dying.

Jessie Mae wished them well with their program and went to be with her group. Vivian and Diane spent the remaining time in the dining hall, sipping tea. The portraits of all the church's pastors were on the walls, and near the door to the kitchen there was the place where Reverend Louis Ritter's picture would be one day.

The congregation applauded generously when the Gospelteers came on. Vivian stepped forward and told the congregation that the group would be singing some of the favorites of Mahalia Jackson, and the congregation broke into applause again. Anita would be singing the first songs solo, and the young woman took Vivian's place in front of the group. She looked briefly at Counsel and he nodded once and began to play. Anita closed her eyes for a few seconds and began to sing as she always did—for God and for her father. Once, as she was singing at the Virgin Mother Baptist Church on Kentucky Avenue, Jesus had come down the aisle and sat down in a pew near the front. He told her that her voice pleased him. He had said no more than that, but she had taken his words to mean that he forgave her for living with John without marriage. And each time she saw her father, who would not forgive her, she wanted to tell him what Jesus had done and said. But she could not create the words. Perhaps the words were in the music, but it did no good, because her father did not come anymore to hear her sing.

The Gospelteers opened with "Consideration":

> *Tide rolling high billows . . .*
> *Lord, when you smile on all creations, consider me,*

Mad winds may blow; mad breakers roar
They beat on every side

By the time they had reached the refrain of "Walk Over God's Heaven," Vivian knew the group had reached that sometimes elusive part of the program when the church belonged to them. Those moments were at the center of her life, those moments when the audience, if given a choice of all the things to do on the earth, would have chosen to go on listening to them forever. If I could pick my time to die . . . she had once thought. When the group reached the end of the program with "What Could I Do if It Wasn't for the Lord," the congregation and Reverend Ritter refused to let them go. And so they sang "Move on up a Little Higher" and "Jesus Met the Woman at the Well," and then they went into "Amazing Grace" all over again.

When it was all over, they had a bite to eat at the church, mingling with those who could not get enough of hearing and talking about the old man. Diane said she had a most important call to make and went off while the others were eating, and when she returned the group made its good-byes. Outside, they hugged Counsel good night, and the four women set off in Vivian's car. It had been snowing, and each of the four was full of the satisfying warmth at knowing the evening had gone so well. Five blocks or so from the church, Diane asked if they could stop a minute at the corner of 14th and Fairmont. There, she stepped out into the night and the snow.

"I be right back," Diane said before closing the door. She did not look before crossing the street and in a few steps she was at the passenger side of a car that was waiting with its motor on. When she opened the door, the light came on, and in that instant, Vivian could see a bit of the driver, a man who took off his hat. It took her breath away to see him do that. And in that instant before the light went out, she saw Diane and the man lean toward each other. The kiss came in the dark, the two figures silhouetted against the dull light in the area behind the car. The kiss lasted but a second, but for Vivian it was a most unkind second.

The three women waited in silence for many minutes, until Maude asked where was Diane and what was taking her so long. Anita told her what she was seeing.

"Could you tell if it's Harry?" Maude said.

"I don't think it is," Anita said. "It sure isn't Harry's car."

At the word *car* Maude seemed to fall to pieces. "Oh, Lord. Oh, Lord," she said. "She sure is playin with fire doin that. What's wrong with her? What in the world is wrong with her?"

Before long, Diane got out of the car, but midway across the empty street, she hesitated and looked back at the man, then she went to him again, and the man rolled down his window. She nodded to him. To Vivian, it was the nod of a woman who had lost her heart, a woman she did not know, had never met in her life. There was an inch or so of snow everywhere, and in the street there were Diane's footprints, coming and going, two intersecting dotted lines on an otherwise unblemished canvas. Vivian looked away when she saw the small clouds their words made.

"I ain't your gotdamn chauffeur!" Vivian said when Diane had returned and shut the door. "I don't get paid for sittin here and waitin for you!"

"Vi, I'm sorry. It took longer than I expected. I'm really sorry."

Vivian started up the car. "If you think all I got to do with my time is sit here with all your foolishness, you got another thought comin."

"Vi, I told you I'm sorry. What more do you want? Jesus!"

"Vi," Maude said, seeking peace, "it's all right. Take it easy. Let's just get out of here."

"Maude, this my car and I'll say what I want in it."

Except for occasional mumblings from Vivian that she was not a chauffeur, they drove the distance to Maude's apartment building without words. Diane was crying quietly. At the building, Vivian double-parked as Maude and Anita, who had decided to stay the night with the old woman, prepared to get out.

"I want you two to make up, y'hear?" Maude said before leaving. "Yall come too far to let somethin come between you."

But Diane got out of the car. "I'll call for a ride from your place, Maude, if it's all right."

"I thought you wanted a ride home." Vivian said.

"I'll call Harry or Cherry to come pick me up," Diane said.

"Now you both goin in the same direction," Maude said. "Why don't you let Vi take you home?" She stood on the sidewalk, her arm through Anita's.

"Suit yourself," Vivian said. She reached across the seat to close the door and drove away.

The streets were empty of life, though the snow was still falling lightly. Vivian circled the block and went down M Street until, at Thomas Circle, she realized that that was not the way home. She could still see him. . . . And when she had turned the car around, it took a while to understand that she was only going in the general direction of home. She turned her windshield wipers up to their fullest speed and made her way through Northwest, Northeast, and then to Southeast, where she pulled into the parking lot of a High's store a few blocks from the Navy Yard and the river Anacostia. She thought it would take only a moment or two to collect herself.

She could still see him, and it came to her as she watched people go in and out of the High's that she had not seen a man take off his hat in that old-fashioned way in a long, long time. It was a respectful gesture out of a country time when a little girl would watch dark young men tall as trees stand respectfully close to young women and say things that made the women put their hands to their mouths to stifle a giggle. The young women's cotton print dresses billowed slightly with the summer breezes, and even the billowing itself seemed to a little girl a part of all the secrets and romance that she could not yet take part in. And the young women always leaned back against the shadiest of trees with such utter self-assurance, holding a glass of lemonade that the men had brought out from the kitchen. And when the young women's parents thought that there was too much in the giggles, they would tell the women to come up to the porch and bring so-and-so and get some more lemonade.

It was a time of perfect lemonade chilled with hunks of ice cut from larger blocks that were covered with straw and kept in root cellars. It was a time of pound cake baked to such a wondrous golden that it must have been a small sin to even cut into it. But perhaps God forgave, as he went on forgiving a little girl who watched the young men courting the young women, who watched them for so long that the flies set up house on her cake and all the ice in her glass melted and made her drink unpalatable.

Where had all such men gone when she herself came of age? Had the same things been said to the other women that were later said to her as she leaned back against her own tree?

In a cheap metal box in her closet in the house where Ralph Slater waited, she kept the licenses from her three marriages, along with the divorce documents. And from the first common-law marriage, she kept a letter, in childlike block letters and misspelled words, that the man had written to her from two thousand miles away, promising that they would be one forever.

She could still see him. . . . How much more grandness, beyond the gesture with the hat, was there to him? Her heart ached to know, and with both hands she held tight to the steering wheel, as if she were in danger of being swept away on some swelling tide. She did not want to think, though the words took shape and went in and sat down beside the man in his car—she did not want to think that God did not make such men anymore. And that if he still did, he should waste them all upon women like Diane McCollough.

She could see him, and slowly the image of him as she knew she would find him took hold. She could see him—asleep in the same chair she had left him in that morning: Perhaps the Sunday newspaper would be scattered at his feet, and maybe the wobbly TV-dinner table would be empty, for he would not want to bring down her wrath by keeping the remains of his dinner in the living room. Perhaps, too, he might have peed on himself again. And the television would be on, as it had been all day, but aside from a football score here and there, he would not be able to remember what he had seen throughout the day. But the wobbly table would not be empty—a few empty beer cans and one that would be half empty, along with his bottles of medicine and a tablespoon with which to take the liquid one.

A few people came and went about her, but the snow now covered the windows of her car and all she could make out were shadows moving about. She could hear voices, but she could not understand any of what people said, as if all sound were being filtered by the snow and turned into garble. She could not anymore read her watch, but she continued to tell herself that in the next minute she would start up the car and go home to Ralph. In the end, it grew cold in the car, and colder still, and at first she did not notice, and then when she did, she thought it was the general condition of the whole world, owing to the snow, and that there was not very much she could do about it.

A NEW MAN

One day in late October, Woodrow L. Cunningham came home early with his bad heart and found his daughter with the two boys. He was then fifty-two years old, a conscientious deacon at Rising Star AME Zion, a paid-up lifetime member of the NAACP and the Urban League, a twenty-five year member of the Elks. For ten years he had been the chief engineer at the Sheraton Park Hotel, where practically every employee knew his name. For longer than he could recall, his friends and lodge members had been telling him that he was capable of being more than just the number-one maintenance man. But he always told them that he was contented in the job, that it was all he needed, and this was true for the most part. He would be in that same position some thirteen years later, when death happened upon him as he bent down over a hotel bathroom sink, about to do a job a younger engineer claimed he could not handle.

The afternoon he came home early and discovered his daughter with the boys, he found a letter in the mailbox from his father in Georgia. He read the letter while standing in the hall of the apartment building. He expected nothing of importance, as usual, and that was what he found. "Alice took me to Buddy Wilson funeral just last week," Woodrow read. "I loaned him the shirt they buried him in. And that tie he had on was one that I give him too. I thought I would miss him but I do not miss him very much. Checkers was never Buddy Wilsons game." As he read, he massaged the area around his heart, an old habit, something he did even when his heart was not giving him trouble. "I hope you and the family can come down before the winter months set in. Company is never the same after winter get here."

He put the letter back in the envelope, and as he absently looked at the upside-down stamp taped in the vicinity of the corner, the pain in his heart eased. He could picture his father sitting at the kitchen table, writing the letter, occasionally touching the pencil point to his tongue. A new mongrel's head would be resting across his lap, across thin legs that could still carry the old man five miles down the road and back. Woodrow, feeling better, considered returning to work, but he knew his heart was deceitful. He folded the envelope and stuck it in his back pocket, and out of the pocket it would fall late that night as he prepared for bed after returning from the police station.

Several feet before he reached his apartment door he could hear the boys' laughter and bits and pieces of their man-child conquer-the-world talk. He could not hear his daughter at first. He stopped at his door and listened for nearly five minutes, and in that time he became so fascinated by what the boys were saying that he would not have cared if someone walking in the hall found him listening. It was only when he heard his daughter's laughter, familiar, known, that he put his key in the door. She stood just inside the door when he entered, her eyes accusing but her mouth set in a small O of surprise. Beyond her he could see the boys with their legs draped over the arms of the couch and gray smoke above their heads wafting toward the open window.

He asked his daughter, "Why ain't you in school?"

"They let us out early today," she said. "The teachers had some kinda meetin."

He did not listen to her, because he had found that she lived to lie. Woodrow watched the boys as they took their time straightening themselves up, and he knew that their deliberateness was the result of something his daughter had said about him. Without taking his eyes from the boys, he asked his daughter again why she wasn't in school. When he finally looked at her, he saw that she was holding the stump of a thin cigarette. The smoke he smelled was unfamiliar, and at first he thought that they were smoking very stale cigarettes, or cigarettes that had gotten wet and been dried. He slapped her. "I told you not to smoke in my house," he said.

She was fifteen, and up until six months or so before, she would have collapsed into the chair, collapsed into a fit of crying. But now she picked up the fallen cigarette from the floor and stamped it out in the ashtray on the tiny table beside the easy chair. Her hand shook, the only reminder of the old days. "We just talkin. We ain't doin nothin wrong," she said quietly.

He shouted to the boys, "Get outta my house!" They stood up quickly, and Woodrow could tell that whatever she had told them about him, such anger was not part of it. They looked once at the girl.

"They my guests, Daddy," she said, sitting in the easy chair and crossing her legs. "I invited em over here."

Woodrow took two steps to the boy nearest him—the tall light-skinned one he would spot from a bus window a year or so later—and grabbed him with one hand by the jacket collar, shook him until the boy raised his hands as if to protect his face from a blow. The boy's eyes widened and Woodrow shook him some more. He had been living a black man's civilized life in Washington and had not felt so coiled and bristled since the days when he worked with wild men in the turpentine camps in Florida. "I ain't done nothin," the boy said. The words sounded familiar, similar to those of a wild man ready to slink away into his cabin with his tail between his legs. Woodrow relaxed. "I swear. I don't want no trouble, Mr. Cunningham." The boy had no other smell but that peculiar cigarette smoke, and it was a shock to Woodrow that a body with that smell should know something that seemed as personal as his name. The other, smaller boy had tiptoed around Woodrow and was having trouble opening the door. After the small boy had gone out, Woodrow flung the light-skinned boy out behind him. Woodrow locked the door, and the boys stood for several minutes, pounding on the door, mouthing off.

"Why you treat my guests like that?" Elaine Cunningham had not moved from the chair.

"Clean up this mess," he told her, "and I don't wanna see one ash when you done."

She said nothing more, but busied herself tidying the couch cushions. Then Woodrow, after flicking the cushions a few times with his handkerchief, sat in the middle of the couch, and the couch sagged with the familiarity of this weight.

When Elaine had returned the room to what it was, her father said, "I want to know what you was doin in here with them boys."

"Nothin. We wasn't doin nothin. Just talkin, thas all, Daddy." She sat in the easy chair, leaned toward him with her elbows on her knees.

"You can do your talkin down on the stoop," he said.

"Why don't you just say you tryin to cuse me a somethin? Why don't you just come out and say it?"

"If you didn't do things, you wouldn't get accused," he said. He talked without thought, because those words and words like them had been spoken so much to her that he was able to parrot himself. "If you start actin like a young lady should, start studyin and what not, and tryin to make somethin of yourself . . ." Woodrow L. Cunningham bein Woodrow L. Cunningham, he thought.

She stood up quickly, and he was sickened to see her breasts bounce. "I could study them stupid books half the damn day and sit in church the other half, and I'd still get the same stuff thrown in my face bout how I ain't doin right."

"Okay, thas anough a that." He felt a familiar rumbling in his heart. "I done heard anough."

"I wanna go out," she stood with her arms folded. "I wanna go out."

"Go on back to your room. Thas the only goin out you gonna be doin. I don't wanna hear another word outta your mouth till your mother get home." He closed his eyes to wait her out, for he knew she was now capable of standing there till doomsday to sulk. When he heard her going down the hall, he waited for the door to slam. But there was no sound and he gradually opened his eyes. He put a cushion at one end of the couch and took off his shoes and lay down, his hands resting on the large mound that was his stomach. All his friends told him that if he lost thirty or forty pounds he would be a new man, but he did not think that was true. He considered asking Elaine to bring his pills from his bedroom, for he had left the vial he traveled with at work. But he suffered the pain rather than suffer her stirring about. He watched his wife's curtains flap gently with the breeze and the movement soothed him.

"I would not say anything bad about mariage," his father had written to Woodrow after Woodrow called to say he was considering marrying Rita Hadley. "It is easier to pick up and walk away from a wife and a family if you don't like it then you can walk away from your own bad cooking." Woodrow had never been inclined to marry anyone, was able, as he would tell his lodge brothers, to get all the trim he wanted without buying some woman a ring and walking down the aisle with her. "Doin it to a woman for a few months was all right," he would say, sounding like his father, "cause that only put the idea of marryin in their heads. Doin it to them any more than that and the idea take root."

It had never crossed his mind to sleep with any of the women at Rising Star AME, for he had discovered in Georgia that the wrath of church women was greater than that of all others, even old whores. He only went out with Rita because the preacher took him aside one Sunday and told him it was unnatural to go about unmarried and that he should give some thought to promenading with Sister Rita sometime. And, too, he was thirty-six and it was beginning to occur to him that women might not go on forever laying down and opening their legs for him. The second time they went out, he put his arm around Rita and pulled her to him there in the Booker-T Theater. She smacked his hand and that made his johnson hard. "I ain't like that, Mr. Cunningham." He had heard those words before. But when he pulled her to him again, she twisted his finger until it hurt. And that was something he had not experienced before.

His father suffered a mild stroke a week before the wedding. "Do not take this sickness to mean that I do not send my blessing to your mariage to Miss Rita Hadley," his father said in a letter he had dictated to Alice, his oldest daughter. "God took pity on you when he send her your way." Even in the unfamiliarity of Alice's handwriting, the familiarity of his father was there in all the lines, right down to the misspelled words. Until some of his father's children learned in their teens, his father had been the only one in the family who could read and write. "This," he said of his reading and writing, "makes me as good as a white man." And before some of his children learned, discovered there was no magic to it, he enjoyed reading aloud at the supper table to his family, his voice stringing out a long monotone of words that often meant nothing to him and even less to his family because the man read so quickly.

His father read anything he could get his hands on—the words on feed bags, on medicine bottles, on years-old magazine pages they used for wallpaper, just about everything except the Bible. He had a fondness for weeks-old newspapers he would find in the streets when he went to town. No one—not even the squirming small kids—was allowed to move from the supper table until he had finished reading, hooking one word to another until it all became babble. Indeed, it was such a babble that some of his sons would joke behind his back that he was lying about knowing how to read. "Few white men can do what I'm doin right now," he would say. "You go bring ten white men in here and I bet nine couldn't read this. Couldn't read it if God commanded em to." Sometimes, to torment his wife, he would hold a scrap of newspaper close to her face and tell her to read the headlines. "I cain't," she would say. "You know I cain't." No matter how many times he did this, his father would laugh with the pleasure of the very first time. Then he would pass the newspaper among his children and tell them to read him the headlines, and each one would hold it uncomfortably and repeat what their mother had said.

*   *   *

When Woodrow woke, it was nearly five o'clock and his wife was sitting on the side of the couch, asking where Elaine was. "She ain't in her room," his wife said and kissed his forehead. A school cafeteria worker, Rita was a very thin woman who, before she met Woodrow, had lived only for her job and her church activities. She was five years older than he was and had resigned herself to the fact that she was not the type of woman men wanted to marry. "I've put it all in God's hands," she once said to a friend before Woodrow came along, "and left it there."

Rita waited until seven o'clock before she began calling her daughter's friends. "Stop worryin," Woodrow told her after the tenth call, "you know how that girl is." At eight-thirty, they put on light coats and went in search, visiting the same houses and apartments that Rita had called. They returned home about ten and waited until eleven, when they put on their coats again and went to the police station at 16th and V Northwest. They did not call the station because somewhere Woodrow had heard that the law wouldn't begin to hear a complaint unless you stood before it in person.

At the station, the man at the front desk did not look up until they had been standing there for some two minutes. Woodrow wanted to tell him that the police chief and the mayor were now black men and that they couldn't be ignored, but when the man behind the desk looked up, Woodrow could see in his eyes that none of that would have mattered to him.

"Our daughter is missing," Rita said.

"How long?" said the man, a sergeant with an unpronounceable name on his name tag. He pulled a form from a pile to his left and then he took up a pen, loudly clicking out the point to write.

"We haven't seen her since this afternoon," Woodrow says.

The sergeant clicked the pen again and set it on the desk, then put the form back on top with the others. "Not long enough," he said. "Has to be gone forty-eight hours. Till then she's missing, but she's not a missing person."

"She only a baby."

"How old?"

"Fifteen," Woodrow said.

"She's just a runaway," the sergeant said.

"She never run away before," Woodrow said. "This ain't like her, sergeant." Woodrow felt that like all white men, the man enjoyed having attention paid to his rank.

"Don't matter. She's probably waiting for you at home right now, wondering where you two buggied off to. Go home. If she isn't home, then come back when she's a missing person."

Woodrow took Rita's arm as they went back, because he sensed that she was near collapsing. "What happened?" she asked as they turned the corner of U and 10th streets. "Did you say somethin bad to her?"

He told her everything that he could remember, even what Elaine was wearing when he last saw her. Answering was not difficult because no blame had yet been assigned. Despite the time nearing midnight, they became confident with each step that Elaine was just at a friend's they did not know about, that the friend's mother, like any good mother, would soon send their daughter home. Rita, in the last blocks before their apartment, leaned into her husband and his warmth helped to put her at ease.

They waited up until about four in the morning, and then they undressed without words in the dark. Rita began to cry the moment her head hit the pillow, for she was afraid to see the sun come up and find that a new day had arrived without Elaine being home. She asked him again what happened, and he told her again, even things that he had forgotten—the logo of the football team on the light-skinned boy's jacket, the fact that the other boy was bald except for a half-dollar-sized spot of hair carved on the back of his head. He was still talking when she dozed off with him holding her.

Before they had coffee later that morning, about seven thirty, they called their jobs to say they would not be in. Work had always occupied a place at the center of their lives, and there was initially something eerie about being home when it was not a holiday or the weekend. They spent the rest of the morning searching the streets together, and in the afternoon, they separated to cover more ground. They did the same thing after dinner, each spreading out farther and farther from their apartment on R Street. That evening, they called neighbors and friends, church and lodge members, to tell them that their child was missing and that they needed their help and their prayers. Their friends and neighbors began searching that evening, and a few went with Woodrow and Rita the next day to the police station to file a missing person's report. A different sergeant was at the desk, and though he was a white man, Woodrow felt that he understood their trouble.

For nearly three months, Woodrow and Rita searched after they came from work, and each evening after they and their friends had been out, the pastor of Rising Star spoke to a small group that gathered in the Cunninghams' living room. "The world is cold and not hospitable," he would conclude, holding his hat in both hands, "but we know our God to be a kind God and that he has provided our little sister with a place of comfort and warmth until she returns to her parents and to all of us who love and treasure her."

In the kitchen beside the refrigerator, Rita tacked up a giant map of Washington, on which she noted where she and others had searched. "I didn't know the city was this big," she said the day she put it up, her fingertips touching the neighborhoods that she had never heard of or had heard of only in passing—foreign lands she thought she would never set eyes on. Petworth. Anacostia. Lincoln Park. And in the beginning, the very size of the city lifted her spirits, for in a place so big, there was certainly a spot that held something as small as her child, and if they just kept looking long enough, they would come upon that place.

"What happened?" Rita would ask as they prepared for bed. What he told her and her listening replaced everything they had ever done in that bed—discussing what future they wanted for Elaine, lovemaking, sharing what the world had done to them that workday. "What happened?" It was just about the only thing she ever asked Woodrow as the months grew colder. "What happened?

Whatcha say to her?" By late February, when fewer and fewer people were going out to search, he had told the whole story, but then he began to tell her things that had not happened. There were three boys, he said at one point, for example. Or, he could see a gun sticking out of the jacket pocket of the light-skinned one, and he could see the outline of a knife in the back pants pocket of the third. Or he would say that the record player was playing so loudly he could hear it from the street. They were small embellishments at first, and if his wife noticed that the story of what happened was changing, she said nothing. In time, with winter disappearing, he was adding more and more so that it was no longer a falseness here and there that was embedded in the whole of the truth, but the truth itself, an ever-diminishing kernel, that was contained in the whole of falseness. And, like some kind of bedtime story, she listened and drifted with his words into a sleep where the things he was telling her were sometimes happening.

By March, Woodrow had written countless letters to his father telling the old man it was not necessary to come to Washington to help look for the girl. "I got a sign from God," the old man kept writing, "that I could help find her." Then, with spring, he began writing that he had received signs that he was not long for the world, that finding the girl was the last thing God wanted him to do. In the longest letters the old man had ever written to the one child of his who responded, he would go on and on about the signs he saw signaling his own death: The mongrel would no longer take food from his hand; the dead visited him at night, sitting down on the side of his bed and telling him things about himself; the rising sun now touched his house last in the morning, though there were houses to the left and right of his.

"You keep telling me that I'll be hurt or lost," the old man wrote Woodrow. "But I know the way that Washington, D.C. is set up. I came there once maybe twice. How could I get lost. Take a chance on me, and we'll have that child home before you can blink one eye. I can bring Sparky he got some bloodhound in him."

In late April, Rita took down the map in the kitchen. The tacks fell to the floor and she left them there. She put the map in the bottom drawer of her daughter's dresser, among the blouses and blue jeans and a diary she would not find the strength to read for another three months. Her days of searching during the week dwindled down to two, then to one. She returned the car a church member had lent her to drive around the city in. Each evening when she got home, Woodrow would be out and she left his dinner in the oven to stay warm. Every now and again, when the hour was late, she went out to look for him, often for no other reason than that there was nothing worth watching on the television. As she put on more and more weight, it became difficult for her to stand and dish out food to the students at lunchtime. Her supervisor and fellow workers sympathized, and, after a week of perfunctory training, she was allowed to sit and work at the cash register.

As he continued going about the city, sometimes on foot, Woodrow told himself and everyone else that he was hunting for his daughter, but this was only a piece of the truth. "I'm lookin for my daughter, who's run away," he said to those opening the doors where he knocked. "She's been gone a long time, and her mama and me are about to lose our minds." He sometimes presented a picture of his daughter, smiling radiantly, that was taken only months before she disappeared. But just as often, he would pull out a photograph of the girl when she was five, standing one Easter between her parents in front of Rising Star. All who looked at the photograph, even the drunks half-blind with alcohol, were touched by the picture of the little girl in her Easter dress who had now gone away from her parents, parents who were now worried sick. Many people invited Woodrow into their homes.

The Easter picture became a passport, and the more places he visited the more places he wanted to see. On U Street, a woman of twenty-five or so with three children put down the child she was holding to get a better look at the picture of the five-year-old girl. Woodrow, in the doorway, noted just over her shoulder that on her wall there was a calendar with a snow-covered mountain, hung with the prominence others would have given a landscape painting. An old woman on Harvard Street, tsk-tsking as she looked at the picture, invited him in for coffee and cake. "My prayers go out to you." Nearly everything in her apartment was covered in plastic, even the pictures on the walls. The old woman sat him on her plastic-covered couch and placed the food on a coffee table covered with a plastic cloth. "And such a sweet-lookin child, too, son." When he asked to use the bathroom (more out of curiosity than for relief), she pointed to a plastic path leading away down the hall. "Stay on the mat, son."

A tottering man in a place on 21st Street just off Benning Road began to cry when Woodrow told him his story. "Dora, Dora," the man called to a woman. "Come see this little angel." The woman, who was also tottering, pulled Woodrow into their house with one hand, while the other hand pressed the picture to her bosom. The man and Woodrow sat on the couch. The woman stood in front of them, swaying trancelike, her eyes closed, the picture still pressed to her. The man put his arm around Woodrow and breathed a sour wine smell into his face. "Let's me and you pray about this situation," he said.

One April evening, a little more than a year and a half after their daughter disappeared, Rita was standing in front of their building, waiting for him. "We have fish tonight. It's in the stove waitin," she said, in the same way she would have said, "I know what you been doin. And who you been doin it with." "We have fish to eat," she said again. She turned around and went back inside. "We have fish, and we have to move from this place," she said.

Woodrow's father died nearly seven years after Elaine Cunningham disappeared. Of the eight children he had had with Woodrow's mother and the five he had had with other women, only Woodrow, Alice, and a half-brother who lived down the road from the old man came to the funeral. It was a frozen day in January, and the gravediggers broke two picks before they had even gone down one foot. They labored seven hours to make a hole for the old man. "Even the ground don't want him," said one of the old man's friends standing at the gravesite.

There was not much in the old man's place to divide among his heirs. In a wooden trunk in one of the back rooms, Woodrow found several pictures of his mother. He had been kneeling down, going through the trunk, and when he saw the pictures, he cried out as if he had been struck. He had not seen his mother's face in more than forty years, had thought his father had destroyed all the pictures of her. "You always looked like her," Alice said, coming up behind him. "Even when you sat at the right hand of the father, you looked like her."

Though he was younger than three other brothers, Woodrow had worked hardest of his father's children. At first, his father had sat his children about the supper table according to their ages, but then he began to seat them according to who did the most work. His best workers sat closest to him, and by the time he was seven, Woodrow had worked his way to the right hand of his father. Woodrow's mother sat at the far end of the table, between two of her daughters. Most of his brothers and sisters, unable to pick the amount of cotton Woodrow could, never forgave him for living only to be close to their father. But he learned to pay them no mind and even learned to enjoy their hostility. He never moved from that right-hand place until the day he went off down the road to work in the turpentine camps.

He also found in the trunk some letters he wrote his father from the camps and from railroad yards and from the places he worked as he made his way up to Washington. They were all of one page or less, and they were all about work, work from sunup to sundown. There were no friends mentioned, there were no descriptions of places where he lived, there were no names of women courted, loved. "I got a two-week job tanning hides," he wrote from a nameless place in South Carolina. "I got work cureing tobacco. I may stay on after the season," he wrote from somewhere near Raleigh. "I have been working in the stables outside

Charlotesvile. The pay is good. I got used to the smell. and the work goes easy."

Woodrow and Rita took the train back to Washington, bringing back a few of the pictures and none of the letters, which he burned in a barrel outside his father's house. Everything along the way back to D.C. was as frozen as Georgia. It was as if the cold had separated the world into three unrelated and distinct parts—the earth, what was on the earth, and the sky above. Nothing moved. Flying birds seemed to freeze in midair, and then the cold would nail them there.

Rita and Woodrow were back in the apartment on Independence Avenue in Southeast by ten o'clock that night. Rita took her usual place at an easy chair near the window. On a table beside the chair was all she needed—the television guide, snacks, the telephone. The chair was very large and had had to be specially ordered, because she could not fit into the regular ones in the store.

Woodrow, even though the hour was late and the weather people were predicting even colder temperatures, quietly put on his heaviest coat and left the apartment. He said nothing to Rita, and she did not look up when the door locked behind him. At the corner of Independence and 15th, Woodrow looked into the grocery store window at the owner he had become friends with since moving to Southeast. No customers went into the store, and the owner was dozing behind the counter, his head back, his mouth open. Woodrow watched him for a very long time. By now he knew everything about the man and his store and the sons who helped the man, and there was no urgency to be inside with him. Having lost so much weight, Woodrow felt that even more of the world had opened up to him. And so he wondered if he should go on down 15th Street, try to find a house he had not visited before, and bring out the picture of the child in her Easter dress.

A DARK
NIGHT

About four that afternoon the thunder and lightning began again. The four women seated about Carmena Boone's efficiency apartment grew still and spoke in whispers, when they spoke at all: They were each of them no longer young, and they had all been raised to believe that such weather was—aside from answered prayers—the closest thing to the voice of God. And so each in her way listened.

They heard an apartment door down the long hall to the right open and close with utter violence, obviously pushed shut by the wind of the storm. Within seconds, they saw Ida Garrett move almost soundlessly past Carmena Boone's open door, a rubber-tipped brown cane in her good hand. She went the few yards to the end of the hall on the left and knocked again and again and again at what everyone in the room knew was the door of Beatrice Atwell's apartment. Beatrice was sitting in the middle of Carmena's couch, snug between the large Frazier sisters from the fifth floor. Then, just as soundlessly, Mrs. Garrett was standing small and silent in Boone's doorway. She could not have looked any more forlorn if she had been out in the storm: breathing as if each breath would be her last, her wig perched haphazardly on her head as if it had been dropped from the ceiling by accident, her pocketbook hanging from the arm that a stroke had permanently folded against her body, her eyeglasses resting near the end of her nose, beyond where they could possibly do her any good.

"I was passin," she said with effort to Carmena, "and I saw your door was open." Leaning against the doorjamb, she blinked in an effort to adjust to a room that was lit by only a forty-watt bulb, another concession to the voice of God. Several times, she shifted the scarred cane from the good hand to the bad, and just when the bad hand seemed about to drop it, she would take it back. "I was passin and saw your door was open, Boone. . . ."

She continued to repeat herself until Carmena stood and went to her, reassured Mrs. Garrett with a light touch of the hand. "You know you always welcome here, Miss Garrett." She took the woman's elbow and led her to a chair at the dining table. "I was thinkin bout you, me and the Fraziers, but somebody said you'd been under the weather, so I thought I shouldn't bother you."

It began to rain, no more than a soft tapping at the window.

"I'm fine, by the help of the Lord," Mrs. Garrett said, sitting. She settled herself, patting her wig and making sure her dress was well down over her knees. Her movements seemed practiced, like those of someone who did everything according to the way it was set out in some book. She placed her cane across her lap and leisurely began to pick pieces of lint off her dress, a silklike, polka-dotted thing that shimmered with what seemed huge green eyes. Then, with a flash of lightning and burst of thunder, she jerked her head up, as if the whole thing had been directed at her personally, the thunder an inch from her ear and the lightning just in front of her eyes. She waited, and when there was quiet for several minutes, she sighed, then began to take note of the four other women. They had been watching her intently, but when she looked at them, they nodded and lowered their eyes or deftly turned their heads away. Only when they were addressed by name did the women look at her, smile, ask how she was keeping. Beatrice, knitting on the couch between the Frazier sisters, did not look up.

"I'm surprised to see you here," Mrs. Garrett said to her. "I thought you might be home." There was a bit of hurt to the last words.

"No," Beatrice said happily. "I'm here. I'm right here." It

seemed to give her so much pleasure to say these words that she repeated them again and again until she raised a thread to her mouth
and bit it in two. "I've come for the prayer meetin."

"So *thas* what all yall hens here for?" Mrs. Garrett said and
turned to Carmena at the other end of the table. Carmena nodded
with a smile. "Oh, but I hope yall ain't gonna have that Reverend
Sawyer again. He ain't nothin but jackleg, Boone. I could tell the
first time I laid eyes on him. 'Jackleg,' I said to myself. 'As jackleg as
they come.' "

Carmena, seeking support, glanced at the others. "It's him. But
he got a church of his own now, Miss Garrett. Out in Northwest,
just off Rhode Island Avenue."

"Havin a church, Boone, don't mount to a hill of beans," Mrs.
Garrett said with exasperation. "It don't make a man a preacher,
called by God. Even I"—she put her good hand over her heart—
"could say I'm a man a God, but that don't make it so. All havin a
church means is you got a little money to rent a hole in the wall and
a few fools to come to the hole and give you their pennies."

"Well, I ain't a member of his church," Carmena said defen-
sively, "and don't plan to be a member. And I ain't never give him
money to come here to pray with us." Mrs. Garrett smiled knowingly. "I do have some food for us all when he get here. But thas a
everyday normal courtesy. Some sandwiches . . . some cake and
punch . . . just things I picked up round the corner . . . whatn't no
trouble. . . ."

Mrs. Garrett looked askance at the food displayed on the table.
"He'll fill hisself up off that, belch once, and look for more," she
said. She leaned down and placed her cane on the floor beside her.
"And what time is this man a God spected on the premises?"

"He said three thirty," Carmena said.

"Three thirty, huh? And all the clocks in the world now sayin
it's way past four."

Carmena shut the window just as the rain began to come in.
With only the forty-watt burning in the lamp on the table, the

room was on the verge of darkness. But each flash of lightning would give a ghastly brightness to the place and for those moments everything in the room could be clearly seen.

"And what you doin over there, Atwell, workin away like a tiny little mouse?" Mrs. Garrett said.

"Sewin," Beatrice said. "Makin somethin for my new grand-child."

"Oh, Lani dropped another one, huh? You didn't even tell me."

"A girl. A little over a month ago." The two Frazier sisters on either side of Beatrice were tall women, each weighing about 200 pounds, and they seemed to spread out much more than when they were standing. Beatrice weighed little more than 110 pounds, and if there had been no words from her, she might well have gone unnoticed.

"And you never told me," Mrs. Garrett said. "Tsk tsk tsk. I always thought well of Lani." She turned slowly to Carmena, and as she turned, her smiled widened. "But that husband of Lani's keeps her havin babies. Who can keep up with how many they have? She's the babiest-havin woman I ever knowed of. One after the other after the other. . . ."

Silent and still except for the motions of her hands, Beatrice never looked up.

Carmena prayed for the Reverend Sawyer to turn up. If nothing stopped her, Mrs. Garrett would sit in that chair and rain down devilment all day and all night and all day some more. Carmena thought it had to do with her being ninety-one years old and thinking she was closer to God than any human being in the world. Mrs. Garrett and Beatrice had once been so close that people joked they would be buried together in the same casket. Now Mrs. Garrett was forever after Beatrice as if the final task standing between her and the key to heaven was to make Beatrice suffer. Beatrice, however, treated Mrs. Garrett as she would a child who didn't know any better.

*   *   *

Toward five thirty, not long after Mrs. Garrett had asked again what time the Reverend Doctor Sawyer was supposed to arrive, the telephone rang. Carmena answered and spoke but a few words before hanging up. She announced that it had been Reverend Sawyer's wife, that his car would not start and that he apologized to everyone for not being able to make the prayer meeting. Waving her hand over the table, she told her guests that there was no need to let the food go to waste, and one by one the women got up and helped themselves. The storm, the thunder and lightning, had stopped, but there was still the rain, a nuisance scratching at the window.

Once the women were seated again, the conversation took varied turns, and the autumn evening wore away. Mrs. Garrett, perhaps dulled by the food, had less to say than anyone. At one point, the Frazier sister nearest the window commented on how particularly bad the weather had been lately. They all agreed, and Mrs. Garrett, capping one hand over her knee, said that she could not remember when Old Man Arthur and the Ritis boys had caused her so much pain, that sometimes she felt she would never walk again. The other women gave sympathetic nods, one or two mentioning their own aches and pains, and then they all began to exchange remedies. Beatrice stuck her needle with finality into the piece she was working on and put it in a cloth bag at her feet. Looking about the room, she said quietly, "It all reminds me of one summer back home. It was kinda like it is now, day after day."

"Oh, now, Atwell, we ain't gonna have one a your down-home, way-back-when stories, are we?" Mrs. Garrett said. "We ain't had a evenin of prayer, but we been tryin to keep it as close to that as we can."

"How, Bea?" Carmena said, ignoring Mrs. Garrett. "How does this remind you of back home?" Mrs. Garrett rubbed the elbow of her bad arm, then put the bad hand in the center of her lap.

Beatrice said nothing for several seconds. "It thundered and lightened a lot then, too," she said. "I guess I was sixteen or seventeen and this fella I was keepin company with was sittin with me and my daddy on my daddy's porch. There was a storm comin on while we were sittin there. There had already been a lotta rain, but not anough to do that much damage to the crops. I remember it was late in the evenin and so dark I could barely make out what was three feet in front a me. It was already rainin when the thunder and lightnin come up, and we was just sittin and talkin.

"Maybe a half hour or more into that storm, I started seein this figure, this thing, that kinda just stood in that corn patch in my mother's garden. If I didn't know the garden, I woulda thought it was a scarecrow or somethin. It was no further than from here to that television there. I looked and looked, tryin to see into all that dark, and then I told myself it was just a big corn stalk leanin out heavy with the rain. It made a move a corn stalk ain't supposed to make but I tried not to think about it. 'It's corn,' I said to myself. But when this thing moved again—moved different from all the other corn—I said this real quiet 'Oh.' I touched the fella I was keepin company with and pointed and we looked together. My daddy looked, too. This corn stalk, this thing, said, 'Uncle . . . Uncle . . . Bea . . .' Then it moved a few steps toward us. It was this cousin a mine, John Henry. He came even closer and just dropped heavy to the ground, cryin like a baby.

"I said, 'John Henry, whas wrong? What is it?' My daddy was already gettin up. 'It's them,' he said. He was cryin so hard that I could barely make out what he was sayin. 'It's them,' he kept sayin. 'They just sittin there.'

"My daddy went down the steps to him, and when he touched John Henry, John Henry just jumped right up, real quick, like he was some doll and somethin had pulled him up by the neck. He took off down the path that led from his place to where we lived. The three of us—my daddy, me and this fella I was keepin company with—took off after him. It was rainin way harder than it is right now and we was soaked through fore we even took a few steps. All the way down there, I kept prayin, 'Lord, don't let me get struck by lightnin.'

"When we got to the house, John Henry was there lookin in

the front door. 'John Henry,' my daddy said, 'John Henry.' We got there and looked in too. Everybody was just sittin around like he had said. My Uncle Joe, his wife Ebbie, her mother, and my Uncle Ray. There was a pipe stickin in Uncle Ray's mouth, not lit, just stickin there like he did sometimes. The only light was from a coal-oil lamp on the mantlepiece and from a real small fire in the fireplace. It never crossed my mind why they would have a fire burnin on a summer evenin. But there it was—this one log that they kept there all spring and all summer, and it was steady burnin right in the center. I think I thought to myself how dark they all looked, but I put that to how feeble the light in the room was. They was all kinda gathered around the hearth, which wasn't too strange cause yall know how some folks use the fireplace for the center of the house all year round. There was a buncha smells in that room. One was the kind you get when wood gets wet, and another was burnt hair. But around all of the smells was this one I hadn't smelled before and ain't smelled since. It was everything dead you had ever come across in your whole life piled at one time in that room.

" 'Joe. Ray,' my daddy said to his bothers. Uncle Joe was sittin in that chair he'd made with his own hands, and he was starin at us. No, not really at us, kinda through us and around us at the same time. 'Joe.' My daddy went over to him. '*Joseph!*' My daddy touched him and my uncle did nothin. Then my daddy pulled on my uncle's shirt front and my uncle fell into my daddy's arms, right into his arms, like some dime-store dummy. And that told us right then that he and everybody else was gone. It told me anyway. The fella I was keepin company with just said, 'Jesus Christ!' I fixed my eyes on him when he said that. I was feelin all kinds of things standin there, and you know, one a them was this feelin that I couldn't ever keep company with that boy again.

"I looked around the room. This long black line that had cut a rut in the floor went from the fireplace through that group a people right out the room to the kitchen—like somebody had took a big fireball of barbed wire and run cross the floor with it.

"They was just sittin there and they was all gone. You could see where Aunt Ebbie's mother had been rockin the crib with Aunt Ebbie's baby in it. A wind was coming down the chimney and through the door, and it was rockin the crib, rockin Aunt Ebbie's mother's hand right along with it. I thought the baby was dead, too, but when I saw a leg twitch, I knowed he was alive. I picked him up and he didn't look surprised to see me, he didn't look happy or sad or anything. Just a baby waiting for the next thing in his life to happen. I put Aunt Ebbie's mother's hand in her lap. I did it calm-like and I was surprised at myself, the way I was actin. I musta been scared somewhere inside, but it was a long time before I knowed it. And then it stayed and never went away.

" 'Lightnin,' the fella I was keepin company with said. 'Lightnin.' My daddy had put his brother back in the chair and he was standin there lookin down at him and my uncle Ray. The fella I was keepin company with pointed at the way the black line ran along the floor and out of the room. 'Just came down the chimney, Mista Davenport,' he said, proud that he knew what he knew. 'Look at it!' And we looked again when he said that, not so much cause a what he said, but cause somethin in our heads told us to make a everlastin memory of it.

"John Henry came into the house and went on out into the kitchen, his mud tracks walkin right over that black line. I followed him and I seen where the black line came to the kitchen table and hopped right up on it, threw everything every which way, then jumped back down to the floor and ran out the back door. One a the straightest lines you'd ever wanna see. John Henry's little sister was sittin at the table. Alma was alive. She was cryin real soft, and I don't think she'd moved since it happened. John Henry sat down and put his head in his hands. He started cryin again. All of a sudden I got weak as that dishrag there. I held the baby and watched them children. Their whole family. My family too. People who'd never done a moment's harm to a soul. Not one moment's harm. Somethin in me was struck by that when I started thinkin of Uncle Ray's pipe stickin in his mouth and when I saw that one of Alma's plaits had come loose, like they do on little girls. I didn't know what else to do so I leaned Alma's head against my stomach. Then I told em that it would be all right, but it didn't mean anything and I knew it. If somebody had told me to say that tomorrow would be Easter, I woulda said that instead. But I kept sayin that everything would be all right until my daddy came in and picked Alma up and told us he was takin us home. . . ."

The other women in Carmena Boone's apartment were all quiet, and they were quiet for a long time. The rain had long since stopped. Finally, Mrs. Garrett said, "The Lord works in mysterious ways." Her dentures made a soft clicking sound as she spoke. "For good or for bad, the Lord seeks you out and finds you. There ain't no two ways about that." She looked about the room as if for confirmation, and when no one said anything, she seemed to fold up into silence.

They were all quiet again, until Mrs. Garrett began to talk about the eleventh of August, 1894, the night she was saved. . . . The others looked knowingly at one another. The story never changed: a huge tent and an itinerant preacher and a little girl who was overcome that night with something she would years later learn to call the Holy Ghost. She had been frightened at first, with this thing that commanded without talking, she said, but it comforted her and led her down the aisle of the tent to the preacher's outstretched arms. The story, after a thousand tellings, had ceased being an experience to share but was more like an incantation she had to chant to reaffirm for herself the importance of that night.

"He said I was the youngest person in five counties to ever be saved, to ever find the Lord," she was saying. "Reverend Dickinson told me that, told everybody in the tent. And I've walked in the light of the Lord ever since. . . ."

"Why don't yall have some more a this cake?" Carmena said. "Or take it with you. I'll never eat it all." She provided aluminum foil and each woman put two slices in the foil and prepared to leave. At the door, as they said their good nights, Carmena asked Beatrice to tell that joke she had heard her tell once, the one about the dark night. Before Beatrice had said a word, Mrs. Garrett made her way through the group and went to her apartment. After they heard Mrs. Garrett lock her door, Carmena asked again to tell about the dark night.

"Well, my daddy," Beatrice said, "my daddy and my uncle Joe would fun around a lot, mostly for us kids, like two fellas on a radio show. Every now and then my daddy would say, 'Joe, what's the darkest night you ever knowed? Tell me, Joe.' My uncle Joe would play with his chin for a bit, like he was thinkin. 'Les see,' he'd say. 'Les see . . . oh, yes. *Oh*, yes. I member this one night I was sittin at home all by my lonesome, nobody for company but the four walls and the memory of company. It commenced to rain and rain, and I heard this knockin at my door. So I get up and opened the door. Well, sir, who was it but these raindrops—a whole passel of raindrops—lookin down at me, lookin scared and cold. And the one in front says to me in this real squeaky voice, 'Mista, it's so dark out here, so very dark. Would you please mind tellin us which way it is to the ground? . . . And *that*,' my uncle would say, 'is the darkest night I ever knowed.' And we all bust out laughin, specially the little kids, who thought it was the funniest thing in the world to have talkin raindrops."

The women laughed, too. Then they all hugged good night, each saying that they would not be long out of bed.

About four that morning the thunder and lightning began again. At the first blast of thunder, a sleeping Mrs. Garrett sprang up in her bed, like a puppet jerked suddenly to life by its master, her head turning first this way and then the other. Her heart, usually so docile, began to throw itself about its cage. "Oh, dear Jesus," she whispered. She flung back the covers with her good arm and swung her legs out of the bed, and in reaching for her glasses, she tipped over the plastic cup that contained her teeth. She did not bother to pick them up, but threw on her robe and took up her cane. The lightning lit her way to the door. Taking her key from a small table, she went out the door, and the wind closed it behind her with such viciousness that she nearly fell to the hall floor.

As she moved down the hall, an enclosed area with no windows, she could hear the clamor of thunder and the whistling of wind coming from under the doors of the apartments. With their half-globe coverings, the ceiling lights provided a long line of moons all the way down the hall. She knocked lightly at Beatrice's door, and when Mrs. Garrett heard a thunder boom come from under the door of the next apartment, she knocked with greater insistence.

"Who is it?" Beatrice asked.

"It's me."

There was a long, long pause, then Beatrice asked again, "Who is it?"

"It's me. *Me!*"

There was a pause again, but Beatrice unlocked the door and took off the chain and cracked the door. Mrs. Garrett avoided Beatrice's eyes and stared into the heart of the flame of the candle Beatrice was holding.

"Bea, it's me," Mrs. Garrett said.

"Why you all the time knockin at my door, woman?" Beatrice said. "We ain't no friends no more, or did you forget that?" The candle's flame swayed with each word she spoke.

"Please, Bea. You know how it can be. Please don't leave me out here. Have some pity."

With two thunderclaps, Beatrice opened the door. "You lucky," she said, shutting and locking her door. "I was just about ready to go in that bathroom, and you know when I go in there I don't come out for a soul." Her hair was in plaits and she wore a nightgown that swept the floor as she moved.

"Thank you," Mrs. Garrett mumbled, still looking only into the flame. "Thank you so much."

Beatrice did not help Mrs. Garrett with her chair, and in the end, Mrs. Garrett had to drop her cane and drag the chair into the bathroom with her good arm. The cane hit the floor with a clatter.

"There are people sleepin!" Beatrice said from inside the bathroom.

When Mrs. Garrett had made her way with the chair into the bathroom, Beatrice closed the door, and as soon as she did there was the ripping sound of thunder that bounded across the outside room and found its way under the door of the windowless bathroom.

Beatrice set the candle in the sink, then she spread a blanket across the door's threshold, Mrs. Garrett put her chair beside the hamper made into the wall. With a sigh Beatrice put down the toilet cover and sat down.

"How long you think it might last, Bea. How long?"

"Why you always ask me such stupid goddamn questions!"

The blanket did nothing to moderate the violence of the thunder, and it continued to sound as if it were outside the door. "Ain't you gonna blow out the candle?" Mrs. Garrett said. Beatrice leaned over and blew lightly, and in the quickest of moments, the room was engulfed in darkness. Mrs. Garrett began to pray, a long, monotonous mumble of words. Once or twice a boom would produce a small yelp of surprise from each woman, but they did not comfort one another. Over time, the intensity of the thunder grew until it was like a pounding at the bathroom door. And each time it pounded, the women would look toward the door as if they were making up their minds whether to get up and answer it.

MARIE

Every now and again, as if on a whim, the federal government people would write to Marie Delaveaux Wilson in one of those white, stampless envelopes and tell her to come in to their place so they could take another look at her. They, the Social Security people, wrote to her in a foreign language that she had learned to translate over the years, and for all the years she had been receiving the letters the same man had been signing them. Once, because she had something important to tell him, Marie called the number the man always put at the top of the letters, but a woman answered Mr. Smith's telephone and told Marie he was in an all-day meeting. Another time she called and a man said Mr. Smith was on vacation. And finally one day a woman answered and told Marie that Mr. Smith was deceased. The woman told her to wait and she would get someone new to talk to her about her case, but Marie thought it bad luck to have telephoned a dead man and she hung up.

Now, years after the woman had told her Mr. Smith was no more, the letters were still being signed by John Smith. Come into our office at 21st and M streets, Northwest, the letters said in that foreign language. Come in so we can see if you are still blind in one eye, come in so we can see if you are still old and getting older. Come in so we can see if you still deserve to get Supplemental Security Income payments.

She always obeyed the letters, even if the order now came from a dead man, for she knew people who had been temporarily cut off from SSI for not showing up or even for being late. And once cut off, you had to move heaven and earth to get back on.

So on a not unpleasant day in March, she rose in the dark in the morning, even before the day had any sort of character, to give herself plenty of time to bathe, eat, lay out money for the bus, dress, listen to the spirituals on the radio. She was eighty-six years old, and had learned that life was all chaos and painful uncertainty and that the only way to get through it was to expect chaos even in the most innocent of moments. Offer a crust of bread to a sick bird and you often drew back a bloody finger.

John Smith's letter had told her to come in at eleven o'clock, his favorite time, and by nine that morning she had had her bath and had eaten. Dressed by nine thirty. The walk from Claridge Towers at 12th and M down to the bus stop at 14th and K took her about ten minutes, more or less. There was a bus at about ten thirty, her schedule told her, but she preferred the one that came a half hour earlier, lest there be trouble with the ten thirty bus. After she dressed, she sat at her dining room table and went over still again what papers and all else she needed to take. Given the nature of life—particularly the questions asked by the Social Security people—she always took more than they might ask for—her birth certificate, her husband's death certificate, doctor's letters.

One of the last things she put in her pocketbook was a seven-inch or so knife that she had, with the use of a small saw borrowed from a neighbor, serrated on both edges. The knife, she was convinced now, had saved her life about two weeks before. Before then she had often been careless about when she took the knife out with her, and she had never taken it out in daylight, but now she never left her apartment without it, even when going down the hall to the trash drop.

She had gone out to buy a simple box of oatmeal, no more, no less. It was about seven in the evening, the streets with enough commuters driving up 13th Street to make her feel safe. Several yards before she reached the store, the young man came from behind her and tried to rip off her coat pocket where he thought she kept her money, for she carried no purse or pocketbook after five o'clock. The money was in the other pocket with the knife, and his hand caught in the empty pocket long enough for her to reach around with the knife and cut his hand as it came out of her pocket.

He screamed and called her an old bitch. He took a few steps up 13th Street and stood in front of Emerson's Market, examining the hand and shaking off blood. Except for the cars passing up and down 13th Street, they were alone, and she began to pray.

"You cut me," he said, as if he had only been minding his own business when she cut him. "Just look what you done to my hand," he said and looked around as if for some witness to her crime. There was not a great amount of blood, but there was enough for her to see it dripping to the pavement. He seemed to be about twenty, no more than twenty-five, dressed the way they were all dressed nowadays, as if a blind man had matched up all their colors. It occurred to her to say that she had seven grandchildren his age, that by telling him this he would leave her alone. But the more filth he spoke, the more she wanted him only to come toward her again.

"You done crippled me, you old bitch."

"I sure did," she said, without malice, without triumph, but simply the way she would have told him the time of day had he asked and had she known. She gripped the knife tighter, and as she did, she turned her body ever so slightly so that her good eye lined up with him. Her heart was making an awful racket, wanting to be away from him, wanting to be safe at home. I will not be moved, some organ in the neighborhood of the heart told the heart. "And I got plenty more where that come from."

The last words seemed to bring him down some and, still shaking the blood from his hand, he took a step or two back, which disappointed her. I will not be moved, that other organ kept telling the heart. "You just crazy, thas all," he said. "Just a crazy old hag." Then he turned and lumbered up toward Logan Circle, and several times he looked back over his shoulder as if afraid she might be following. A man came out of Emerson's, then a woman with two little boys. She wanted to grab each of them by the arm and tell them she had come close to losing her life. "I saved myself with this here thing," she would have said. She forgot about the oatmeal and took her raging heart back to the apartment. She told herself that she should, but she never washed the fellow's blood off the knife, and over the next few days it dried and then it began to flake off.

Toward ten o'clock that morning Wilamena Mason knocked and let herself in with a key Marie had given her.

"I see you all ready," Wilamena said.

"With the help of the Lord," Marie said. "Want a spot a coffee?"

"No thanks," Wilamena said, and dropped into a chair at the table. "Been drinkin so much coffee lately, I'm gonna turn into coffee. Was up all night with Calhoun."

"How he doin?"

Wilamena told her Calhoun was better that morning, his first good morning in over a week. Calhoun Lambeth was Wilamena's boyfriend, a seventy-five-year-old man she had taken up with six or so months before, not long after he moved in. He was the best-dressed old man Marie had ever known, but he had always appeared to be sickly, even while strutting about with his gold-tipped cane. And seeing that she could count his days on the fingers of her hands, Marie had avoided getting to know him. She could not understand why Wilamena, who could have had any man in Claridge Towers or any other senior citizen building for that matter, would take such a man into her bed. "True love," Wilamena had explained. "Avoid heartache," Marie had said, trying to be kind.

They left the apartment. Marie sought help from no one, lest she come to depend on a person too much. But since the encounter with the young man, Wilamena had insisted on escorting Marie. Marie, to avoid arguments, allowed Wilamena to walk with her from time to time to the bus stop, but no farther.

Nothing fit Marie's theory about life like the weather in Washington. Two days before the temperature had been in the forties, and yesterday it had dropped to the low twenties then warmed up a bit, with the afternoon bringing snow flurries. Today the weather people on the radio had said it would warm enough to wear just a sweater, but Marie was wearing her coat. And tomorrow, the weather people said, it would be in the thirties, with maybe an inch or so of snow.

Appointments near twelve o'clock were always risky, because the Social Security people often took off for lunch long before noon and returned sometime after one. And except for a few employees who seemed to work through their lunch hours, the place shut down. Marie had never been interviewed by someone willing to work through the lunch hour. Today, though the appointment was for eleven, she waited until one thirty before the woman at the front of the waiting room told her she would have to come back another day, because the woman who handled her case was not in.

"You put my name down when I came in like everything was all right," Marie said after she had been called up to the woman's desk.

"I know," the woman said, "but I thought that Mrs. Brown was in. They told me she was in. I'm sorry." The woman began writing in a log book that rested between her telephone and a triptych of photographs. She handed Marie a slip and told her again she was sorry.

"Why you have me wait so long if she whatn't here?" She did not want to say too much, appear too upset, for the Social Security people could be unforgiving. And though she was used to waiting three and four hours, she found it especially unfair to wait when there was no one for her at all behind those panels the Social Security people used for offices. "I been here since before eleven."

"I know," the woman behind the desk said. "I know. I saw you there, ma'am, but I really didn't know Mrs. Brown wasn't here." There was a nameplate at the front of the woman's desk and it said Vernelle Wise. The name was surrounded by little hearts, the kind a child might have drawn.

Marie said nothing more and left.

The next appointment was two weeks later, eight thirty, a good hour, and the day before a letter signed by John Smith arrived to remind her. She expected to be out at least by twelve. Three times before eleven o'clock, Marie asked Vernelle Wise if the man, Mr. Green, who was handling her case, was in that day, and each time the woman assured her that he was. At twelve, Marie ate one of the two oranges and three of the five slices of cheese she had brought. At one, she asked again if Mr. Green was indeed in that day and politely reminded Vernelle Wise that she had been waiting since about eight that morning. Vernelle was just as polite and told her the wait would soon be over.

At one fifteen, Marie began to watch the clock hands creep around the dial. She had not paid much attention to the people about her, but more and more it seemed that others were being waited on who had arrived long after she had gotten there. After asking about Mr. Green at one, she had taken a seat near the front, and as more time went by, she found herself forced to listen to the conversation that Vernelle was having with the other receptionist next to her.

"I told him . . . I told him . . . I said just get your things and leave," said the other receptionist, who didn't have a nameplate.

"Did he leave?" Vernelle wanted to know.

"Oh, no," the other woman said. "Not at first. But I picked up some of his stuff, that Christian Dior jacket he worships. I picked up my cigarette lighter and that jacket, just like I was gonna do something bad to it, and he started movin then."

Vernelle began laughing. "I wish I was there to see that." She was filing her fingernails. Now and again she would look at her fingernails to inspect her work, and if it was satisfactory, she would blow on the nail and on the file. "He back?" Vernelle asked.

The other receptionist eyed her. "What you think?" and they both laughed.

Along about two o'clock Marie became hungry again, but she did not want to eat the rest of her food because she did not know how much longer she would be there. There was a soda machine in the corner, but all sodas gave her gas.

"You know-who gonna call you again?" the other receptionist was asking Vernelle.

"I hope so," Vernelle said. "He pretty fly. Seemed decent too. It kinda put me off when he said he was a car mechanic. I kinda like kept tryin to take a peek at his fingernails and everything the whole evenin. See if they was dirty or what."

"Well, that mechanic stuff might be good when you get your car back. My cousin's boyfriend used to do that kinda work and he made good money, girl. I mean real good money."

"Hmmmm," Vernelle said. "Anyway, the kids like him, and you know how peculiar they can be."

"Tell me about it. They do the job your mother and father used to do, huh? Only on another level."

"You can say that again," Vernelle said.

Marie went to her and told her how long she had been waiting.

"Listen," Vernelle said, pointing her fingernail file at Marie. "I told you you'll be waited on as soon as possible. This is a busy day. So I think you should just go back to your seat until we call your name." The other receptionist began to giggle.

Marie reached across the desk and slapped Vernelle Wise with all her might. Vernelle dropped the file, which made a cheap tinny sound when it hit the plastic board her chair was on. But no one heard the file because she had begun to cry right away. She looked at Marie as if, in the moment of her greatest need, Marie had denied her. "Oh, oh," Vernelle Wise said through the tears. "Oh, my dear God . . ."

The other receptionist, in her chair on casters, rolled over to Vernelle and put her arm around her. "Security!" the other receptionist hollered. "We need security here!"

The guard at the front door came quickly around the corner, one hand on his holstered gun and the other pointing accusatorially at the people seated in the waiting area. Marie had sat down and was looking at the two women almost sympathetically, as if a stranger had come in, hit Vernelle Wise, and fled.

"She slapped Vernelle!" the other receptionist said.

"Who did it?" the guard said, reaching for the man sitting beside Marie. But when the other receptionist said it was the old lady in the blue coat, the guard held back for the longest time, as if to grab her would be like arresting his own grandmother. He stood blinking and he would have gone on blinking had Marie not stood up.

She was too flustered to wait for the bus and so took a cab home. With both chains, she locked herself in the apartment, refusing to answer the door or the telephone the rest of the day and most of the next. But she knew that if her family or friends received no answer at the door or on the telephone, they would think something had happened to her. So the next afternoon, she began answering the phone and spoke with the chains on, telling Wilamena and others that she had a toothache.

For days and days after the incident she ate very little, asked God to forgive her. She was haunted by the way Vernelle's cheek had felt, by what it was like to invade and actually touch the flesh of another person. And when she thought too hard, she imagined that she was slicing through the woman's cheek, the way she had sliced through the young man's hand. But as time went on she began to remember the man's curses and the purplish color of Vernelle's fingernails, and all remorse would momentarily take flight. Finally, one morning nearly two weeks after she slapped the woman, she woke with a phrase she had not used or heard since her children were small: You whatn't raised that way.

It was the next morning that the thin young man in the suit knocked and asked through the door chains if he could speak with her. She thought that he was a Social Security man come to tear up her card and papers and tell her that they would send her no more checks. Even when he pulled out an identification card showing that he was a Howard University student, she did not believe.

In the end, she told him she didn't want to buy anything, not magazines, not candy, not anything.

"No, no," he said. "I just want to talk to you for a bit. About your life and everything. It's for a project for my folklore course. I'm talking to everyone in the building who'll let me. Please . . . I won't be a bother. Just a little bit of your time."

"I don't have anything worth talkin about," she said. "And I don't keep well these days."

"Oh, ma'am, I'm sorry. But we all got something to say. I promise I won't be a bother."

After fifteen minutes of his pleas, she opened the door to him because of his suit and his tie and his tie clip with a bird in flight, and because his long dark-brown fingers reminded her of delicate twigs. But had he turned out to be death with a gun or a knife or fingers to crush her neck, she would not have been surprised. "My name's George. George Carter. Like the president." He had the kind of voice that old people in her young days would have called womanish. "But I was born right here in D.C. Born, bred, and buttered, my mother used to say."

He stayed the rest of the day and she fixed him dinner. It scared her to be able to talk so freely with him, and at first she thought that at long last, as she had always feared, senility had taken hold of her. A few hours after he left, she looked his name up in the telephone book, and when a man who sounded like him answered, she hung up immediately. And the next day she did the same thing. He came back at least twice a week for many weeks and would set his cassette recorder on her coffee table. "He's takin down my whole life," she told Wilamena, almost the way a woman might speak in awe of a new boyfriend.

One day he played back for the first time some of what she told the recorder:

> . . . My father would be sittin there readin the paper. He'd say whenever they put in a new president, "Look like he got the chair for four years." And it got so that's what I saw—this poor man sittin in that chair for four long years while the rest of the world went on about its business. I don't know if I thought he ever

did anything, the president. I just knew that he had to sit in that chair for four years. Maybe I thought that by his sittin in that chair and doin nothin else for four years he made the country what it was and that without him sittin there the country wouldn't be what it was. Maybe thas what I got from listenin to my father readin and to my mother askin him questions bout what he was readin. They was like that, you see. . . .

George stopped the tape and was about to put the other side in when she touched his hand.

"No more, George," she said. "I can't listen to no more. Please . . . please, no more." She had never in her whole life heard her own voice. Nothing had been so stunning in a long, long while, and for a few moments before she found herself, her world turned upside down. There, rising from a machine no bigger than her Bible, was a voice frighteningly familiar and yet unfamiliar, talking about a man whom she knew as well as her husbands and her sons, a man dead and buried sixty years. She reached across to George and he handed her the tape. She turned it over and over, as if the mystery of everything could be discerned if she turned it enough times. She began to cry, and with her other hand she lightly touched the buttons of the machine.

Between the time Marie slapped the woman in the Social Security office and the day she heard her voice for the first time, Calhoun Lambeth, Wilamena's boyfriend, had been in and out the hospital three times. Most evenings when Calhoun's son stayed the night with him, Wilamena would come up to Marie's and spend most of the evening, sitting on the couch that was catty-corner to the easy chair facing the big window. She said very little, which was unlike her, a woman with more friends than hairs on her head and who, at sixty-eight, loved a good party. The most attractive woman Marie knew would only curl her legs up under herself and sip whatever Marie put in her hand. She looked out at the city until she took herself to her apartment or went back down to Calhoun's place. In the beginning, after he returned from the hospital the first time, there was the desire in Marie to remind her friend that she wasn't married to Calhoun, that she should just get up and walk away, something Marie had seen her do with other men she had grown tired of.

Late one night, Wilamena called and asked her to come down to the man's apartment, for the man's son had had to work that night and she was there alone with him and she did not want to be alone with him. "Sit with me a spell," Wilamena said. Marie did not protest, even though she had not said more than ten words to the man in all the time she knew him. She threw on her bathrobe, picked up her keys and serrated knife, and went down to the second floor.

He was propped up on the bed, and he was surprisingly alert and spoke to Marie with an unforced friendliness. She had seen this in other dying people—a kindness and gentleness came over them that was often embarrassing for those around them. Wilamena sat on the side of the bed. Calhoun asked Marie to sit in a chair beside the bed and then he took her hand and held it for the rest of the night. He talked on throughout the night, not always understandable. Wilamena, exhausted, eventually lay across the foot of the bed. Almost everything the man had to say was about a time when he was young and was married for a year or so to a woman in Nicodemus, Kansas, a town where there were only black people. Whether the woman had died or whether he had left her, Marie could not make out. She only knew that the woman and Nicodemus seemed to have marked him for life.

"You should go to Nicodemus," he said at one point, as if the town was only around the corner. "I stumbled into the place by accident. But you should go on purpose. There ain't much to see, but you should go there and spend some time there."

Toward four o'clock that morning, he stopped talking and moments later he went home to his God. Marie continued holding the dead man's hand and she said the Lord's prayer over and over until it no longer made sense to her. She did not wake Wilamena. Eventually, the sun came through the man's venetian blinds and she heard the croaking of the pigeons congregating on the window ledge. When she finally placed his hand on his chest, the dead man expelled a burst of air that sounded to Marie like a sigh. It occurred to her that she, a complete stranger, was the last thing he had known in the world and that now that he was no longer in the world all she knew of him was that Nicodemus place and a lovesick woman asleep at the foot of his bed. She thought that she was hungry and thirsty, but the more she looked at the dead man and the sleeping woman, the more she realized that what she felt was a sense of loss.

Two days later, the Social Security people sent her a letter, again signed by John Smith, telling her to come to them one week hence. There was nothing in the letter about the slap, no threat to cut off her SSI payments because of what she had done. Indeed, it was the same sort of letter John Smith usually sent. She called the number at the top of the letter, and the woman who handled her case told her that Mrs. White would be expecting her on the day and time stated in the letter. Still, she suspected the Social Security people were planning something for her, something at the very least that would be humiliating. And, right up until the day before the appointment, she continued calling to confirm that it was okay to come in. Often, the person she spoke to after the switchboard woman and before the woman handling her case was Vernelle. "Social Security Administration. This is Vernelle Wise. May I help you?" And each time Marie heard the receptionist identify herself she wanted to apologize. "I whatn't raised that way," she wanted to tell the woman.

George Carter came the day she got the letter to present her with a cassette machine and copies of the tapes she had made about her life. It took quite some time for him to teach her how to use the machine, and after he was gone, she was certain it took so long because she really did not want to know how to use it. That evening, after her dinner, she steeled herself and put a tape marked "Parents; Early Childhood" in the machine.

... My mother had this idea that everything could be done in Washington, that a human bein could take all they troubles to Washington and things would be set right. I think that was all wrapped up with her notion of the govment, the Supreme Court and the president and the like. "Up there," she would say, "things can be made right." "Up there" was her only words for Washington. All them other cities had names, but Washington didn't need a name. It was just called "up there." I was real small and didn't know any better, so somehow I got to thinkin since things were on the perfect side in Washington, that maybe God lived there. God and his people. . . . When I went back home to visit that first time and told my mother all about my livin in Washington, she fell into such a cry, like maybe I had managed to make it to heaven without dyin. Thas how people was back in those days. . . .

The next morning she looked for Vernelle Wise's name in the telephone book. And for several evenings she would call the number and hang up before the phone had rung three times. Finally, on a Sunday, two days before the appointment, she let it ring and what may have been a little boy answered. She could tell he was very young because he said "Hello" in a too-loud voice, as if he was not used to talking on the telephone.

"Hello," he said. "Hello, who this? Granddaddy, that you? Hello. Hello. I can see you."

Marie heard Vernelle tell him to put down the telephone, then another child, perhaps a girl somewhat older than the boy, came on the line. "Hello. Hello. Who is this?" she said with authority. The boy began to cry, apparently because he did not want the girl to talk if he couldn't. "Don't touch it," the girl said. "Leave it alone." The boy cried louder and only stopped when Vernelle came to the telephone.

"Yes?" Vernelle said. "Yes." Then she went off the line to calm the boy who had again begun to cry. "Loretta," she said, "go get his bottle. . . . Well, look for it. What you got eyes for?"

There seemed to be a second boy, because Vernelle told him to help Loretta look for the bottle. "He always losin things," Marie heard the second boy say. "You should tie everything to his arms." "Don't tell me what to do," Vernelle said. "Just look for that damn bottle."

"I don't lose nofin. I don't," the first boy said. "You got snot in your nose."

"Don't say that," Vernelle said before she came back on the line. "I'm sorry," she said to Marie. "Who is this? . . . Don't you dare touch it if you know what's good for you!" she said. "I wanna talk to Granddaddy," the first boy said. "Loretta, get me that bottle!"

Marie hung up. She washed her dinner dishes. She called Wilamena because she had not seen her all day, and Wilamena told her that she would be up later. The cassette tapes were on the coffee table beside the machine, and she began picking them up, one by one. She read the labels. "Husband No. 1." "Working." "Husband No. 2." "Children." "Race Relations." "Early D. C. Experiences." "Husband No. 3." She had not played another tape since the one about her mother's idea of what Washington was like, but she could still hear the voice, her voice. Without reading its label, she put a tape in the machine.

. . . I never planned to live in Washington, had no idea I would ever even step one foot in this city. This white family my mother worked for, they had a son married and gone to live in Baltimore. He wanted a maid, somebody to take care of his children. So he wrote to his mother and she asked my mother and my mother asked me about goin to live in Baltimore. Well, I was young. I guess I wanted to see the world, and Baltimore was as good a place to start as anywhere. This man sent me a train ticket and I went off to Baltimore. Hadn't ever been kissed, hadn't ever been anything, but here I was goin farther from home than my mother and father put together. . . . Well, sir, the train stopped in Washington, and I thought I heard the conductor say we would be stoppin a bit there, so I got off. I knew I probably wouldn't see no

more than that Union Station, but I wanted to be able to say I'd
done that, that I step foot in the capital of the United States. I
walked down to the end of the platform and looked around, then I
peeked into the station. Then I went in. And when I got back, the
train and my suitcase was gone. Everything I had in the world on
the way to Baltimore. . . .

    . . . I couldn't calm myself anough to listen to when
the redcap said another train would be leavin for Baltimore, I was
just that upset. I had a buncha addresses of people we knew all the
way from home up to Boston, and I used one precious nickel to call a
woman I hadn't seen in years, cause I didn't have the white people
in Baltimore number. This woman come and got me, took me to her
place. I member like it was yesterday, that we got on this streetcar
marked 13th and D NE. The more I rode, the more brighter
things got. You ain't lived till you been on a streetcar. The further
we went on that streetcar—dead down in the middle of the street—
the more I knowed I could never go live in Baltimore. I knowed I
could never live in a place that didn't have that streetcar and them
clackety-clack tracks. . . .

 She wrapped the tapes in two plastic bags and put them in the
dresser drawer that contained all that was valuable to her—birth
and death certificates, silver dollars, life insurance policies, pictures
of her husbands and the children they had given each other, and the
grandchildren those children had given her and the great-grands
whose names she had trouble remembering. She set the tapes in a
back corner of the drawer, away from the things she needed to get
her hands on regularly. She knew that however long she lived, she
would not ever again listen to them, for in the end, despite all that
was on the tapes, she could not stand the sound of her own voice.

[Originally published in THE NEW YORKER and to appear
in the forthcoming ALL AUNT HAGAR'S CHILDREN]

A RICH
MAN

Horace and Loneese Perkins—one child, one grandchild—lived most unhappily together for more than twelve years in Apartment 230 at Sunset House, a building for senior citizens at 1202 13th Street NW. They moved there in 1977, the year they celebrated forty years of marriage, the year they made love for the last time—Loneese kept a diary of sorts, and that fact was noted on one day of a week when she noted nothing else. "He touched me," she wrote, which had always been her diary euphemism for sex. That was also the year they retired, she as a pool secretary at the Commerce Department, where she had known one lover, and he as a civilian employee at the Pentagon, as the head of veteran records. He had been an Army sergeant for ten years before becoming head of records; the Secretary of Defense gave him a plaque as big as his chest on the day he retired, and he and the Secretary of Defense and Loneese had their picture taken, a picture that hung for all those twelve years in the living room of Apartment 230, on the wall just to the right of the heating-and-airconditioning unit.

A month before they moved in, they drove in their burgundy-and-gold Cadillac from their small house on Chesapeake Street in Southeast to a Union Station restaurant and promised each other that Sunset House would be a new beginning for them. Over blackened catfish and a peach cobbler that they both agreed could have been better, they vowed to devote themselves to each other and become even better grandparents. Horace had long known about the

Commerce Department lover. Loneese had told him about the man two months after she had ended the relationship, in 1969. "He worked in the mail room," she told her husband over a spaghetti supper she had cooked in the Chesapeake Street home. "He touched me in the motel room," she wrote in her diary, "and after it was over he begged me to go away to Florida with him. All I could think about was that Florida was for old people."

At that spaghetti supper, Horace did not mention the dozens of lovers he had had in his time as her husband. She knew there had been many, knew it because they were written on his face in the early years of their marriage, and because he had never bothered to hide what he was doing in the later years. "I be back in a while. I got some business to do," he would say. He did not even mention the lover he had slept with just the day before the spaghetti supper, the one he bid good-bye to with a "Be good and be sweet" after telling her he planned to become a new man and respect his marriage vows. The woman, a thin school-bus driver with clanking bracelets up to her elbows on both arms, snorted a laugh, which made Horace want to slap her, because he was used to people taking him seriously. "Forget you, then," Horace said on the way out the door. "I was just tryin to let you down easy."

Over another spaghetti supper two weeks before moving, they reiterated what had been said at the blackened-catfish supper and did the dishes together and went to bed as man and wife, and over the next days sold almost all the Chesapeake Street furniture. What they kept belonged primarily to Horace, starting with a collection of 639 record albums, many of them his "sweet babies," the 78s. If a band worth anything had recorded between 1915 and 1950, he bragged, he had the record; after 1950, he said, the bands got sloppy and he had to back away. Horace also kept the Cadillac he had painted to honor a football team, paid to park the car in the underground garage. Sunset had once been intended as a luxury place, but the builders, two friends of the city commissioners, ran out of money in the middle and the commissioners had the city-government people buy it off them. The city-government people completed Sunset, with its tiny rooms, and then, after one commissioner gave a speech in Southwest about looking out for old people, some city-government people in Northeast came up with the idea that old people might like to live in Sunset, in Northwest.

Three weeks after Horace and Loneese moved in, Horace went down to the lobby one Saturday afternoon to get their mail and happened to see Clara Knightley getting her mail. She lived in Apartment 512. "You got this fixed up real nice," Horace said of Apartment 512 a little less than an hour after meeting her. "But I could see just in the way that you carry yourself that you got good taste. I could tell that about you right off." "You swellin my head with all that talk, Mr. Perkins," Clara said, offering him coffee, which he rejected, because such moments always called for something stronger. "Whas a woman's head for if a man can't swell it up from time to time. Huh? Answer me that, Clara. You just answer me that." Clara was fifty-five, a bit younger than most of the residents of Sunset House, though she was much older than all Horace's other lovers. She did not fit the city people's definition of a senior citizen, but she had a host of ailments, from high blood pressure to diabetes, and so the city people had let her in.

Despite the promises, the marriage, what little there had been of it, came to an end. "I will make myself happy," Loneese told the diary a month after he last touched her. Loneese and Horace had fixed up their apartment nicely, and neither of them wanted to give the place up to the other. She wanted to make a final stand with the man who had given her so much heartache, the man who had told her, six months after her confession, what a whore she had been to sleep with the Commerce Department mail-room man. Horace, at sixty, had never thought much of women over fifty, but Clara—and, after her, Willa, of Apartment 1001, and Miriam, of Apartment 109—had awakened something in him, and he began to think that women over fifty weren't such a bad deal after all. Sunset House had dozens of such women, many of them attractive widows, many of them eager for a kind word from a retired Army sergeant who had so many medals and ribbons that his uniform could not carry them. As far as he could see, he was cock of the walk: many of the men in Sunset suffered from diseases that Horace had so far escaped, or they were not as good-looking or as thin, or they were encumbered by wives they loved. In Sunset House he was a rich man. So why move and give that whore the satisfaction?

They lived separate lives in a space that was only a fourth as large as the Chesapeake Street house. The building came to know them as the man and wife in 230 who couldn't stand each other. People talked about the Perkinses more than they did about anyone else, which was particularly upsetting to Loneese, who had been raised to believe family business should stay in the family. "Oh, Lord, what them two been up to now?" "Fight like cats and dogs, they do." "Who he seein now?" They each bought their own food from the Richfood on 11th Street or from the little store on 13th Street, and they could be vile to each other if what one bought was disturbed or eaten by the other. Loneese stopped speaking to Horace for nine months in 1984 and 1985, when she saw that her pumpkin pie was a bit smaller than when she last cut a slice from it. "I ain't touch your damn pie, you crazy woman," he said when she accused him. "How long you been married to me? You know I've never been partial to pumpkin pie." "That's fine for you to say, Horace, but why is some missing? You might not be partial to it, but I know you. I know you'll eat anything in a pinch. That's just your dirty nature." "My nature ain't no more dirty than yours."

After that, she bought a small icebox for the bedroom where she slept, though she continued to keep the larger items in the kitchen refrigerator. He bought a separate telephone, because he complained that she wasn't giving him his messages from his "associates." "I have never been a secretary for whores," she said, watching him set up an answering machine next to the hide-a-bed couch where he slept. "Oh, don't get me started bout whores. I'd say you wrote the damn book." "It was dictated by you."

Their one child, Alonzo, lived with his wife and son in Baltimore. He had not been close to his parents for a long time, and he could not put the why of it into words for his wife. Their boy,

Alonzo, Jr., who was twelve when his grandparents moved into Sunset, loved to visit them. Horace would unplug and put away his telephone when the boy visited. And Loneese and Horace would sleep together in the bedroom. She'd put a pillow between them in the double bed to remind herself not to roll toward him.

Their grandson visited less and less as he moved into his teenage years, and then, after he went away to college, in Ohio, he just called them every few weeks, on the phone they had had installed in the name of Horace and Loneese Perkins.

In 1987, Loneese's heart began the countdown to its last beat and she started spending more time at George Washington University Hospital than she did in the apartment. Horace never visited her. She died two years later. She woke up that last night in the hospital and went out into the hall and then to the nurses' station but could not find a nurse anywhere to tell her where she was or why she was there. "Why do the patients have to run this place alone?" she said to the walls. She returned to her room and it came to her why she was there. It was nearing three in the morning, but she called her own telephone first, then she dialed Horace's. He answered, but she never said a word. "Who's this playin on my phone?" Horace kept asking. "Who's this? I don't allow no playin on my phone." She hung up and lay down and said her prayers. After moving into Sunset, she had taken one more lover, a man at Vermont Avenue Baptist Church, where she went from time to time. He was retired, too. She wrote in her diary that he was not a big eater and that "down there, his vitals were missing."

Loneese Perkins was buried in a plot at Harmony Cemetery that she and Horace had bought when they were younger. There was a spot for Horace and there was one for their son, but Alonzo had long since made plans to be buried in a cemetery just outside Baltimore.

Horace kept the apartment more or less the way it was on the last day she was there. His son and daughter-in-law and grandson took some of her clothes to the Goodwill and the rest they gave to other women in the building. There were souvenirs from countries that Loneese and Horace had visited as man and wife—a Ghanaian carving of men surrounding a leopard they had killed, a brass menorah from Israel, a snow globe of Mt. Fuji with some of the snow stuck forever to the top of the globe. They were things that did not mean very much to Alonzo, but he knew his child, and he knew that one day Alonzo, Jr., would cherish them.

Horace tried sleeping in the bed, but he had been not unhappy in his twelve years on the hide-a-bed. He got rid of the bed and moved the couch into the bedroom and kept it open all the time.

He realized two things after Loneese's death: His own "vitals" had rejuvenated. He had never had the problems other men had, though he had failed a few times along the way, but that was to be expected. Now, as he moved closer to his seventy-third birthday, he felt himself becoming ever stronger, ever more potent. God is a strange one, he thought, sipping Chivas Regal one night before he went out: he takes a man's wife and gives him a new penis in her place.

The other thing he realized was that he was more and more attracted to younger women. When Loneese died, he had been keeping company with a woman of sixty-one, Sandy Carlin, in Apartment 907. One day in February, nine months after Loneese's death, one of Sandy's daughters, Jill, came to visit, along with one of Jill's friends, Elaine Cunningham. They were both twenty-five years old. From the moment they walked through Sandy's door, Horace began to compliment them—on their hair, the color of their fingernail polish, the sharp crease in Jill's pants ("You iron that yourself?"), even "that sophisticated way" Elaine crossed her legs. The young women giggled, which made him happy, pleased with himself, and Sandy sat in her place on the couch. As the ice in the Pepsi-Cola in her left hand melted, she realized all over again that God had never promised her a man until her dying day.

When the girls left, about three in the afternoon, Horace offered to accompany them downstairs, "to keep all them bad men away." In the lobby, as the security guard at her desk strained to hear, he made it known that he wouldn't mind if they came by to see him sometime. The women looked at each other and giggled some more. They had been planning to go to a club in Southwest that evening, but they were amused by the old man, by the way he had his rap together and put them on some sort of big pedestal and shit, as Jill would tell another friend weeks later. And when he saw how receptive they were he said why not come on up tonight, shucks, ain't no time like the present. Jill said he musta got that from a song, but he said no, he'd been sayin that since before they were born, and Elaine said thas the truth, and the women giggled again. He said I ain't gonna lie bout bein a seasoned man, and then he joined in the giggling. Jill looked at Elaine and said want to? And Elaine said what about your mom? And Jill shrugged her shoulders and Elaine said O.K. She had just broken up with a man she had met at another club and needed something to make the pain go away until there was another man, maybe from a better club.

At about eleven-thirty, Jill wandered off into the night, her head liquored up, and Elaine stayed and got weepy—about the man from the not-so-good club, about the two abortions, about running away from home at seventeen after a fight with her father. "I just left him nappin on the couch," she said, stretched out on Horace's new living-room couch, her shoes off and one of Loneese's throws over her feet. Horace was in the chair across from her. "For all I know, he's still on that couch." Even before she got to her father, even before the abortions, he knew that he would sleep with her that night. He did not even need to fill her glass a third time. "He was a fat man," she said of her father. "And there ain't a whole lot more I remember."

"Listen," he said as she talked about her father, "everything's gonna work out right for you." He knew that, at such times in a se-duction, the more positive a man was, the better things went. It would not have done to tell her to forget her daddy, that she had done the right thing by running out on that fat so-and-so; it was best to focus on tomorrow and tell her that the world would be brighter in the morning. He came over to the couch, and before he sat down on the edge of the coffee table he hiked up his pants just a bit with his fingertips, and seeing him do that reminded her vaguely of something wonderful. The boys in the club sure didn't do it that way. He took her hand and kissed her palm. "Everything's gonna work out to the good," he said.

Elaine Cunningham woke in the morning with Horace sleeping quietly beside her. She did not rebuke herself and did not look over at him with horror at what she had done. She sighed and laid her head back on the pillow and thought how much she still loved the man from the club, but there was nothing more she could do: not even the five-hundred-dollar leather jacket she had purchased for the man had brought him around. Two years after running away, she had gone back to where she had lived with her parents, but they had moved and no one in the building knew where they had gone. But everyone remembered her. "You sure done growed up, Elaine," one old woman said. "I wouldna knowed if you hadn't told me who you was." "Fuck em," Elaine said to the friends who had given her a ride there. "Fuck em all to hell." Then, in the car, heading out to Capitol Heights, where she was staying, "Well, maybe not fuck my mother. She was good." "Just fuck your daddy then?" the girl in the backseat said. Elaine thought about it as they went down Rhode Island Avenue, and just before they turned onto New Jersey Avenue she said, "Yes, just fuck my daddy. The fat fuck."

She got out of Horace's bed and tried to wet the desert in her mouth as she looked in his closet for a bathrobe. She rejected the blue and the paisley ones for a dark green one that reminded her of something wonderful, just as Horace's hiking up his pants had. She smelled the sleeves once she had it on, but there was only the strong scent of detergent.

In the half room that passed for a kitchen, she stood and drank most of the orange juice in the gallon carton. "Now, that was stupid, girl," she said. "You know you shoulda drunk water. Better for the thirst." She returned the carton to the refrigerator and marveled at all the food. "Damn!" she said. With the refrigerator door still open, she stepped out into the living room and took note of all that Horace had, thinking, A girl could live large here if she did things right. She had been crashing at a friend's place in Northeast, and the friend's mother had begun to hint that it was time for her to move on. Even when she had a job, she rarely had a place of her own. "Hmm," she said, looking through the refrigerator for what she wanted to eat. "Boody for home and food. Food, home. Boody. You shoulda stayed in school, girl. They give courses on this. Food and Home the first semester. Boody Givin the second semester."

But as she ate her eggs and bacon and Hungry Man biscuits, she knew that she did not want to sleep with Horace too many more times, even if he did have his little castle. He was too tall, and she had never been attracted to tall men, old or otherwise. "Damn! Why couldn't he be what I wanted and have a nice place, too?" Then, as she sopped up the last of the yolk with the last half of the last biscuit, she thought of her best friend, Catrina, the woman she was crashing with. Catrina Stockton was twenty-eight, and though she had once been a heroin addict, she was one year clean and had a face and a body that testified not to a woman who had lived a bad life on the streets but to a nice-looking Virginia woman who had married at seventeen, had had three children by a truck-driving husband, and had met a man in a Fredericksburg McDonald's who had said that women like her could be queens in D.C.

Yes, Elaine thought as she leaned over the couch and stared at the photograph of Horace and Loneese and the Secretary of Defense, Catrina was always saying how much she wanted love, how it didn't matter what a man looked like, as long as he was good to her and loved her morning, noon, and night. The Secretary of Defense was in the middle of the couple. She did not know who he was, just that she had seen him somewhere, maybe on the television. Horace was holding the plaque just to the left, away from the Secretary. Elaine reached over and removed a spot of dust from the picture with her fingertip, and before she could flick it away a woman said her name and she looked around, chilled.

She went into the bedroom to make sure that the voice had not been death telling her to check on Horace. She found him sitting up in the bed, yawning and stretching. "You sleep good, honey bunch?" he said. "I sure did, sweetie pie," she said and bounded across the room to hug him. A breakfast like the one she'd had would cost at least four dollars anywhere in D.C. or Maryland. "Oh, but Papa likes that," Horace said. And even the cheapest motels out on New York Avenue, the ones catering to the junkies and prostitutes, charged at least twenty-five dollars a night. What's a hug compared with that? And, besides, she liked him more than she had thought, and the issue of Catrina and her moving in had to be done delicately. "Well, just let me give you a little bit mo, then."

Young stuff is young stuff, Horace thought the first time Elaine brought Catrina by and Catrina gave him a peck on the cheek and said, "I feel like I know you from all that Elaine told me." That was in early March.

In early April, Elaine met another man at a new club on F Street Northwest and fell in love, and so did Horace with Catrina, though Catrina, after several years on the street, knew what she was feeling might be in the neighborhood of love but it was nowhere near the right house. She and Elaine told Horace the saddest of stories about the man Elaine had met in the club, and before the end of April he was sleeping on Horace's living-room floor. It helped that the man, Darnell Mudd, knew the way to anyone's heart, man or woman, and that he claimed to have a father who had been a hero in the Korean War. He even knew the name of the Secretary of Defense in the photograph and how long he had served in the Cabinet.

By the middle of May, there were as many as five other people, friends of the three young people, hanging out at any one time in Horace's place. He was giddy with Catrina, with the blunts, with the other women who snuck out with him to a room at the motel across 13th Street. By early June, more than a hundred of his old records had been stolen and pawned. "Leave his stuff alone,"

Elaine said to Darnell and his friends as they were going out the door with ten records apiece. "Don't take his stuff. He loves that stuff." It was eleven in the morning and everyone else in the apartment, including Horace, was asleep. "Sh-h-h," Darnell said. "He got so many he won't notice." And that was true. Horace hadn't played records in many months. He had two swords that were originally on the wall opposite the heating-and-air-conditioning unit. Both had belonged to German officers killed in the Second World War. Horace, high on the blunts, liked to see the young men sword-fight with them. But the next day, sober, he would hide them in the bottom of the closet, only to pull them out again when the partying started, at about four in the afternoon.

His neighbors, especially the neighbors who considered that Loneese had been the long-suffering one in the marriage, complained to the management about the noise, but the city-government people read in his rental record that he had lost his wife not long ago and told the neighbors that he was probably doing some kind of grieving. The city-government people never went above the first floor in Sunset. "He's a veteran who just lost his wife," they would say to those who came to the glass office on the first floor. "Why don't you cut him some slack?" But Horace tried to get a grip on things after a maintenance man told him to be careful. That was about the time one of the swords was broken and he could not for the life of him remember how it had happened. He just found it one afternoon in two pieces in the refrigerator's vegetable bin.

Things toned down a little, but the young women continued to come by and Horace went on being happy with them and with Catrina, who called him Papa and pretended to be upset when she saw him kissing another girl. "Papa, what am I gonna do with you and all your hussies?" "Papa, promise you'll only love me." "Papa, I need a new outfit. Help me out, willya please?"

Elaine had become pregnant not long after meeting Darnell, who told her to have the baby, that he had always wanted a son to carry on his name. "We can call him Junior," he said. "Or Little

Darnell," she said. As she began showing, Horace and Catrina became increasingly concerned about her. Horace remembered how solicitous he had been when Loneese had been pregnant. He had not taken the first lover yet, had not even thought about anyone else as she grew and grew. He told Elaine no drugs or alcohol until the baby was born, and he tried to get her to go to bed at a decent hour, but that was often difficult with a small crowd in the living room.

Horace's grandson called in December, wanting to come by to see him, but Horace told him it would be best to meet someplace downtown, because his place was a mess. He didn't do much cleaning since Loneese died. "I don't care about that," Alonzo, Jr., said. "Well, I do," Horace said. "You know how I can be bout these things."

In late December, Elaine gave birth to a boy, several weeks early. They gave him the middle name Horace. "See," Darnell said one day, holding the baby on the couch. "Thas your grandpa. You don't mind me callin you his granddad, Mr. Perkins? You don't mind, do you?" The city-government people in the rental office, led by someone new, someone who took the rules seriously, took note that the old man in Apartment 230 had a baby and his mama and daddy in the place and not a single one of them was even related to him, though if one had been it still would have been against the rules as laid down in the rule book of apartment living.

By late February, an undercover policeman had bought two packets of crack from someone in the apartment. It was a woman, he told his superiors at first, and that's what he wrote in his report, but in a subsequent report he wrote that he had bought the rocks from a man. "Start over," said one of his superiors, who supped monthly with the new mayor, who lived for numbers, and in March the undercover man went back to buy more.

It was late on a warm Saturday night in April when Elaine woke to the crackle of walkie-talkies outside the door. She had not seen Darnell in more than a month, and something told her that she should get out of there because there might not be any more good times. She thought of Horace and Catrina asleep in the bedroom. Two men and two women she did not know very well were asleep in various places around the living room, but she had dated the brother of one of the women some three years ago. One of the men claimed to be Darnell's cousin, and, to prove it to her, when he knocked at the door that night he showed her a Polaroid of him and Darnell at a club, their arms around each other and their eyes red, because the camera had been cheap and the picture cost only two dollars.

She got up from the couch and looked into the crib. In the darkness she could make out that her son was awake, his little legs kicking and no sound from him but a happy gurgle. The sound of the walkie-talkie outside the door came and went. She could see it all on the television news—"Drug Dealing Mama in Jail. Baby Put in Foster Care." She stepped over the man who said he was Darnell's cousin and pushed the door to the bedroom all the way open. Catrina was getting out of bed. Horace was snoring. He had never snored before in his life, but the drugs and alcohol together had done bad things to his airway.

"You hear anything?" Elaine whispered as Catrina tiptoed to her.

"I sure did," Catrina said. Sleeping on the streets required keeping one eye and both ears open. "I don't wanna go back to jail."

"Shit. Me, neither," Elaine said. "What about the window?"

"Go out and down two floors? With a baby? Damn!"

"We can do it," Elaine said, looking over Catrina's shoulder to the dark lump that was Horace mumbling in his sleep. "What about him?"

Catrina turned her head. "He old. They ain't gonna do anything to him. I'm just worried bout makin it with that baby."

"Well, I sure as hell ain't gonna go without my child."

"I ain't said we was," Catrina hissed. "Down two floors just ain't gonna be easy, is all."

"We can do it," Elaine said.

"We can do it," Catrina said. She tiptoed to the chair at the foot of the bed and went through Horace's pants pockets. "Maybe fifty dollars here," she whispered after returning. "I already got about three hundred."

"You been stealin from him?" Elaine said. The lump in the bed turned over and moaned, then settled back to snoring.

"God helps them that helps themselves, Elaine. Les go." Catrina had her clothes in her hands and went on by Elaine, who watched as the lump in the bed turned again, snoring all the while. Bye, Horace. Bye. I be seein you.

The policeman in the unmarked car parked across 13th Street watched as Elaine stood on the edge of the balcony and jumped. She passed for a second in front of the feeble light over the entrance and landed on the sloping entrance of the underground parking garage. The policeman was five years from retirement and he did not move, because he could see quite well from where he sat. His partner, only three years on the job, was asleep in the passenger seat. The veteran thought the woman jumping might have hurt herself, because he did not see her rise from the ground for several minutes. I wouldn't do it, the man thought, not for all a rich man's money. The woman did rise, but before she did he saw another woman lean over the balcony dangling a bundle. Drugs? he thought. Nah. Clothes? Yeah, clothes more like it. The bundle was on a long rope or string—it was too far for the man to make out. The woman on the balcony leaned over very far and the woman on the ground reached up as far as she could, but still the bundle was a good two feet from her hands.

Just let them clothes drop, the policeman thought. Then Catrina released the bundle and Elaine caught it. Good catch. I wonder what she looks like in the light. Catrina jumped, and the policeman watched her pass momentarily in front of the light, and then he looked over at his partner. He himself didn't mind filling out the forms so much, but his partner did, so he let him sleep on. I'll be on a lake fishin my behind off and you'll still be doin this. When he looked back, the first woman was coming up the slope of the entrance with the bundle in her arms and the second one was limping after her. I wonder what that one looks like in a good light. Once on the sidewalk, both women looked left, then right, and headed down 13th Street. The policeman yawned and watched through his sideview mirror as the women crossed M Street. He yawned again. Even at three o'clock in the morning people still jay-walked.

The man who was a cousin of Darnell's was on his way back from the bathroom when the police broke through the door. He frightened easily, and though he had just emptied his bladder, he peed again as the door came open and the light of the hallway and the loud men came spilling in on him and his sleeping companions.

Horace began asking about Catrina and Elaine and the baby as soon as they put him in a cell. It took him that long to clear his head and understand what was happening to him. He pressed his face against the bars, trying to get his bearings and ignoring everything behind him in the cell. He stuck his mouth as far out of the bars as he could and shouted for someone to tell him whether they knew if the young women and the baby were all right. "They just women, y'all," he kept saying for some five minutes. "They wouldn't hurt a flea. Officers, please. Please, Officers. What's done happened to them? And that baby . . . That baby is so innocent." It was a little after six in the morning, and men up and down the line started hollering for him to shut up or they would stick the biggest dick he ever saw in his mouth. Stunned, he did quiet down, because, while he was used to street language coming from the young men who came and went in his apartment, no bad words had ever been directed at him. They talked trash with the filthiest language he had ever heard but they always invited him to join in and "talk about how it really is," talk about his knowing the Secretary of Defense and the Mayor. Usually, after the second blunt, he was floating along with them. Now someone had threatened to do to him what he and the young men said they would do to any woman that crossed them.

Then he turned from the bars and considered the three men he was sharing the two-man cell with. The city-jail people liked to make as little work for themselves as possible, and filling cells beyond their capacity meant having to deal with fewer locks. One man was cocooned in blankets on the floor beside the tiered metal beds. The man sleeping on the top bunk had a leg over the side, and because he was a tall man the leg came down to within six inches of the face of the man lying on the bottom bunk. That man was awake and on his back and picking his nose and staring at Horace. His other hand was under his blanket, in the crotch of his pants. What the man got out of his nose he would flick up at the bottom of the bunk above him. Watching him, Horace remembered that a very long time ago, even before the Chesapeake Street house, Loneese would iron his handkerchiefs and fold them into four perfect squares.

"Daddy," the man said, "you got my smokes?"

"What?" Horace said. He recalled doing it to Catrina about two or three in the morning and then rolling over and going to sleep. He also remembered slapping flies away in his dreams, flies that were as big as the hands of policemen.

The man seemed to have an infinite supply of boogers, and the more he picked, the more Horace's stomach churned. He used to think it was such a shame to unfold the handkerchiefs, so wondrous were the squares. The man sighed at Horace's question and put something from his nose on the big toe of the sleeping man above him. "I said do you got my smokes?"

"I don't have my cigarettes with me," Horace said. He tried the best white man's English he knew, having been told by a friend who was serving with him in the Army in Germany that it impressed not only white people but black people who weren't going anywhere in life. "I left my cigarettes at home." His legs were aching and he wanted to sit on the floor, but the only available space was in the general area of where he was standing and something adhered to his shoes every time he lifted his feet. "I wish I did have my cigarettes to give you."

"I didn't ask you bout *your* cigarettes. I don't wanna smoke them. I ask you bout *my* cigarettes. I wanna know if you brought *my* cigarettes."

Someone four cells down screamed and called out in his sleep: "Irene, why did you do this to me? Irene, ain't love worth a damn anymore?" Someone else told him to shut up or he would get a king-sized dick in his mouth.

"I told you I do not have any cigarettes," Horace said.

"You know, you ain't worth shit," the man said. "You take the cake and mess it all up. You really do. Now, you know you was comin to jail, so why didn't you bring my goddam smokes? What kinda fuckin consideration is that?"

Horace decided to say nothing. He raised first one leg and then the other and shook them, hoping that would relieve the aches. Slowly, he turned around to face the bars. No one had told him what was going to happen to him. He knew a lawyer, but he did not know if he was still practicing. He had friends, but he did not want any of them to see him in jail. He hoped the man would go to sleep.

"Don't turn your fuckin back on me after all we meant to each other," the man said. "We have this long relationship and you do this to me. Whas wrong with you, Daddy?"

"Look," Horace said, turning back to the man. "I done told you I ain't got no smokes. I ain't got your smokes. I ain't got my smokes. I ain't got nobody's smokes. Why can't you understand that?" He was aware that he was veering away from the white man's English, but he knew that his friend from Germany was probably home asleep safely in his bed. "I can't give you what I don't have." Men were murdered in the D.C. jail, or so the *Washington Post* told him. "Can't you understand what I'm sayin?" His back stayed as close to the bars as he could manage. Who was this Irene, he thought, and what had she done to steal into a man's dreams that way?

"So, Daddy, it's gonna be like that, huh?" the man said, raising his head and pushing the foot of the upper-bunk man out of the way so he could see Horace better. He took his hand out of his crotch and pointed at Horace. "You gon pull a Peter-and-Jesus thing on me and deny you ever knew me, huh? Thas your plan,

Daddy?" He lowered his head back to the black-and-white-striped pillow. "I've seen some low-down dirty shit in my day, but you the lowest. After our long relationship and everything."

"I never met you in my life," Horace said, grabbing the bars behind him with both hands, hoping, again, for relief.

"I won't forget this, and you know how long my memory is. First, you don't bring me my smokes, like you know you should. Then you deny all that we had. Don't go to sleep in here, Daddy, thas all I gotta say."

He thought of Reilly Johnson, a man he had worked with in the Pentagon. Reilly considered himself something of a photographer. He had taken the picture of Horace with the Secretary of Defense. What would the bail be? Would Reilly be at home to receive his call on a Sunday morning? Would they give him bail? The policemen who pulled him from his bed had tsk-tsked in his face. "Sellin drugs and corruptin young people like that?" "I didn't know nothin about that, Officer. Please." "Tsk tsk. An old man like you."

"The world ain't big enough for you to hide from my righteous wrath, Daddy. And you know how righteous I can be when I get started. The world ain't big enough, so you know this jail ain't big enough."

Horace turned back to the bars. Was something in the back as painful as something in the stomach? He touched his face. Rarely, even in the lost months with Catrina, had he failed to shave each morning. A man's capable demeanor started with a shave each morning, his sergeant in boot camp had told him a thousand years ago.

The man down the way began calling for Irene again. Irene, Horace called in his mind. Irene, are you out there? No one told the man to be quiet. It was about seven and the whole building was waking up and the man calling Irene was not the loudest sound in the world anymore.

"Daddy, you got my smokes? Could use my smokes right about now."

Horace, unable to stand anymore, slowly sank to the floor. There he found some relief. The more he sat, the more he began to play over the arrest. He had had money in his pocket when he took off his pants the night before, but there was no money when they booked him. And where had Catrina and Elaine been when the police marched him out of the apartment and down to the paddy wagon, with the Sunset's female security guard standing behind her desk with an "Oh, yes, I told you so" look? Where had they been? He had not seen them. He stretched out his legs and they touched the feet of the sleeping man on the floor. The man roused. "Love don't mean shit anymore," the man on the lower bunk said. It was loud enough to wake the man on the floor all the way, and that man sat up and covered his chest with his blanket and looked at Horace, blinking and blinking and getting a clearer picture of Horace the more he blinked.

Reilly did not come for him until the middle of Monday afternoon. Somebody opened the cell door and at first Horace thought the policeman was coming to get one of his cellmates.

"Homer Perkins," the man with the keys said. The doors were supposed to open electronically, but that system had not worked in a long time.

"Thas me," Horace said and got to his feet. As he and the man with the keys walked past the other cells, someone said to Horace, "Hey, Pops, you ain't too old to learn to suck dick." "Keep moving," the man with the keys said. "Pops, I'll give you a lesson when you come back."

As they poured his things out of a large manila envelope, the two guards behind the desk whispered and laughed. "Everything there?" one of them asked Horace. "Yes." "Well, good," the guard said. "I guess we'll be seein you on your next trip here." "Oh, leave that old man alone. He's somebody's grandfather." "When they start that old," the first man said, "it gets in their system and they can't stop. Ain't that right, Pops?"

He and Reilly did not say very much after Reilly said he had been surprised to hear from Horace and that he had wondered what had happened to him since Loneese died. Horace said he was eternally grateful to Reilly for bailing him out and that it was all a mistake as well as a long story that he would soon share with him. At Sunset, Reilly offered to take him out for a meal, but Horace said he would have to take a rain check. "Rain check?" Reilly said, smiling. "I didn't think they said that anymore."

The key to the apartment worked the way it always had, but something was blocking the door, and he had to force it open. Inside, he found destruction everywhere. On top of the clothes and the mementos of his life, strewn across the table and the couch and the floor were hundreds and hundreds of broken records. He took three steps into the room and began to cry. He turned around and around, hoping for something that would tell him it was not as bad as his eyes first reported. But there was little hope—the salt and pepper shakers had not been touched, the curtains covering the glass door were intact. There was not much beyond that for him to cling to.

He thought immediately of Catrina and Elaine. What had he done to deserve this? Had he not always shown them a good and kind heart? He covered his eyes, but that seemed only to produce more tears, and when he lowered his hands the room danced before him through the tears. To steady himself, he put both hands on the table, which was covered in instant coffee and sugar. He brushed broken glass off the chair nearest him and sat down. He had not got it all off, and he felt what was left through his pants and underwear.

He tried to look around but got no farther than the picture with the Secretary of Defense. It had two cracks in it, one running north to south and the other going northwest to southeast. The photograph was tilting, too, and something told him that if he could straighten the picture it all might not be so bad. He reached out a hand, still crying, but he could not move from the chair.

He stayed as he was through the afternoon and late into the evening, not once moving from the chair, though the tears did stop around five o'clock. Night came and he still did not move. My name is Horace Perkins, he thought just as the sun set. My name is

Horace Perkins and I worked many a year at the Pentagon. The apartment became dark, but he did not have it in him to turn on the lights.

The knocking had been going on for more than ten minutes when he finally heard it. He got up, stumbling over debris, and opened the door. Elaine stood there with Darnell, Jr., in her arms.

"Horace, you O.K.? I been comin by. I been worried about you, Horace."

He said nothing but opened the door enough for her and the baby to enter.

"It's dark, Horace. What about some light?"

He righted the lamp on the table and turned it on.

"Jesus in Heaven, Horace! What happened! My Lord Jesus! I can't believe this." The baby, startled by his mother's words, began to cry. "It's O.K.," she said to him, "It's O.K.," and gradually the baby calmed down. "Oh, Horace, I'm so sorry. I really am. This is the worst thing I've ever seen in my life." She touched his shoulder with her free hand, but he shrugged it off. "Oh, my dear God! Who could do this?"

She went to the couch and moved enough trash aside for the baby. She pulled a pacifier from her sweater pocket, put it momentarily in her mouth to remove the lint, then put it in the baby's mouth. He appeared satisfied and leaned back on the couch.

She went to Horace, and right away he grabbed her throat. "I'm gonna kill you tonight!" he shouted. "I just wish that bitch Catrina was here so I could kill her, too." Elaine struggled and sputtered out one "please" before he gripped her tighter. She beat his arms but that seemed to give him more strength. She began to cry. "I'm gonna kill you tonight, girl, if it's the last thing I do."

The baby began to cry, and she turned her head as much as she could to look at him. This made him slap her twice, and she started to fall, and he pulled her up and, as he did, went for a better grip, which was time enough for her to say, "Don't kill me in front of my son, Horace." He loosened his hands. "Don't kill me in front of my boy, Horace." Her tears ran down her face and over and into his hands. "He don't deserve to see me die. You know that, Horace."

"Where, then!"

"Anywhere but in front of him. He's innocent of everything."

He let her go and backed away.

"I did nothin, Horace," she whispered. "I give you my word, I did nothin." The baby screamed, and she went to him and took him in her arms.

Horace sat down in the same chair he had been in.

"I would not do this to you, Horace."

He looked at her and at the baby, who could not take his eyes off Horace, even through his tears.

One of the baby's cries seemed to get stuck in his throat, and to release it the baby raised a fist and punched the air, and finally the cry came free. How does a man start over with nothing? Horace thought. Elaine came near him, and the baby still watched him as his crying lessened. How does a man start from scratch?

He leaned down and picked up a few of the broken albums from the floor and read the labels. "I would not hurt you for anything in the world, Horace," Elaine said. Okeh Phonograph Corporation. Domino Record Co. RCA Victor. Darnell, Jr.'s crying stopped, but he continued to look down at the top of Horace's head. Cameo Record Corporation, N.Y. "You been too good to me for me to hurt you like this, Horace." He dropped the records one at a time: "It Takes an Irishman to Make Love." "I'm Gonna Pin a Medal on the Girl I Left Behind." "Ragtime Soldier Man." "Whose Little Heart Are You Breaking Now." "The Syncopated Walk."

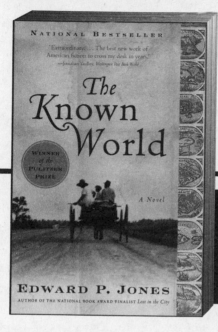